Freiburger Schriften zur Forst- und Umweltpolitik
Band 11

Capacities of rural forest-dependent communities in the northern Bolivian Amazon in times of legal reforms

Carmen Gottwald

Verlag Dr. Kessel
Remagen-Oberwinter 2006

1. Auflage 2006
Tel.: 02228-493
Fax: 01212-512382426
eMail: nkessel@web.de

Homepage: www.forstbuch.de

Druck: www.business-copy.com

ISBN: 3-935638-76-0

This thesis is lovingly dedicated to

Harold Ibañez Vaca

&

Jaro

Donde existe un gran amor

siempre se producen milagros

Acknowledgements

Many coincidences came together providing me with the opportunity to write this thesis. I want to thank the 'Amazonian sisters' Jana and Sonja for the hints made at the time and the Freiburg crew for accepting my application after the closing date.

I am deeply grateful to Prof. Dr. Michel Becker, who always left me the necessary space to develop my own ideas and guided me at the appropriate times with his constructive criticisms and the advice given along the winding road that was this dissertation. In particular, I want to thank him for his commitment and support in securing the finances necessary for this study, without which I could not have finished.

Thanks to the German Ministry for Economic Co-operation and Development (BMZ) and the Centre for International Forestry Research (CIFOR) for providing the funds for the major part of this study and to the women's representative with the administration department of Albert-Ludwigs-University Freiburg for the scholarship needed to finish.

I want to thank all of the colleagues and friends that contributed to creating a good atmosphere and provided help and advice during my time in Freiburg. Many thanks especially to Dietmar for his initial thesis orientation, Steffi for providing a long-term roof for a homeless mother, Carol for her manifold support and positive philosophy of life, Gregor for being the move manager, Juán for his *enchufes*, providing work for my husband, David for the extensive English corrections and Barbara for being the good soul in the office.

Many thanks to Wil De Jong for all of his input, advice and the opportunities he provided the CIFOR project and me. Muchas gracias to the staff of the *Centro de Investigación y Promoción del Campesinado* (CIPCA) in Riberalta, Bolivia, for granting me a space in their office, a platform for discussion, helping me with the infrastructural issues and warmly integrating me into Bolivian life and their volleyball team. I also thank Sergio and his family for the part they shared in the Riberalta experience and their company, especially in the aftermath of the burglar attack. Yolanda, you are so kind, thanks for your support in the embassy and at the airport.

I would particularly like to thank all of the people in the Bolivian communities who received me so kindly and provided their time and experience all in the name of this study. May the current political events not harm Bolivia's delicate target for improvement and may the future offer you more opportunities. Stay brave.

My innermost gratefulness is dedicated to my family;

Harold, I am infinitely grateful to you for everything you did enabling me to finish this thesis; coming to Germany and starting a new life, caring for our son during countless hours and always believing in me. *No hay palabras para todo eso.*

Jaro, you spent so many hours without me, but now this will all change!

Finally, I wish to thank my parents and friends for their support. Especially Jaro's *padrinos* Jutta & Gregor, Sergio (el Malagueño), Katja & Ralf, Antje & Andreas, and the childminders Maka and Brigitte for caring so well for Jaro and in so doing allowing me to write this thesis.

Contents

Figures

Tables

Maps

ZUSAMMENFASSUNG

Die vorliegende Dissertation entstand im bolivianischen Amazonasgebiet im Rahmen eines gemeinsamen Forschungsprojektes des *Centre for International Forestry Research* (CIFOR), des Instituts für Forst- und Umweltpolitik, Arbeitsbereich Markt und Marketing, Universität Freiburg, und des *Centro de Investigación y Promoción del* Campesinado (CIPCA) als Partnerinstitution in Riberalta. Das Projekt wurde durch das Bundesministerium für wirtschaftliche Entwicklung und Zusammenarbeit (BMZ) und CIFOR finanziert. Das Beenden der Dokorarbeit wurde durch ein Stipendium der Frauenbeauftragten und des Rektorates der Albert-Ludwigs-Universität Freiburg ermöglicht.

Diese Studie analysiert waldnutzende Siedlungen im ländlichen Raum des nordboliviansichen Amazonasgebietes zu einer Zeit, in der die Implementierung der umfassenden Gesetzesreformen der neunziger Jahre im Gebiet stattfindet. Die Hauptziele sind 1) das Wissen über die Art und Weise, wie Dezentralisierungspolitik und Ressourcenmanagement auf lokaler Ebene verknüpft sind, und welche Faktoren das Ergebnis bestimmen, zu erweitern; 2) zu einem besseren Verstehen ländlicher Siedlungen beizutragen, indem interne Unterschiede, Prozesse und Institutionen mit dem Ziel berücksichtigt werden, universelle Behauptungen zu überwinden; und 3) zu einem besseren Verständnis der institutionellen, strukturellen and sozio-historischen Einflüsse beizutragen, die die Waldnutzung und das Wohlergehen von ‚unabhängigen' Gemeinden beeinflussen.

Es wurde ein Fallstudienansatz gewählt, um die Forschungsziele zu erreichen. Da es viele unterschiedliche Siedlungen im Untersuchungsgebiet gibt, wurden Kriterien aufgestellt, um diese auszuwählen. Anhand dieser Kriterien wurden vier Dörfer mit unterschiedlicher Variablenausprägung ausgesucht. Durch diese Auswahl soll sichergestellt werden, daß die vier Fallstudien die Bandbreite des vorhandenen Spektrums abdecken. Die empirische Datenerhebung stützt sich auf die Methoden der qualitativen Beobachtung, Haushaltsinterviews und die Anwendung von Zukunftsszenarien. Die Forscherin besuchte die Dörfer mehrmals mit einer durchschnittlichen Aufenthaltsdauer von einer Woche pro Besuch.

Die Dissertation besteht aus fünf Kapiteln:

Kapitel 1 als Einleitungskapitel besteht aus der Problemstellung, den Forschungszielen und Forschungsfragen, Methodik und Methoden, Untersuchungsregion sowie theoretischem Ansatz im Allgemeinen.

Kapitel 2 analysiert, wie ländliche Bewohner den Prozess von Dezentralisierung und Reform wahrnehmen, sich im politischen Bereich verhalten und formal am lokalen Ressourcenmanagement teilnehmen. Es wird gezeigt, dass es ländlichen Bewohnern an Wissen über die neuen Institutionen auf Gesetzesebene mangelt. Manchen fehlt eine Interessenvertretung auf politischer Ebene, anderen fehlt lokales Engagement oder Vertrauen zu den gewählten Vertretern, oder sie können auf formeller Ebene nicht partizipieren, da ihnen persönliche Ausweispapiere fehlen. Dörfer erfahren je nach wahltaktischer Wichtigkeit unterschiedliche Zuwendung auf politischer Ebene. Demzufolge werden Gelegenheiten zur Verbesserung der lokalen Selbstverwaltung nur zögerlich genutzt.

Kapitel 3 untersucht das Vermächtnis historischer Organisation und Ressourcennutzung in nordbolivianischen Dörfern und dessen Folgen für Organisation und Ressourcennutzung in diesen Dörfern heute. Es wird dargelegt, dass institutionelle Pfadabhängigkeiten durch lokale sozio-historische Bedingungen bedingt sind. Dies hat im Zuge der Gesetzesreformen, die in den neunziger Jahren verabschiedet wurden und für alle Dörfer gleich gelten, zu unterschiedlicher Ausgestaltung der Organisation und Ressourcennutzung geführt. Die Fallstudien zeigen auf, wie Siedlungsgeschichte die Gegenwart beeinflusst.

Kapitel 4 bezieht sich theoretisch auf soziales Kapital, soziales Vermögen und Wohlergehen im Sinn von Wahlmöglichkeiten und wahrgenommenen Gelegenheiten. Empirisch werden spezifische soziale Vermögenswerte wie Organisationen, Institutionen, Netzwerke und Vertrauen sowie Elemente des Funktionsverhaltens der Dörfer analysiert. Von diesen Ergebnissen wird ein relatives kommunales Leistungsvermögen jedes Dorfes im Vergleich zu den anderen abgeleitet. Obwohl alle untersuchten ländlichen Siedlungen arm nach UN Kriterien sind und denselben gesetzlichen Rahmenbedingungen unterliegen, zeigen die Ergebnisse, wie deren ‚interne Welt' sich unterscheidet. Politische Vertretung der Basis, Zugang zu natürlichen Ressourcen usw. funktionieren unterschiedlich aufgrund der variierenden instrumentellen Ausgestaltung durch die Bewohner dieser Siedlungen. Dies hat auch Auswirkung auf das kommunale Funktionsverhalten und das kommunale Leistungsvermögen.

Darüber hinaus wird eine explorative Studie über die Verbindung zwischen Bildung und Häufigkeit organisationeller Mitgliedschaft auf Individualebene durchgeführt und für alle Befragten in allen vier Siedlungen vergleichend dargestellt. Die Ergebnisse zeigen, dass im Allgemeinen Männer mit höherer Bildung auch eine höhere Anzahl von Organisationsmitgliedschaften aufweisen als dies Männer mit geringerer Bildung tun. Dies gilt allerdings nicht für die Frauen in den Gemeinden.

Kapitel 5 enthält die Schlußfolgerungen. Während der neue gesetzliche Rahmen eine formale Dorfarena definiert, basieren die Interaktionen in dieser Arena fast ausschließlich auf dem Informellen. Obwohl informelle Regeln normalerweise durch einen langfristigen Einfluß gekennzeichnet sind, sind sie auch in Kurzzeituntersuchungen von Relevanz. Das Informelle, welches die politische Interessenvertretung, Ressourcennutzung und viele andere Dinge im ländlichen Bolivien von heute regelt, ist im Evolutions- und Veränderungsprozeß, bleibt aber das Hauptmittel, das die Interaktionen im ländlichen, waldabhängingen Siedlungen ermöglicht. Die Ergebnisse zeigen, daß Dezentralisierung und Partizipation voranschreiten. Allerdings gibt es Hindernisse auf Mikro- und Mesoebene sowie Defizite im Zugang zu Informationen und anderen Dienstleistungen. Dörfer und ihre Einwohner vermögen das lokale System zu gestalten und zu betreiben um das Zusammenleben zu regeln, den Ressourcenzugang zu sichern und diese zu verteilen, um Härten abzumildern, Verbesserungen zu erreichen und Interessen auf Munizipalebene zu vertreten. Der Umfang dieses Leistungsvermögens hängt von verschiedenen Faktoren ab und wird durch Macht und Informationsasymmetrien beeinflußt.

SUMMARY

This doctoral thesis documents a study executed in the Bolivian Amazon within the framework of a joint research project between the Centre for International Forestry Research (CIFOR), the Institute of Forest and Environmental Policy, Markets and Marketing Section, at the University of Freiburg, and the partner institution Centro de Investigación y Promoción del Campesinado (CIPCA) in Riberalta. The project was financed by the German Ministry of Economic Cooperation and Development (BMZ) and CIFOR. The completion of the dissertation was made possible with the granting of a scholarship by the women's representative of the administration department of the University of Freiburg.

The study provides an analysis of rural forest-dependent settlements in the northern Bolivian Amazon at a time during which the implementation of wide reaching legal reforms initiated in the nineties was taking place in the region. The main objectives are 1) to enhance knowledge of the manner in which decentralisation policies and resource management at local level are intertwined and what factors determine the outcomes; 2) to contribute to a better understanding of community, taking into account internal differences, processes and institutions with the aim of overcoming universal claims; and 3) to contribute to a better understanding of institutional, structural and socio-historical influences shaping forest use and the well-being of 'independent communities'.

In order to achieve the research objectives, a case study approach was used. As there are many different rural forest-dependent settlements in the region, criteria were established for the selection of the case study settlements. Four settlements with differing variables were selected on the basis of these criteria. This selection assured that the four case studies represent the broad spectrum of heterogeneous communities in the region. Empirical data collection is based on the methodological pillars of qualitative observation, household interviews and future scenario exercises. The researcher visited each community on numerous occasions for stays lasting an average of one week each.

The dissertation is organised into five chapters:

Chapter 1, the introductory chapter, includes the problem statement, research objectives and questions, methods and methodology, a presentation of the study region and a general theoretical approach.

Chapter 2 contains an analysis of how people in rural settlements perceive the ongoing process of decentralisation and reform, their place in the political sphere, and their participation in the management of resources. It is demonstrated that rural inhabitants in Bolivia lack knowledge of the new state institutions. Some do not feel that their interests are represented at the formal political level, others lack local engagement, trust in their representatives or cannot fully participate due to the lack of personal documentation. The political support a community receives depends on its the electoral importance. As a result, opportunities to improve local resource management are used hesitantly.

Chapter 3 contains a discussion of the legacy of past organisation and resource use in rural communities in the northern Bolivian Amazon and the consequences for organisation and resource use in these communities today. It is argued that institutional path dependencies are determined by the local socio-historical conditions. This has led to varying outcomes in terms of organisation and resource use today under the umbrella of legal reforms undertaken in the 1990s. These case studies illustrate how settlement history impacts upon the present.

Chapter 4 concerns the significance for the region of the theories of social capital, social assets and well-being in terms of the range of choices and opportunities. Specific social assets in the communities, namely organisations, institutions, networks and trust, are analysed empirically and elements of community performance investigated. From the results a relative community capacity level for each community is derived and compared for each community. Although all of the communities investigated are poor in UN-terms and are subject to the same legal conditions, the results show how their internal worlds differ. Political representation, natural resource access, etc., function differently due to the varying tools employed by the inhabitants of these communities, which also has repercussions for their performance and overall capacity.

In addition, an explorative study into the link between education and the frequency of organisation membership is carried out at the level of individuals and comparatively presented for all interviewees in the four communities. The results show that generally men with a higher level of education engage in more organisations than less well educated men. However, this does not hold true for women in the respective communities.

In chapter 5 the conclusions of the study are presented. While the new legal framework in Bolivia creates a community space, the interactions within this space, namely at community level, are based almost exclusively on the informal institutions. Although informal institutions usually have a long-term influence, they are also relevant in short-term investigations. These informal structures, which have to date regulated political representation and resource use as well as many other things in rural communities in Bolivia, are in a process of evolution and adaptation, but remain the leading tool for the facilitation of interaction in rural forest-dependent settlements. The results show that decentralisation processes and participation are increasing and that historical path dependencies have an influence on these processes. However, there are stumbling blocks at micro and meso level, as well as deficiencies in terms of access to information and other services. Communities and their inhabitants are capable of designing and running the local system in order to regulate social interaction, secure resource access and distribution, buffer hardships, bring about improvements and lobby interests at municipality level. The amplitude of this capacity depends on various factors and is influenced by power and information asymmetries. Further investigation into the processes related to the formation, change and influence of local systems and the influence of the asset endowment of individuals within this system is required.

GLOSSARY

altura	upland area which is not flooded during the rainy season; synonymous with → terra firme (Portuguese), as opposed to → bajío
bajío	floodplain; temporarily flooded site
barraca	formerly 'rubber estate'; once synonymous with estación, hacienda gomera, and siringal or seringal (Portuguese). Now a unit of forest exploitation yielding various forest products under the control of a → patrón
barraquero	owner or claimant of a → barraca; synonymous with → patrón
caja	unit of measure for Brazil nut in-shell; the wooden box (51x27x35 cm) contains 22 (-26) kg
camba	mestizo smallholder of Bolivian tropical lowland origin
campesino	the most apt translation of a campesino of the Bolivian Amazon would be 'agro-extractive small producer' (e.g. see Stoian 2000: xii), which adheres to the self-designation of independent rural inhabitants. In this study, the term 'peasant' is used to refer to campesino. The author would like to emphasise that she does NOT share the view that the term 'peasant' implies a person existing exclusively from agriculture, is generally poor and forms a kind of proletariat (with other peasants). Here the term peasant stands for the agro-extractive small producer of the Bolivian Amazon, without any negative or contemptuous valuations. The author would also point out that there are different types of peasants all over the world, but that they share a common peasant habit, following the definition of the dynamic habit concept by Bourdieu (1976)
chaco	agricultural field of typically 1-2 ha, cleared through slash-and-burn
colla	colla is the term for a person from the Bolivian Andes, the highlands and valleys. The term also applies to a person of these origins living in the lowlands. It implies a cultural connotation
corregidor	in post-independence Bolivia a corregidor was an official (usually white or cholo) charged with administering local Indian affairs. Today corregidor refers to the lowest authority in the hierarchy of

	the national executive, which is structured as follows: president, prefect (departmento), subprefect (province), mayor (municipality) and corregidor (canton)
estrada	rubber trail, typically consisting of 80-200 rubber trees in a natural forest. Abandoned nowadays or, alternatively, used for Brazil nut harvest
galpón	shed used for the storage of Brazil nuts
gringo/gringa	the term gringo, or gringa (female) is used to denote a foreigner in Latin America, especially a North American or British person. Sometimes it can be used as a disparaging term. People in the Bolivian lowlands refer to every foreigner (not necessarily North American or English) as gringo. Depending on the context, it is used in a neutral, negative or even positive way
Junta Vecinal	neighbourhood union in urban areas, is at the same time → OTB.
Kataristas	the first activists to play a significant role in the indigenous movements; they were young Aymaras (a big indigenous group in Bolivia). Named after the eighteenth century indigenous rebel Tupaj Katari, this group began to make a clear reference to the ethnic basis of the discrimination suffered by the native peoples. It was in effect an attempt "to unravel the Bolivian project for mestizo hegemony", as they sought to rescue and revitalise their alternative history of Bolivia. Indeed, the Aymara flag, the wiphala, became an important symbol of the movement. By the late 1970s they began to conceive the idea that they would need to form their own political parties, which would represent their own particular needs. At this point the Movimiento Indio Tupaj Katari (MITKA) split from the main Kataristas and presented itself as a political party (McKee 1999: 2)
latifundio	A latifundio is a very large property characterised by: - large size, from several hundred hectares to tens of thousands of hectares - very low productivity of the land, which is often devoted to extensive grazing - supplemented by subsistence crops provided by the people living on the land and tied to the landlord on whom they are both personally and financially dependent (FAO 2003: 154)
mestizo	person of mixed European and native ancestry

MNR	Movimiento Nacional Revolucionario, political party
OTB	Organización Territorial de Base, smallest territorial administration unit in the national government hierarchy. Different in situ organisations like those of peasant communities, indigenous people with their organisational forms (Cabildos, Capitanias etc.) or urban neighbourhood unions are recognised as OTBs
Participación Popular	this expression refers not only to the Popular Participation Law, the details of which are given below, but also implies other laws, such as the Administrative Decentralisation Law and others, which taken together represent the comprehensive process of decentralisation in Bolivia
patrón	formerly 'rubber baron'. Now individual or corporate patron, estate owner or claimant, synonymous with → barraquero
PDM	Plan de Desarollo Municipal, municipal development plan with a time horizon of five years
peon	day-labourer
plaza	public square
POA	Plan Operativo Annual, annual operation plan of the municipality. This plan is drafted each year in order to achieve the implementation of goals fixed in the →PDM
pulpería	merchandise store; on a → barraca the monopoly facility for the sale of basic necessities
saneamiento	all technical and juridical activities necessary for the regulation and consolidation of land rights
TCO	Tierra Comunitaria de Origen, indigenous communal land, constituted by law with specific property rights
zafra	the collection period for Brazil nuts in northern Bolivia, lasting from December to March; in the southern Bolivian Amazon, the harvesting period for sugarcane
zafrero	in northern Bolivia a temporary worker hired to gather Brazil nuts during the → zafra, in the southern Bolivian Amazon a harvester of sugarcane

1 INTRODUCTION

1.1 Problem statement

Decades of intrusive resource management strategies and planned policies have resulted in poor development and conservation statuses in developing countries. As a consequence, the perception of the role of communities in the international development debate as a 'hindrance to progressive social change' shifted, becoming a key factor of decentralisation, meaningful participation, cultural autonomy and conservation (Chambers and McBeth 1992; Chitere 1994, Etzioni 1996, Agrawal/Gibson 1999: 630). In the course of the debate authors have used different concepts of community. Many of these approaches exhibited weaknesses. Agrawal and Gibson (ibid.) explored the conceptual origins of the community, and the ways in which the term has been employed in writings pertaining to resource use. They then analysed those aspects of community most important in terms of advocating its role in resource management. Their results suggested that a more political approach is necessary. In the context of development and conservation, community must be examined "(...) by focusing on the multiple interests and actors within the communities, on how these actors influence decision-making, and on the internal and external institutions that shape the decision-making process. A focus on institutions rather than 'community' is likely to be more fruitful for those interested in community-based natural resource management" (ibid. 629).

The beginnings of a shift of emphasis away from central authority in favour of local authorities were evident in Asia, Latin America and Africa in the 1970s (Rondinelli and Cheema, 1983; Brillantes and Cuachon 2002). In the 1990s natural resource management in developing countries became increasingly decentralised, whereas in countries like Switzerland, Canada and India this had been common practice for decades. "Decentralisation, it is hoped, will make decision-making more democratic, help to distribute the benefits which flow from forests more fairly, and ensure that the forests are used more efficiently" (CIFOR 2003). The countries of Latin America in which this trend can be seen include Bolivia, Honduras, Guatemala, Nicaragua, Brazil and Costa Rica. Examples from Africa include Burkina Faso, Cameroon, Guinea, Malawi, Mali, Niger, Uganda, Gambia and Zimbabwe (Ribot 2003: 54), and in Asia Bangladesh, Cambodia, Indonesia, Laos, the Philippines, and very recently Nepal.

With the implementation of measures geared towards decentralisation in every possible aspect, local communities became the main focus of policy and scientists. Previous unsuccessful development and conservation policies, which had overlooked the role of the communities, shifted towards a pro-community-orientated attitude, fostering their lead role in resource management without taking into account possible constraints.

Forest and woodland resources play an important role in the economies of rural dwellers, low income traders, and in national economies of many developing countries (Campbell and Byron 1996; Stoian and Henkemans 2000; Stoian 2000; Bojanic 1999). Whereas a few decades ago, colonial and post-colonial governments controlled the major areas of natural forests in developing countries de jure, but not necessarily de facto, today in most developing countries a quarter of the forest estate is said to be owned or controlled by indigenous and rural communities (White and Martin 2002, cited in Scherr et. al. 2003: 16).

In Bolivia a similar development has taken place; under a wide range of reforms in the nineties pertaining to land, forests, decentralisation, education, etc., rural communities were granted property rights over land and forests in an official titling and (re)distribution process. In order to receive land titles the communities were required to organise themselves and meet certain requirements for local governance and resource management. The following table contains data on the forest ownership classification in Bolivia from 2002:

Table 1-1: Forest ownership classification in Bolivia

Administered by government	Reserved for community and indigenous groups	Community/indigenous	Individual/firm
28.2 (53.2)	16.6 (31.3)	2.8 (5.3)	5.4 (10.2)

Note: Numbers indicate area in millions of hectares (percentage of total area of Bolivia)

Source: Extracted and adapted from White and Martin 2002: table 1

Bolivia is in the midrange of the thirty most forested countries by area of forest cover[1] in the world. However, it is second only to Haiti as the poorest country in Latin America and ranks number 114 on the UN Human Development Index 2003[2]. This contrast of richness in natural resources, but poverty among many of its inhabitants is directly visible in Bolivia. This holds especially true for the northern Bolivian Amazon, the research area[3] discussed in this study. This region provides Bolivia's second largest 'agro-industrial export product' (WTO/UNIDO 2004: 17), namely the non-timber forest product Brazil nuts. These nuts are gathered in the forests and processed for exportation in the regional urban centres (unshelled and shelled nuts). The extraction of the nuts takes place in the northern Bolivian Amazon, which covers an area of 100000 km² with a forest cover of about 90%, and inhabited by 200000 people (30% in rural areas, 70% concentrated in urban centres). The infrastructure of the region is poor; 80% of households are below the poverty line (ibid.). The extraction and processing of Bolivian Brazil nuts generates an export value of US$ 32.8 million (2000), constituting the single most important forest product exported from the country (CFB 2001). The gathering of NTFPs has proved not to be environmentally harmful over the past two hundred years[4]. The

[1] Identified by FAO 2001.

[2] UNDP 2003, based on data from 2001.

[3] Details on the history of the research area and the extracted NTFPs are provided in 2.3.

[4] However, a recent ecological study of Brazil nut stands in the Amazon region indicated reproduction problems due to insufficient juvenile recruitment, affecting tree densities in stands in areas where collection has been intensive (Peres et al. 2003: 2112). Up to the turn of the millennium, official timber extraction in the region occurred at a very low level (illegal logging has taken place, but the lack of a transport infrastructure and the remote location prevented large scale activities). Therefore, the regional forest cover is still high, and the forest composition largely reflects that of primary forests. However, infrastructure is improving, and the regional authorities (such as the Prefectura of the Pando Department) have started to foster activities such as cattle ranching and lack forest-orientated policies. Timber

region under discussion is shaped by an extractive economy[5]. Approximately 50% of the economically active population is directly involved in Brazil nut 'production'; about 7500 families in harvesting and additional 4500 in processing (WTO/UNIDO 2004: 17). Thousands of rural and peri-urban dwellers make their living by gathering and trading Brazil nuts.

The research project[6] preceding this study revealed that little was known of the rules governing rural communities and their use of resources (Stoian 2000). Based on previous research and literature sources (for example, Peluso 1992; Neumann 1992; Bebbington et al 1997; Campbell et al. 1999; Matose and Wily 1996; Nhira 1995), it was assumed for the purposes of this study that problems related to poverty and benefit-capturing in resource use were in part the result of inadequate institutional arrangements (CIFOR 1999: 3).

It must be assumed that institutions (rules) and organisation play an important role in the performance of rural settlements and the benefits derived from NTFP extraction and trade, as well as for natural resource use in general. Data collected by Stoian showed that collectors, and in particular those living in independent[7] communities, were able to augment their 'piece of the cake'. Nevertheless, the absolute benefit for them remains low. Despite the importance of NTFPs to the regional and national economy as products for exportation, an average of 72.4% (Pando) to 86.5% (Beni) of regional inhabitants is deemed poor by United Nations

export from Bolivia is also on the rise. As other regions have already been harvested to a great extent, there is a growing shift towards the Amazon region for the supply of resources.

[5] The definition of extractive economy refers in general to any economy reliant upon the extraction of natural resources. For the purposes of the study region presented here, the author adhered to the definition elaborated by Stoian (2000: 20): "In the context of this study, the term refers to the extraction of forest products, be they timber or non-timber forest products. That is to say that the term here excludes the removal of tree cover on land destined for conversion to non-forest land use, as well as mining of mineral deposits (…). The term includes all levels of commercial transactions within the context of forest product sale. Households gathering and selling forest products are as much part of an extractive economy, as are middlemen, processors, and wholesalers."

[6] Jointly undertaken by the Center of International Forestry Research (CIFOR), the Institute of Forest Policy, Markets and Marketing Section, at the University of Freiburg and various partner institutions in the northern Bolivian Amazon from 1996 to 2000.

[7] When referring to 'independent' communities, one must bear in mind the change in settlement patterns in the Bolivian Amazon. With the disintegration of the Suárez Company there was an increase in the number of independent communities after 1940. Smallholders installed themselves in areas previously unoccupied (Assies 1997: 44), and to a lesser extent on abandoned *barracas* (formerly 'rubber estates'; nowadays units of forest exploitation yielding various forest products under the control of a *patrón* (Stoian 2000: xii)). Despite the land reform of 1953, very few smallholders received legal title for their plot due to changes of the legal authorities, the non-registration of permits and exploitation based on traditional claims (DHV 1993e, cited in Assies 1997: 44, 81).
At present, independent communities principally establish along roads (see Stoian 2000: 188). This process has been going on for some time and increased as a result of the improved roads in the late 1980s. Previously, communities often tended to establish along rivers (Assies 1997: 45).
In order to attain an adequate view of the present circumstances of such independent communities, it is necessary to make further distinctions. Stoian developed a typology of six types of independent community by taking into account "the relative importance of wage labour, commercial agriculture, and Brazil nut extraction, as well as ethnic composition and the infrastructure available" (Stoian 2000: 185). In all but one community immigration outweighed emigration for the period between 1977 and 1995, to varying degrees. These independent communities are a crucial and growing element of the economic, social and political landscape in the region. They perform a vital role in the ongoing transformation process.

poverty indicator standards (PNUD 2003: 62). Due to their remote geographic location, the level of poverty in rural settlements closest to collection centres amounts to 100%[8], with 94.7% living in extreme poverty. These data were derived from the Census 2001, the most complete to have been carried out in the history of the country. Under the land titling and (re)distribution process, many of these impoverished households were recently granted legal access to land and forest resources because they are located in peasant (and indigenous[9]) communities. The reforms and the current regulations permit the allocation of at least 500 hectares per peasant family[10]. As Bolivia is currently undergoing a process of decentralisation and democratisation (CDR 1999:1), it is of even greater research interest to attempt to understand the role of institutions and organisation, and the effects of changes in these forest-dependent communities in northern Bolivia.

In the context of this process the forest use situation in the Bolivian Amazon is subject to site-specific dynamics due to the interrelation of (external) legislative change and conditions in situ. There are different forest use stakeholders in the region. Of these, the rural campesino communities, which according to the definition are at the same time independent communities (see footnote 7), were granted the opportunity to legally lay claim to large areas of land in the region, also implying access to the forests situated on these lands, as well as their products. The national land administration office estimated (on the basis of titled land and land surveyed under the titling process) that about 30% of the northern Bolivian Amazon would ultimately be in the hands of peasant and indigenous communities.

Before the implementation of the reforms, the Bolivian Amazon was marked by national isolation[11] and the absence of state influence until as late as the 1990s. In 1985, the physical isolation was ameliorated by the construction of the Riberalta – La Paz road, but de facto isolation remained. Land tenure and resource access were regulated mainly by the local elite according to informal institutions while other inhabitants were severely restricted in their access to natural and financial resources, education, health, etc. With the reform process in the nineties the state began to show its presence at local level and triggered the integration of the region, as well as the formalisation and redistribution of rights and obligations of Bolivian citizens inhibiting this part of the country. It was only once the region became more

---

[8] For example, Manuripi Province, Municipality of San Pedro, where the Loma Velarde case study is located.

[9] The focus of the research was on peasant communities, and not on indigenous communities.

[10] This is only possible in areas with enough available space. For communities close to urban centres in particular this cannot be achieved on their immediate territory. Under the *Decreto* 27572 from 6.17.2004, though, the possibility to obtain additional territory for the community in other areas has been opened up, if there is not enough space available in the immediate vicinity. However, the 500 hectare mark is the outcome of a successful strategy of demands made to the government by indigenous and peasant grassroots movements at a time of nationwide social strife, where government officials were under pressure to re-establish social peace quickly, exposed to several trouble spots all over the country involving many different issues. Originally, the law provided for 50 hectares, but this was subsequently expanded to 500.

[11] The Bolivian Amazon borders with Peru and Brazil. The export of NTFPs always focussed on the USA and Europe. Processed foods, fuel and other industrial products were mainly imported from Brazil.

integrated into the rest of the country that the central government managed to institute a stronger link between the Amazon and the state (PNUD, 2003).

However, there currently exist in the Bolivian Amazon communities (depending on their location) rich in terms of natural resources, but poor in terms of income, access to health, education, infrastructure, etc. In adherence to the concept of human poverty proposed by the UNDP, the reality is characterised by shortcomings in terms of equity, social inclusion, women's empowerment and respect for the human rights of the Bolivian citizens in this area.

The arrival of legal reforms formally tackled these issues to some extent. The reforms established a platform upon which further improvements can be built. Rural communities can demand projects from the relevant municipalities and improve their situations by means of the greater internal organisation and the work of their elected representatives. At the same time, this platform varies according to local circumstances. In the case of the independent rural communities, there is a range of different actor groups, which organise and function in different ways and are endowed with varying degrees of knowledge and skills. This leads to different outcomes in terms of resource use and benefit capturing.

Land redistribution and the associated access to the forests and the legal land titling process have been achieved for campesino families in many parts of the region. Moreover, under the reforms the municipalities received financial support to implement projects to improve the infrastructure, health, education etc. needs of the rural communities. However, project planning and implementation is deficient in many respects. The following should be noted in relation to the forests situated on community land: though there are legal regulations governing forest management (especially for commercial purposes), the management of the vast areas of 'community' forests depends primarily on the respective community regimes.

Based on literature review, the current perception of the author is that the role of community in the process of decentralisation, resource management and development has been integrated in the research agenda without the prior definition of a concept of community that adequately takes into account decisive factors such as information asymmetries amongst the inhabitants, internal rule-making, power-structure, accountability of representatives etc. and other specifications important to that community, which may influence the resulting outcome.

1.2 Objectives

There is a growing volume of literature on community-based forestry stemming from academics and NGOs. Analyses of socio-political aspects at local level are rare. Communities in northern Bolivia are on the verge of entering the age of community-based forestry as a result of the recent land titling process. The kind of forestry to be practiced in these settlements remains open, as well as whether and how benefits will result for the communities. To account for the heterogeneous forest user group this requires an investigation of socio-political preconditions in situ, and the manner in which they differ between settlements. Institutions and organisation at the local level, and their impact under the new legal situation on resource use and community development in the Bolivian Amazon have not been investigated in any great detail.

Formulated on the basis of the problems stated above, the aim of this research study was to meet the following objectives:

- Enhance knowledge of the manner in which decentralisation policies and resource management at local level are intertwined and what factors determine the outcome.
- Contribute to a better understanding of community, taking into account internal differences, processes and institutions with the aim to overcome universalist claims.
- Contribute to a better understanding of institutional, structural and socio-historical influences shaping forest use and the well-being of 'independent communities'.

1.3 Research Questions

In order to meet the objectives and address the problems outlined above, the investigation was guided by the following research questions:

- How do citizens in forest-dependent communities perceive decentralisation policies and the new legal framework?
- How do socio-historical factors govern citizens and their resource use at local level?
- How do citizens organise, interact and set rules within independent communities in order to secure livelihoods and well-being? What are the critical determinants?
- How are these three aspects intertwined? Are there parallels between heterogeneous communities or distinctions between similar communities?

1.4 Organisation of the dissertation

The dissertation comprises this introductory chapter with problem statement, research objectives and questions, as well as a methodology drawn on information on the study region, an overview of the theoretical approach and a section on data analysis. Three thematic chapters follow, all of which refer to divergent theoretical or analytical frameworks. Chapter 2 refers to decentralisation in the northern Bolivian Amazon, political participation at community level and how rural inhabitants perceive the new legal framework, which represents external institutional change. Chapter 3 draws on the concept of path dependency as an element of institutionalism (for definition see section 1.5.7) to analyse socio-historical aspects in community formation and resource use. The focus lies on internal rule making, indicators for the potential for community management of common property and agri'culture'. Chapter 4 draws on the combination of concepts related to social assets (with institutions) and social capital in order to analyse the capacity of the communities. Chapter five provides overall conclusions.

The following figure depicts the community as a legal unit (circle), of which four have been studied. The eyeglasses (chapter 2) represent how inhabitants perceive the new legal framework, and the arrows stand for perception and political participation, as feedback from and to this external institutional change. The assumed socio-historical influence on the community is represented by an arrow to the community (chapter 3). Over the course of time there is mutual influence, so the arrows would ultimately point in both directions, indicating a circle. As the study takes place at a certain point in time, though, in this case the direction of the arrow is only towards the community. Situated within the circle is the internal world at the time of research of the communities investigated. This implies the study of certain social assets, community performance, relative capacity and of an asset link of individuals.

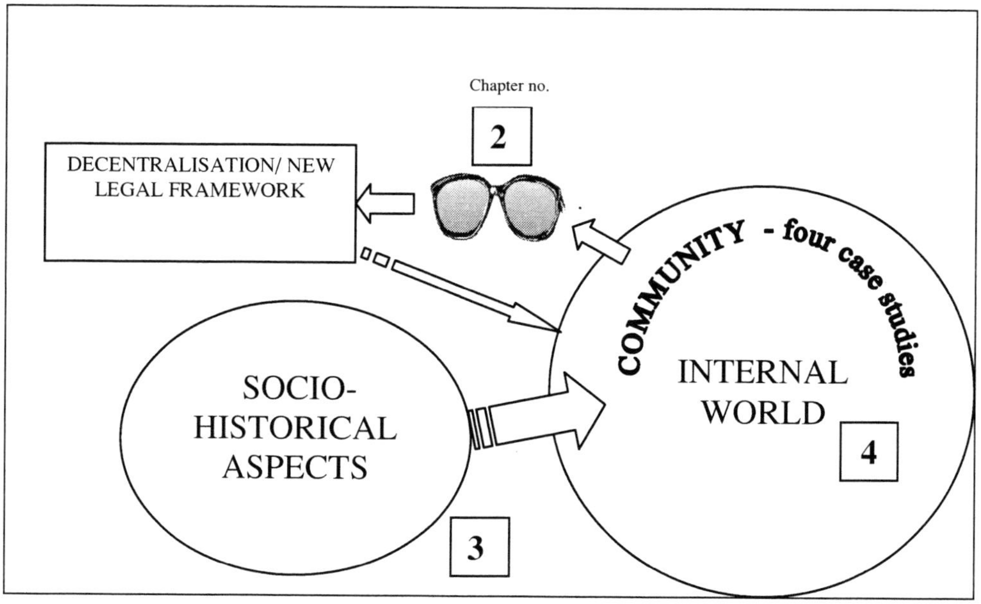

Figure 1-1: Overview of and relationship between thematic chapters

1.5 Methodology and Methods

1.5.1 General methodological aspects

Methodology in the social sciences requires the consideration of aspects related to human life:

- Structures characterise social reality and have to be considered in an appropriate way.
- 'Objective truth' changes over time.
- The objectivity of the scientist is constrained when collecting data, as the specific ideas and beliefs predominant in the society to which the scientist belongs will affect or even determine what he or she discovers.

- The assumption of deep – often hidden –structures that are the lives of human beings (and not an objective reality), which can only be addressed by a qualitative research method and an interpretative approach following the post-positivistic/post-modern paradigm.
- Field research based on interaction between the researcher and interviewees is the only method for comprehending and learning more about human existence, because the researcher as a human being is the only instrument able to 'measure' other human beings (Burgess 1984, Lave & Kvale 1995).

(Fink 2000: 5-7)

The author refutes the positivistic paradigm within social science, because it regards social reality as an objective entity and data as independent, indifferent and unconnected to the researcher who collects them (Fink 2000: 1). This may hold true in many cases in the natural sciences, but not in social research. The author favours the connivance of multiple perspectives on the same issue, which is inherent to post-modernism[12.] Certain critics claim post-modernism lacks objectivity, a view not shared by the author. Objectivity is a utopia due to the ever-present interference of the normative and personal influence of society, researcher and interviewee. However, this study follows principles which shall lead to inter-subjectivity. The aim was the attainment of knowledge independent of the author's particular perceptions. Transparency is necessary in order to successfully pursue the goal of inter-subjectivity despite hindrances. Transparency in all aspects of data collection, analysis and interpretation will help the reader to evaluate the quality of the study.

For the purposes of this study a qualitative approach was pursued, for reasons outlined above, and the nature of the research questions of 'how', but mainly due to the author's personal preference for anthropological research approaches. Quantitative questions such as 'how many' were subordinate. Qualitative and quantitative approaches can complement, not substitute each other. Here the main approach was qualitative, although there are also some quantitative elements, which were integrated to answer the proposed questions. It must be stressed that any investigation can only capture sections of reality, and sections only become meaningful if the data are collected systematically and theory-orientated (Atteslander 2000: 4). 'Systematically' means to establish rules for data collection. These rules will be outlined in the following sections. With respect to theory, the general orientation will be presented in the introductory chapter, whereas specific theoretical approaches and details are presented in the chapters 2 to 4 in association with the related empirical data.

[12] The post-modernists argued (contrary to enlightment rethoric) that rational was neither as certain nor as clear as rationalists supposed, and that knowledge was inherently linked to time, place, social position and other factors from which individuals *construct* their view of knowledge. So post-modernists called for an escape from constructed knowledge by criticising it, which leads to a deconstruction of the asserted knowledge. They encouraged fractured, fluid and multiple perspectives and were marked by an increasing importance of ideas from the sociology of knowledge (Wikipedia 2004).

1.5.2 Overview of field research

While formulating the research concept, the author had the opportunity to spend one month gathering first hand information in Bolivia through interviewing experts. Another goal of the preliminary trip was to search for collaboration partners for the later fieldwork phase. The collection of primary data took place in Bolivia over the course of one year, from August 2001 until July 2002.

After a meeting in Santa Cruz with the project coordinator Wil de Jong from Indonesia, the author established a main residence for the field phase in Riberalta, located in the Bolivian Amazon. Once in place, collaboration with the *Centro Investigación y Promoción del Campesinado Norte* - CIPCA (northern office) began. CIPCA provided a workspace in their offices, computer access and other amenities wherever possible, as well as a platform for discussion. The first months were used to attain an overview of the communities by searching databases, carrying out interviews and making fieldtrips. At the same time, guiding questions for household interviews used in the later case studies were prepared and pre-tested with members of different communities participating in a training course for chicken breeding. The four case studies began in November 2001.

The familiarisation phase was followed by research periods with several visits to the communities. The duration of a visit to a community was on average one week (from three to ten days plus two days travelling). After each stay, the author returned to Riberalta from where the next visit was undertaken with a short break in between. The four communities were visited in turns, sometimes in different orders, depending on infrastructure conditions and events that were about to take place in the communities, etc. This scheme of repeated one week stays was selected in order to demonstrate to the local people a presence, to become familiar with local conditions, and to avoid simply showing up, collecting data and disappearing again. A number of short trips to each community were preferred over a single long stay in order to facilitate visiting all four communities within the same phase of the livelihood cycle of the year like, for example, during the Brazil nut season. In the case of long-term stays, whereby one community followed the other, all four case studies would have taken place in different seasons.

After two months of community stays, the author remained for a break in Riberalta, and began to process the collected data. From mid-January to June 2002, the four communities were again visited in turns. The only interruption came when a week was spent participating in future scenario training exercises, a workshop offered by CIFOR in April in the vicinity of Santa Cruz. Apart from the case studies (for details see the section on the methodology at the village-level) and the other activities outlined, the author participated in meetings of relevance to the study subject in Riberalta whenever the opportunity arose, as well as a congress of two regional *campesino* federations, and engaged in exchanges with different organisations working with *campesino* communities. The author left Riberalta for La Paz in late June. Over the course of two weeks several organisations and libraries in La Paz and Cochabamba were visited in order to access literature locally before returning to Germany.

1.5.3 Selection criteria for case studies

The author did not select the study region in the northern Bolivian Amazon, as the location was determined by the aforementioned BMZ/CIFOR project, which had already undergone a first research phase in the region prior to the author's integration into the project. The author was drawn to the Bolivian Amazon as there is, to date, less scientific knowledge available for this region than for the Brazilian and the Peruvian Amazon.

As it was only possible to investigate a limited number of case studies, it was necessary to determine the appropriate number and subsequently select the suitable rural communities for study within the general region. Given the time frame of the fieldwork, the number of case studies was limited to four.

The rural population of the northern Bolivian Amazon is distributed amongst independent communities, of which there are some 500[13], or as labourers in *barracas* (Stoian 2000: xii). Stoian and Henkemans (2000) differentiated between six types of independent community and four types of barraca. The six community types differed on the basis of five attributes: the relative importance of paid labour, commercial agriculture and Brazil nut extraction, the ethnic composition and the existing infrastructure (Stoian 2000: 185). The four barraca types varied according to access to resources, infrastructure, social relations and labour organisation.

The definition of community employed for the purposes of this study is explained in the following: under Bolivian law, community is the smallest territorial unit of representation in the Bolivian government hierarchy and, therefore, defined in both geographic and political/administrative terms. This study adheres to this definition but with some additional conditions: a community consists of a group of people who live in the respective territorial unit. When boundaries are not yet fixed, people living on the margins and who regard themselves as members of the group located in the core area are counted also. According to the law, the smallest territorial unit of representation is denominated *Organización Territorial de Base* or *OTB*. In Bolivian parlance the term *OTB* is used synonymously with the geographical 'community' and the political representative body of this community. As the political representative body of the community, the *OTB* does not necessarily represent all of those belonging to the community, this study uses the terms community, village and rural settlement when addressing the territorial unit and/or the group of people living there. The term *OTB* is only used for the political representative body, which was legally established under the reforms in the nineties.

To select the four communities for the case studies, the following criteria were established and applied. They ensured that the selected communities covered as wide a range of the rural settlement spectrum of communities as possible:

[13] Estimate by NGOs. Other experts estimate less.

- Each community must belong to a different type within the typology developed by Stoian and Henkemans (2000).
- Each community is to be situated in a different geopolitical location with respect to a reference point (an urban centre).
- Each community should vary in size, number of families and hectares of land.
- The history of community foundation must differ.
- Internal resource access rights must differ between the communities.

The reason for the inclusion of the widest possible range of communities was to secure the representation of different community types across the rural spectrum in the research area and to provide a broader insight.

Although the research objectives of this study relate to communities, the research questions relate to citizens. The methodological motivations for this were:

- The geographical unit and legal body 'community' is a microsystem, which consists of a group of individuals, the 'citizens'.
- For the success of 'in-depth' case studies, it is methodologically more fruitful and exact to have smaller units of investigation (individuals as representatives of households) and then aggregate data than it is to collect data directly at the community level (e.g. through group interviews). Moreover, there is no such entity 'community' that could be directly and adequately addressed for the purpose of this analysis.
- For further insights and data triangulation with respect to objectivity, reliability and validity, household interviews were supplemented with participation in meetings and other activities in order to grasp elements of (inter)action within the microsystem community.
- Conclusions have been drawn from data obtained from the investigation unit 'citizens' living within one community, as well as the (inter)action observed amongst them. Conclusions based on communities with a higher number of inhabitants are statistically less representative for the total community than is the case for smaller communities, as the ratio of data collection in this study was higher in the smaller communities. Data are not representative, but relevant. This holds especially true for individual statements on networks etc. However, data on community organisations and institutions, as well as community performance, have validity without the necessity of complete data collection from all citizens (or households respectively).

The author first chose one urban centre from the two important centres as a reference point; Riberalta in the Beni Department, and Cobija in the Pando Department[14]. Subsequent to the four week trip to Bolivia during the formulation of the concept the choice fell on Riberalta

[14] The third urban centre in the Bolivian Amazon region, Guajaramirín, is of minor importance in many respects in comparison to Riberalta and Cobija.

due to better availability of data on rural communities. Moreover, the CIPCA[15] Norte team in Riberalta expressed its willingness to collaborate with the project (which was not evident to the same extent from other organisations contacted in Cobija). However, both urban centres would have served the purposes of the investigation.

In order to address the fact that the majority of all rural settlements in the Bolivian Amazon are located in the Pando Department, the author fixed a quota of three case studies in the Pando Department and one in the Beni Department. With respect to criterion number two (geopolitical location), Riberalta, which is located close to the department border with Pando, was the reference point for all four communities, each with varying travelling distances respectively degrees of remoteness.

The selection of the communities included several steps. First, the researcher took part in a project distributing tools and seedlings to the communities along the River Beni affected by a flood catastrophe during the previous rainy season, with the aim of becoming familiar with the reality of the region[16]. Then an intensive search for communities meeting the established criteria began. For this, the author consulted different databases. Stoian prepared one for his study from 2000, which covered a part of the existing settlements. CIPCA Norte compiled the other. This organisation had a database on communities covering several hundred settlements, yet was still incomplete. No single complete database for the whole region existed in 2001. Moreover, the databases consulted did not provide all of the information necessary to apply all of the criteria. Therefore, the author had to interview various individuals with knowledge of rural communities, such as native people with family links to the rural area, representatives of other NGOs working there, etc. If a community was found to meet some of the criteria, more information on the community was sought through interviews with experts familiar with the particular community, in order to check that the other criteria were also met. Communities that did not appear in the database were also sought by asking people whether they knew a community with certain features. By means of the described selection process, the communities for the following analysis were found.

[15] Centro de Investigación y Promoción del Campesinado, Bolivia. National NGO with six offices, one of which is located in Riberalta, northern Bolivia.

[16] The researcher already had practical experience in another part of the Beni Department garnered during four months of field research carried out for a diploma thesis.

1.5.4 Research methods at village level

The stays in the community were characterised by the use of the method of qualitative observation. Bortz and Döring (1995: 297) highlighted the properties of this method:

- Observation in the natural environment of the interviewees
- Active participation of the observer in everyday life
- Concentration on major units and behaviour patterns
- Openness for new insights

This qualitative observation technique is especially useful when the research object is embedded in a social situation, the object is barely visible from outside and the set of questions is of a more explorative nature (Mayring 1999: 64). Since these criteria are met by the research questions presented, qualitative observation made up one important pillar of this study. During research a field book was used to note observations and information that was provided in informal talks, etc.

The other important pillar was household interviews, as well as future scenario exercises. Investigation in the field is a process that can be divided into different steps, the first of which is particularly important (*ibid.* 41, Weinberg and Williams 1973, Girtler 1984, Burgess 1984). To place the process in a broader picture, the role of the researcher changes from intruder at the beginning to that of a community visitor and finally to that of an advocate (*ibid.* 41). The following sections provide an insight in the embeddedness of the investigation process.

Introduction of the researcher to the communities

Once the communities were selected using the aforementioned criteria, a first contact was established with a community authority by radio. This was followed by a reconnaissance trip to the community. The purpose was to present the researcher to the community inhabitants and to receive official permission from their assembly to live in their community for a while and to carry out a study. This approach was applied in three communities. In the fourth (where no such assembly existed or could be called – El Sena), the purpose of the visit was announced to the authorities and permission was sought, and an explanation was given to individuals.

The researcher emphasised her status as a student, writing a thesis funded by means of a scholarship, and conceived independently of any local influences, but with infrastructural support provided by the NGO CIPCA. It was important to point out the academic nature of the study in order to avoid raising expectations in the settlements that there might be a material benefit to the community as a result of the project. Furthermore, the aspect of the student learning from the community was stressed. As far as possible, the researcher tried to give something in return for everything provided by the interviewees, for example responding to all their questions, etc.

One case study community (San Juan km 27) collaborated frequently with the NGO providing the researcher with infrastructural support. Therefore, the inhabitants perceived the researcher as some kind of colleague of the team. The fact that the community was located near Riberalta and the inhabitants occasionally paid visits to the office reinforced this perception. Since the perception of this NGO was overwhelmingly positive in the community, this posed no apparent disadvantages for the research. Nevertheless, this can imply a bias. In fact, it appeared that people were more willing to cooperate.

In two other communities, which at the time of research were both difficult to access due to the lack of infrastructure (means of transportation, as well as roads), the researcher arrived on the first occasion in vehicles provided by the NGO. In both communities, cooperation with this particular NGO had been very low or only started at the same time as the research carried out for this study (Trinidadcito/Loma Velarde). They were aware of the difficult transport situation and had more contact with the researcher than with any NGO representative. Subsequent transport was organised by other means and, therefore, they did not perceive a very close link to the NGO. If this was the case, it was perceived positively due to the help expected from that organisation. Only one person in Loma Velarde was mistrustful of the researcher's intentions. However, this former *patron* also proved courteous when urging the researcher to erect her tent on his property directly by the wharf immediately upon arrival in the community. People throughout the study area received the researcher well. Due to their remote location they seldom received visitors and were quick to express their pleasure. After a few days, it was made clear that living on the grounds of the former patron does not mean any bias in favour of this person. People were aware of his custom to house all visitors from outside the community.

In Trinidadcito the welcome was open and friendly. After seeking the permission of all the inhabitants at a meeting, the author was invited to come back soon in order to participate in the annual community anniversary celebrations. Through participation in this event, which was also attended by regional politicians and personnel from two municipalities, the researcher gained many insights valuable for the research. The inhabitants drew up a diversified cultural programme into which the researcher was integrated. After this event, peoples' doors were always open to the researcher and trust had been established.

In El Sena, on the other hand, the position of the researcher was unclear. As the community did not dispose of an assembly incorporating all of the local population, it was only possible to transmit information about the study to individuals initially. The former *patrón* was sceptical of research in the community. After open talks about the study, he expressed his discomfort with the planned household interviews[17]. This uneasy position influenced data collection in many ways, some people close to this person were wary of providing any information. Other people regarded the interview as means to discuss things they were

[17] On one occasion, upon seeing the researcher leave a house carrying questionnaires, he asked cynically, "What did you spy out today?" (Author's translation).

unhappy about, but had previously lacked the opportunity to express. To sum up, the inhabitants' perception of the researcher was polarised.

The role of the researcher in the communities

The researcher's introduction to the community has been outlined briefly already. The reaction of the inhabitants was influenced by their perception of the researcher. It was claimed earlier that every human being's view of the world is influenced by the beliefs and norms of the society to which they belong. The scope of this claim is even broader when one is referring to human beings stemming from different cultures. In this study, a female researcher arrives from a rich European country, where equal opportunities for men and women are not absolute, but in an advanced state. Perceptions of what role a woman can and should fulfil are flexible. Bolivia, on the other hand, is a country with many different cultures, and as everywhere else in the world there are always individuals who do not share the attitudes of others within the same group of people. In spite of this high degree of heterogeneity the author dares to suggest that in the *campesino* communities of the northern Bolivian Amazon the arrival of a *gringa*[18] constitutes something exceptional, and draws attention. Especially when she comes from so far away, travels alone, stays in the village and poses questions.

Conscious of the fact that the researcher will always remain in some kind of exceptional position in the eyes of the community inhabitants, it was at the same time necessary to do everything possible to adapt to and integrate into village life in order to make these disparities smoother, become accepted and trusted, and leave a positive impression on the people who provided their time, knowledge and hospitality. The transport used corresponded to that of the locals – which sometimes implied two day trips by motorbike, boat or truck in the rainy season in order to reach the village. Accommodation was a tent erected either on communal ground or the property of a family. In both cases food was always shared with a family, provided alternately by either the researcher or the family and prepared together. One might argue that this led other inhabitants to perceive a bias in favour of one family, but this did not appear to be the case; primarily because it was recognised that the researcher was not reliant upon any particular family for food and accommodation. Indeed, the locals would have perceived it as strange if a visitor were to dine in isolation; integration into a family coincides with the local culture. In any case, over the course of the fieldwork the researcher was afforded the opportunity to dine with different families, without ever changing campsite. The researcher also brought presents including cooking oil, sugar, salt and coca leaves, items used by most *campesino* families. Oil, sugar and salt can generally only be purchased in urban centres, or from intermediaries at high prices or through barter, meaning that the local people welcome these kinds of present. The same is true for exercise books for the schoolchildren.

[18] The term *gringo*, or *gringa* (female) is used as term for a foreigner in Latin America, especially a North American or British person. Sometimes it can be used as a disparaging term. People in the Bolivian lowlands refer to every foreigner (not necessarily North American or English) as *gringo*. Depending on the context it is used in a neutral, negative or even positive way.

The researcher always endeavoured to maintain a neutral position in conflict situations such as quarrels between inhabitants. In the case of invitations to religious events, it seemed important to emphasise respect for all of the different congregations and to accept invitations issued by each of them. Whenever opportunities arose, the researcher partook in social activities such as playing the role of spectator at the communities' weekend football events together with local women, as well as birthday and community celebrations, school events, etc. At political level, the researcher was permitted to attend all communal meetings that took place within the timeframe of the research. These meetings provided a valuable basis for this study as did other events, which provided information through informal talks and observation. Practical insights into livelihood activities were gained through participation in the planting of seedlings and the trip to a Brazil nut recollection centre.

As a woman, the researcher was able to establish good contact to female interviewees without any problems. Nor was there any major impediment to the interviews with the men, although some were not used to discussing with a female student the issues broached in the interviews. The only limitation posed by gender was on activities like fishing in Trinidadcito. Many of the local men embark on fishing trips lasting several days and return only for weekends. This also made it more difficult to interview the fishermen because on Saturdays they were engaged in community work, and on Sundays they went to mass, and wanted to relax spending time with their families (and in certain cases were inebriated). It was not possible to accompany the fishermen during the week as this would have been contrary to accepted cultural behaviour, and may have had negative repercussions for a female researcher in the community, possibly even causing conflicts with the fishermen's spouses. In order to find out more about the local fishing practice, a student engaged in an anthropological study in a neighbouring indigenous community, under the auspices of the same University of Freiburg project, accompanied the men on one such fishing trip and collected data on behalf of the researcher. Although the fishermen's association is closed to non-associates, they granted the researcher permission to participate in their meetings in the community.

Research activities in the communities

As mentioned previously, several field trips were made to each of the selected communities with an average duration of one week. The participation in the meetings organised by the community representative bodies, and in the case of El Sena also at municipality level, proved a valuable source of information. The meetings of other associations were also beneficial. The participation in social events such as festivities and sports facilitated the integration of the researcher into the community. These issues were elements of the constant qualitative observation during the stays. Another important pillar on which this study was based were the household interviews. As a supplementary source of information, in two communities the author applied the method of future scenario exercises in the form of a community workshop. Informal talks held within and outside the community helped in the re-evaluation and reinforcement of the collected data and improved the understanding of the overall context.

Qualitative observation

The method of qualitative observation is one important pillar for the obtainment of empirical data for this study. It was used frequently during the researcher's stay in the communities. It made it possible to get to know people, attain insights into dynamics, shared meanings and conflicts of the setting, which are necessary to understand the social world and parts of its complexity. As the researcher is there as another human being and a further element of the overall setting, there are interrelations between the observer and the observed.

The most valuable data for answering the research questions was provided by the participation in community meetings, to observe discussions, relationships and decision-making processes. In each community the frequency of such meetings varied. The researcher was permitted to participate in all meetings taking place during the research period. Apart from meetings in the form of assemblies, the researcher had the opportunity to make qualitative observations on various other occasions. These included the annual community foundation celebrations where politicians and other influential individuals visit the respective community, municipal planning workshops, meetings in the community organised by externals such as NGOs, religious events and services, meetings of professional associations, sports events, communal bingo evenings, birthday celebrations, etc. On a more individual level, qualitative observation took place during every day life in the community. The researcher made notes of observations in a field book, usually in the tent when no one was present in order to avoid making the subjects feel uncomfortable.

Household interviews

Bender (1967) pointed out the importance of segregating the concepts of family and household, and within the concept of household differentiating between the co-residence and the domestic function of a group. In the case of the field study it turned out that in most cases co-residence and domestic functions – for example, the satisfaction of daily needs like supply and preparation of food – coincided within one household; this was not the case for one family. In many cases family members belonged to different households as they were from different generations, were married, etc. For this reason, the household approach to interviews was chosen. In order to avoid causing undue stress in the households, only one person was interviewed per household (for selection criteria see later in this section).

The four case study communities varied in terms of inhabitant numbers. The following table gives an overview over the community size in terms of families and households, as well as the number of household interviews with the respective coverage in percent. While the numbers for three communities are reliable, it was not possible to determine the real number of families and households in El Sena due to different data derived from different sources of information. Due to the size of the community it was not possible for the researcher to carry out an independent census.

Table 1-2: Households per community covered by sample

	Families	**Households**	**Household Interviews (N)**	**Coverage from total households in%[19]**
El Sena	~ 80 to 120	~ 90	30	33
Loma Velarde	13	9	9	100
San Juan km 27	32	27	23	85
Trinidadcito	67	45	30	67

***Note: The total number of households interviewed in the aforementioned form was** n=92.*

Data were collected on the basis of stratified sampling. The entire population (households) was divided into geographic subgroups, and then a random sample was taken from each subgroup

The stratification of households into subgroups ensured that households from all 'quarters' or parts of the sometimes widespread communities were taken into account. The interviews were consequently not concentrated on households close to the community centre

In order to divide all households into geographically defined subgroups, the author drew up community housing maps in collaboration with community members and on the basis of existing information obtained, for example, from the authorities. This complete inventory of the community households ensured that no household was omitted, for example, due to its remote location in the forest. In the case of El Sena, the exact number of households is not known. However, the author possessed a map of the community provided by the municipality, which was supplemented with other information on the locations of houses.

The sole condition for the selection of the one and only interview partner from amongst all the members of each household was that the person be at least 16 years of age. If there was only one person at home, this person was interviewed. If there were several options, the household members decided who was to be interviewed. In most cases, this was the male or female head of the household.

In order to ensure equal representation of the genders the author sought to interview as many men as women. Due to practical limitations, however, this quota was only partially met:

Table 1-3: Gender ratio of interviewees

	Female	Male
El Sena	n=13	n=17
Loma Velarde	n=5	n=4
San Juan km 27	n=9	n=14
Trinidadcito	n=15	n=15

[19] Rounded value.

An average household consisted of two adults and several children. However, the scope ranged from one adult to four adults, from zero to 13 children.

The following table provides the average interviewee household size per community. The right column shows the range of the number of people living within the sampled households in each community:

Table 1-4: Average household size

	Average size of sampled households (number of people)[20]	Number of people in sampled households
El Sena	6	3-11
Loma Velarde	7	2-12
San Juan km 27	6	1-10
Trinidadcito	7	3-15

All interviews were carried out by the researcher personally, without an assistant. The authority claim made by the researcher (in adherence to Bortz/Döring 1995: 217) was 'soft' (low). The degree of standardisation of the interviews can be summed up as semi-structured. However, the interviews also contained some strongly structured parts such as the personal data of the interviewees (date of birth, sex, etc.) and some unstructured elements (such as migration history of the interviewee).

The questionnaire used by the researcher was pre-tested with inhabitants of other communities in order to eradicate questions that were likely to be either misunderstood or not understood at all. As many people in rural communities in Bolivia can neither read nor write, the interviews were carried out orally. The researcher read from the questionnaire and wrote the answers down during the interview. This did not appear to cause any discomfort for the interviewees. The interview language was Spanish. The interviewees did not belong to a specific indigenous population, but can be denominated *mestizos*; Spanish was their mother tongue. The researcher spoke Spanish fluently so communication problems were limited to general misunderstandings and colloquialisms. The language employed and the formulation of the questions was adapted to local conditions and the interviewees. The household interviews lasted an hour and a half on average; the shortest lasted 45 minutes, the longest nearly two hours.

Depending on the interview situation, the researcher intended to cover all topics as far as these were relevant to each particular interviewee. Questions pertaining to agricultural plots were left out if the interviewee had none. The questions were not adhered too rigidly, rather there was room to speak openly about issues covered by other questions later in the questionnaire, or to even bring in new aspects. However, if the content drifted too far from the original design, the researcher intervened subtly to bring the discussion back on track. The

[20] Rounded value.

questions asked were a mixture of open and closed questions, with open questions the more frequent.

The content of the questionnaire was divided into six segments:

a) Personal and household data and migration history
b) Organisations (membership, internal rules)
c) Property rights and natural resources
   (resource endowment, plot description and production)
d) Leadership (governance issues, trust)
e) New legislation (information, external rules, decentralisation)
f) Strategy and networks

There are very different approaches used to assess property rights, and some of them may lead to a misleading description of real circumstances because they do not consider the complexity and differences between tenure types. Moreover, it is necessary to identify links between natural resource tenures and the performance or behaviour of resource users. In order to cope with these problems, the author chose a concept, which incorporated the relevant attributes of tenure and accommodated the behavioural consequences of the existing variety of tenure types. Kundhlande and Luckert (2001)[21] presented a concept consisting of eleven characteristics, which provided a framework facilitating the linking of tenure to economic behaviour. The questions posed in relation to tenure issues addressed the eleven characteristics: Comprehensiveness, Exclusiveness, Use Designation, Duration, Allotment Type, Size, Transferability, Fees, Operational Requirements, Operational Control, and Security. A definition for each of these characteristics can be found in annex 1. The author used these eleven characteristics for the drafting of questions contained in the property rights segment of the questionnaire suitable in the research context.

Future scenario exercises

Scenarios "(...) are tools for planning and decision-making that are appropriate for situations where complexity and uncertainty are high (situations that typically characterise the management of tropical forest ecosystems)" (Nemarundwe et al. 2003: 9). The researcher applied future scenario exercises in two communities as an additional element in the final phase of data collection.

The application of these scenarios in the research communities took place as a means of doing something potentially beneficial for the community on the one hand, and at the same time useful for the researcher by providing practical insights into current trends and future options from the community inhabitants' point of view. The scenario workshops provided a forum for discussion and reflection. Afterwards the researcher invited community inhabitants to a communal meal to thank them for their time and hospitality during the research.

[21] Building on work carried out by Haley and Luckert (1990) and Scott and Johnson (1983).

1.6 Study Region

The study region is the northern Bolivian Amazon. This northern part of Bolivia is bordered by Peru to the west, and Brazil to the north and east. Although two thirds of Bolivia is located in the Amazon Basin, moist evergreen tropical forests can only be found in the northern part of the country. The region is home to Bolivia's rubber and Brazil nut resources and covers an expanse of about 100,000 km². On an administrative level the area comprises the entire Departamento de Pando with its five provinces, as well as the province Vaca Diez in the Departamento del Beni and the province Iturralde in the Departamento de La Paz.

The study area has an estimated population of about 160,000 people, two thirds of which live in one of the three towns, Cobija, Guayaramerín or Riberalta[22]. The remaining third lives in the rural areas of the region. Only 5% are considered indigenous, the majority of the population being *mestizos*; offspring of migrants, who came to the region during the rubber boom, in many cases of European origin, and traditional indigenous inhabitants.

In view of the very low population density and the great distance to larger markets, the pressure on forest resources is still relatively low[23]. About 90%[24] of the land surface is covered by mostly intact forest. The remaining 10% is forest fallow, agricultural and pastoral land, water bodies, patches of savannas and urban spaces. The number of rural settlements (*barracas* included) is an estimated 700, of which two thirds are permanently inhabited (Stoian 1999).

At present, the main economic activity in the region is the extraction, processing and exportation of Brazil nuts with an export value of about 30 million dollars per year. During the harvesting season, the inhabitants of rural settlements and seasonal migrant workers from urban areas extract Brazil nuts from the forests, which then are processed for exportation in urban areas. In the Bolivian Amazon, resource use takes place under adverse circumstances, such as the lack of infrastructure, limited access to health services and education, low incomes, food shortages and the highly volatile nature of the global markets for NTFPs, upon which the economy of the whole region relies. The trade in internationally marketed NTFPs (rubber and Brazil nuts, as well as quinine and palm hearts in certain periods) has shaped the economy of the northern Bolivian Amazon for about two hundred years and is likely to do so for many years to come.

Rural settlements were in the past characterised by a close dependency relationship between collectors and the *patrones*, the *de facto* owners of natural resources in a *barraca*; a system prevalent in the first half of the twentieth century when mainly rubber was extracted, which was in effect a feudal system. Today, rural settlements are heterogeneous and range from

[22] The population of Riberalta exceeds 70,000 (Census 2001).

[23] The pressure is rising, however, due to road construction projects and resource deprivation in other parts of the country, as well as immigration into the region.

[24] Stoian (2000) mentioned 94% based on data from 1992; 90% is a value currently deemed realistic by experts.

small and large-sized *barracas*, whose owners struggle for legal status under the reforms, to independent communities, whose inhabitants' access to land and forest resources on common property has been legalised. If they comply with the requirements set by law, communities can benefit from the distribution of land, the area of which is calculated on the basis of the number of families living in the respective community.

The region is embedded in a national process of reforms, which have brought about decentralisation, as well as reform laws pertaining to the land, forests and other aspects of life such as education. After a long absence of the state from the region, the implementation of the reforms in the region has started and is creating new roles, opportunities and obligations for all stakeholders in the area.

Information in relation to the reform laws, regional history and other details relevant for this study on rural forest-dependent communities of the type 'independent' community will be presented in the respective thematic chapters. For a detailed analysis of institutional change and aspects in relation to the different stakeholders involved in regional forest use, as well as conflicts between them, see Ruiz 2005 (in preparation).

The locations of the four selected case studies are indicated on two maps with Riberalta as the reference point. Map 1 shows the location of Riberalta and the case study community El Sena. Map 2 shows the location of Riberalta and of the other three case study communities, Loma Velarde, San Juan km 27 and Trinidadcito.

Map 1 The northern Bolivian Amazon, comprising the Department of Pando, the Province of Vaca Diez (Beni Department) and the northernmost part of the Province of Iturralde (La Paz Department)

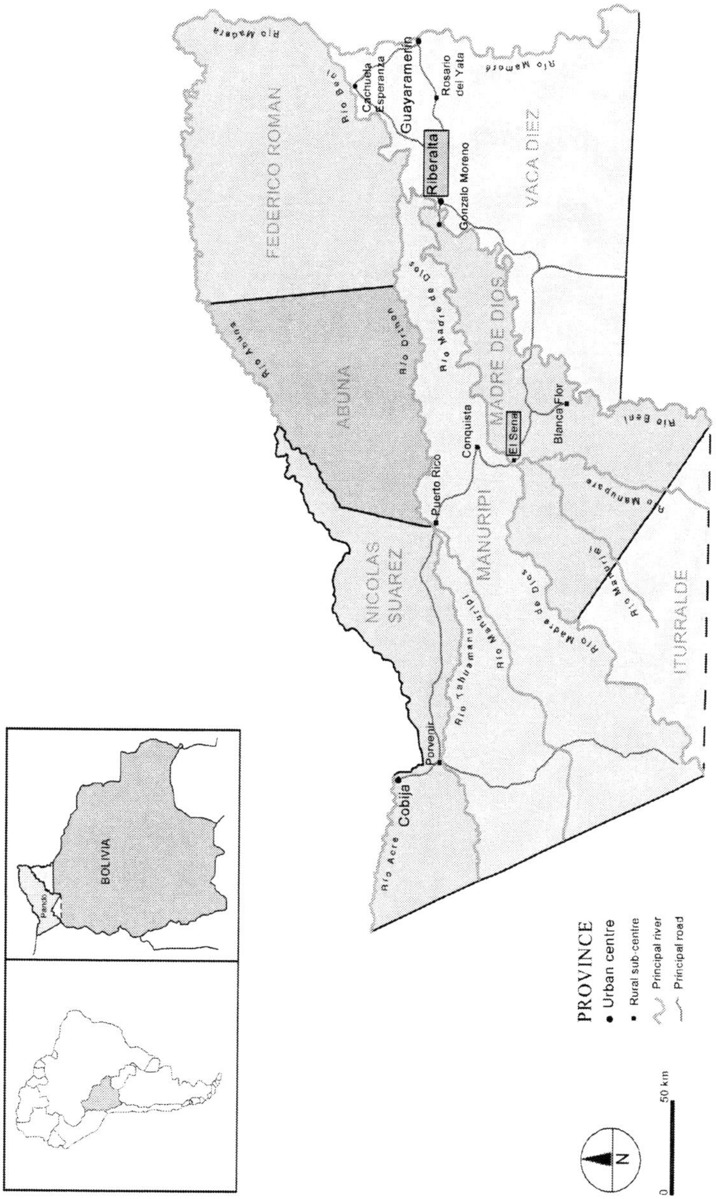

Note:
Riberalta, the reference point for the study, is highlighted as is El Sena, where one of the case studies took place. The location of the other three case study communities can be seen in map 2, Map by Stoian (2000: 48)

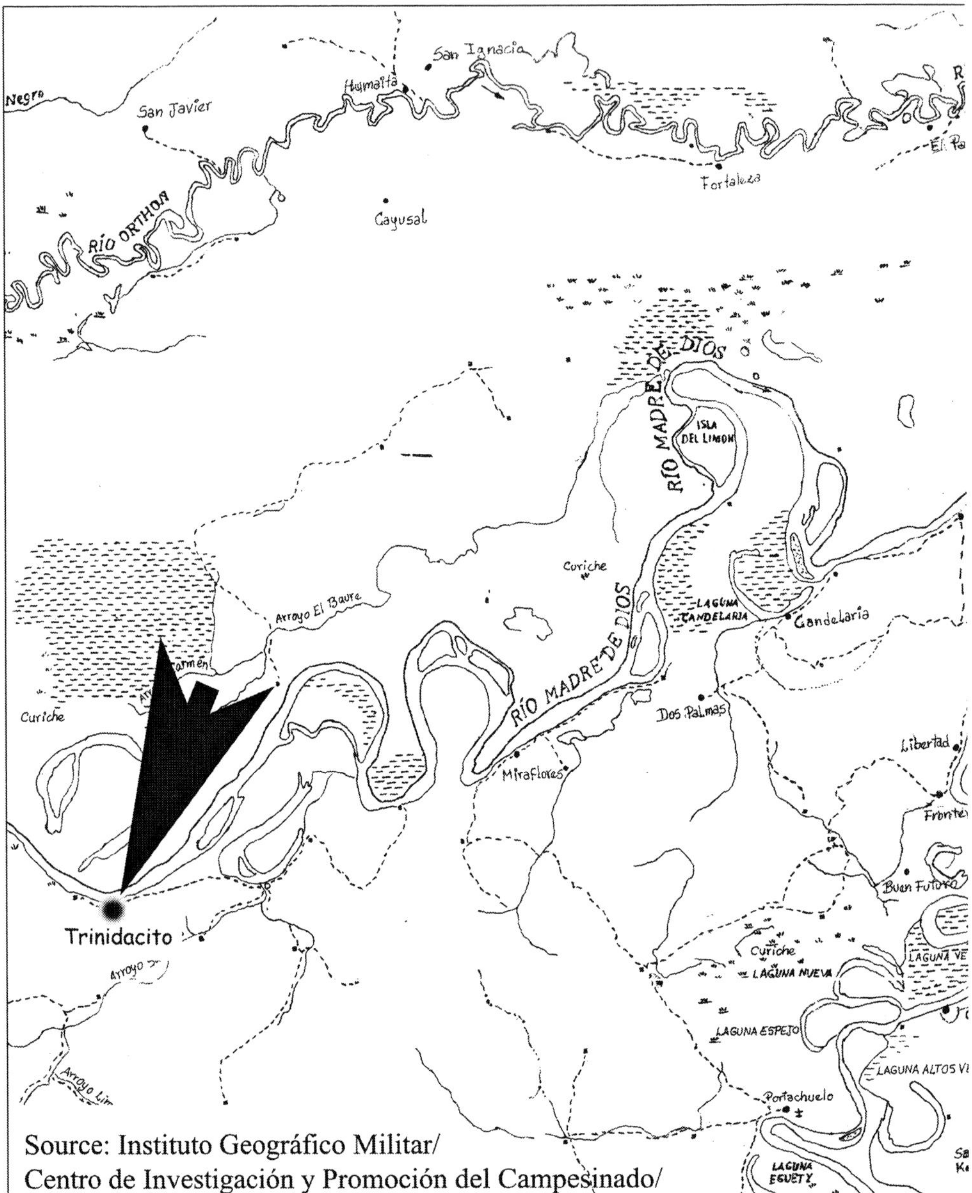

Map 2 Location of three research communities and reference point Riberalta

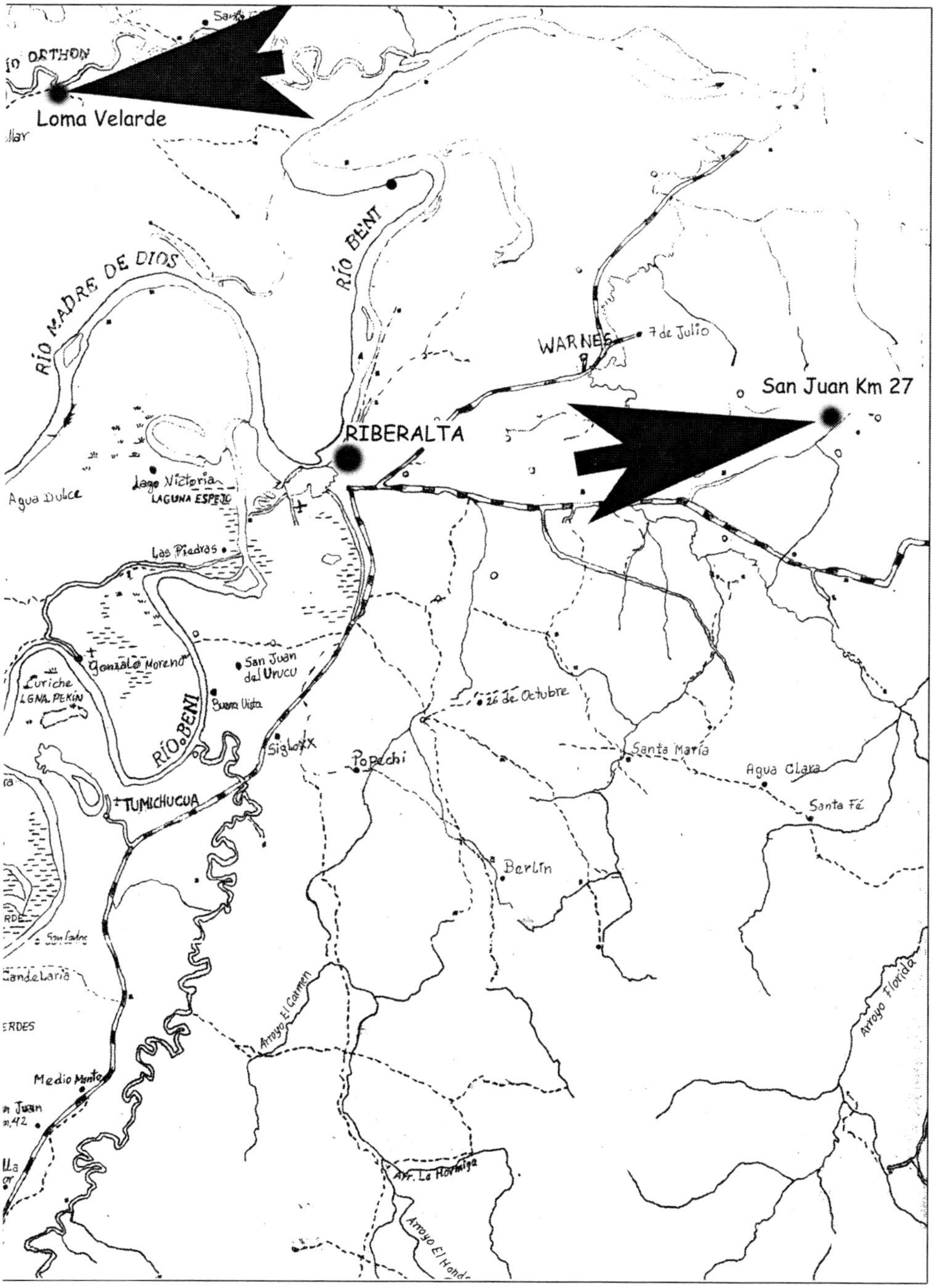
RÍO ORTHON
Loma Velarde
RÍO BENI
RÍO MADRE DE DIOS
WARNES
7 de Julio
San Juan Km 27
RIBERALTA
Lago Victoria
LAGUNA ESPEJO
Agua Dulce
Las Piedras
Gonzalo Moreno
San Juan del Urucu
Curiche
LGNA. PEKIN
Buena Vista
RÍO BENI
Siglo XX
Popechi
26 de Octubre
Santa María
Agua Clara
Santa Fé
TUMICHUCUA
Berlin
Candelaria
Arroyo El Carmen
Arroyo Florida
Medio Monte
Arr. La Hormiga
Arroyo El Hondo

1.7 Theoretical framework

The theoretical framework of this study combines different theoretical approaches, mostly related to institutions. The reason for this was the results of previous research identifying the lack of knowledge of institutions and organisation among people living in rural forest-dependent settlements in the Bolivian Amazon, and at the same time recognition that local institutions and organisation are assumed to be important to the outcomes of the reforms, resource use and their potential role in poverty alleviation.

As this study addresses different research questions and follows different objectives, specific approaches were selected (corresponding to different thematic chapters) and were combined. This theoretical framework provides an overview of aspects of institutions-related theory that are generally relevant to this study. However, each of the three thematic chapters will provide specific theoretical information on the approaches applied. This is especially true for chapter four, where the research goes beyond institutions. Therefore it contains an extensive theoretical part on social capital, social assets and capabilities, and functioning.

Definition of Institution

Neo-institutionalists (for example, North 1986; 1990; 1991; Eggertson 1990) and common property theorists[25] (for example, Ostrom 1994; 1997) view institutions as property rights, rules of conduct, and more formalised regulations and laws; in short instruments that condition behaviour in the economic and social sphere. Commons wrote as early as 1931, "the difficulty in defining a field for the so-called institutional economics is the uncertainty of the meaning of an institution" (*ibid.*: 1). Nabli and Nugent (1989: 1335) defined an institution as "(…) a set of constraints, which governs the behavioural relations among individuals or groups". One of the most frequently cited definitions is that of North (1990: 3): "Institutions are the rules of the game in a society or, more formally, are the human devised constraints that shape human interaction." Lin and Nugent (1995: 2306) expanded upon their definition from 1989 to include "a set of humanly devised behavioural rules that govern and shape interactions of human beings, in part by helping them to form expectations of what other people will do. In so constraining behaviour, institutions may be reflected in the appearance of certain behavioural regularities or norms". According to Mummert (1999: 2), institutions are "commonly shared rules that are endowed with an enforcement mechanism" and which play a central role in mediating environment-society relationships such as natural resource use. The connection between institutions and resource use also plays a role in the considerations of Leach et al. (1999: 236), which is not directly evident in their more general definition of institutions as "regularised patterns of behaviour between individuals and groups in society". Whereas North emphasised that these rules are constraints that shape human interaction, Lin and Nugent emphasised that these rules help to form expectations of the behaviour of others. These views do not contradict one another, but simply reflect a different

[25] New Institutionalism, New Institutional Economics and Common Property all relate to institutions, but combine with different fields of science.

perspective. When fitted with an effective enforcement mechanism, institutions regulate human interaction in all kinds of aspects.

Institutions have the function to economise: In the ideal case they allow one or more of the agents to improve their welfare without making others worse off. They also allow them to attain a higher level of their objectives within their constraints. Within this basic economising function they perform the function of risk and uncertainty reduction. Institutions play a key role in redistribution matters, for example, private law concerning property rights. All these functions are interdependent of each other.

In this study, the author adhered to the general basis shared by all these definitions, namely institutions as rules of conduct, regulations and laws. Organisations are not included in the definition of institutions, but treated separately. Organisations imply actors/people and can be regarded as the bearers and enforcers of rules and regulations. Each organisation usually disposes of institutions, though, as do networks. For the purposes of the study, the consideration of institutions, organisations and organisation is crucial. In the Bolivian Amazon one encountered rural forest-dependent communities whose inhabitants were faced with new legal rules and at the same time disposed of local rules established by local authorities or the inhabitants themselves. The reforms in many cases required changes to the local forms of organisation; but internal organisation and resource use regulations, as well as the question of whether the community attracted projects and developed, depended on the inhabitants themselves.

It is useful to distinguish between formal and informal institutions. Formal institutions shall be defined here as rules made by the state; in other words laws, decrees, regulations, etc., which usually exist in a written form. Informal institutions are 'private' rules, made by the citizens, and exist in either oral or written form. However, these are two extremes on a continuum, with some variations in between. Particularly in developing countries, informal institutions are more common than formal ones (North 1992: 43). Whereas a change of formal institutional arrangements can take place quickly, a change of informal institutions usually takes more time as these relate to aspects such as tradition, culture, religion and power structures. The relationship between formal and informal institutions may be neutral, supplementary, strengthening or conflictive. While the state approves and enforces formal institutions to solve collective action problems, informal rules emerge from society as an outcome of conflicts, such as benefit distribution, and are enforced through ongoing social relationships (Knight 1992: 123-124; Nee and Ingram 1998: 19 *et seqq.*, Ibarra 2002: 63). Their enforcement and monitoring occurs within the group as a by-product of social action (Nee 1998: 86-87). It is assumed that as mere mortals the actors cannot understand completely their environment, nor do they possess an entirely logical mode of conduct. They act according to their perceptions and experience (Mummert 1995: 53).

Williamson provided an overview of institutions-related research by proposing a four-level structure for social analysis:

Table 1-5: Four level structure of social analysis

Level	Feature	Related theory*
Level 1	INFORMAL INSTITUTIONS	Social theory
Level 2	FORMAL INSTITUTIONS	Positive political theory/ Economics of property rights
Level 3	GOVERNANCE STRUCTURES	Transaction cost economics
Level 4	RESSOURCE ALLOCATION AND EMPLOYMENT	Neoclassical economics/agency theory

Source: Adapted from Williamson 2000: 597 ****indicated by Williamson***

In the theories indicated on the right, institutions perform a different role due to different underlying assumptions. So there is an intersection of vast lines of investigations, the majority of which are interdisciplinary and allow synergy-effects. Williamson's list is not exhaustive, nor are the theoretical delineations sharp. However, the structuring of institutions into four social analysis levels is useful in the wide field of institutions-related research. This structure provides approaches facilitating an understanding of the existence, formation and evolution of institutions, which could not be explained by the assumptions of neoclassical theory because of the existence of bounded rationality, incomplete information, changing preferences, trust, multiple equilibriums and dynamics, non-repetitive choices, etc.

The research agenda of this study refers to pan-disciplinary research related to institutions and focuses more on social than economic aspects. Therefore, the term 'Institutionalism' is favoured over 'Institutional Economics'26. As institutionalism can be misunderstood and is also used to refer to the early institutionalist schools, the author would like to clarify that in the context of this study the term institutionalism refers to theoretical approaches related to institutions from different branches as developed to date.

[26] Institutional Economics is connected with the names Hamilton, Veblen, Mitchell and Commons. The first use of the term is recorded to have been in a paper entitled 'The Institutional Approach to Economic Theory' by Walton H. Hamilton in 1918 (Tool 1993: 14). He regarded neoclassical economics as too mechanistic because it tried to encompass economic activity in a set of principles that implied an equilibrium postulate. Veblen and Mitchell were also inherently opposed to mechanistic equilibriums, the common emphasis of all lies on process (Tool 1993: 15). Each sought in his own way for an approach that was man more germane to the economic problems of the day. John Commons enumerated the various aspects that appear to be related to institutional economics and their diversity. The ultimate unit of economic investigation is a relation of to man (*ibid.* 3). Commons, as a social scientist, was influenced by the German Historical School and was convinced that 'sound economic analysis had to be grounded in a set of societal values' (Tool 1993: 16). Thorstein Veblen, John R. Commons, Wesley Mitchell and Clarence Ayres represent the earlier Institutionalist School as an important forerunner of New Institutional Economics. The term 'New Institutional Economics' was introduced explicitly for the first time in the work of Oliver Williamson in 1975 (Döring 1998: 8).

This study focuses on rural forest-dependent communities. They are settlements and they are legal bodies characterised by rules and human actors. Rural communities in the Bolivian Amazon are characterised by local community rules and 'external' rules. The use of institutions-related approaches shall provide insights into the shape of institutions, their interaction and factors that influence their evolution. If institutions are applied, they have effects as they coordinate action in relation to resource use, etc. In the following, issues discussed in the institutional literature and important within the study setting will be presented.

Common property

Within the new legal framework, rural communities in the Bolivian Amazon had the opportunity to obtain titles to land which they already had access to, and to demand further entitlement to land by means of a surveying and redistribution process. The natural resources accessed in this way are a common pool resource belonging to the community, which consists of various families. In the context of natural resource use and institutions, common property regimes received much attention in the nineties as a potentially suitable means of resource management. These common property regimes managed to overcome Hardin's 'Tragedy of the commons' by distinguishing between open access regimes and common pool resources. Common property theory emanated from the assumption that common property management allows for a controlled use of natural resources if the group is organised and designs and enforces rules (Arnold 1998; De Jong 1999). Particular circumstances are needed if such institutional arrangements are to operate successfully (Ostrom 1990). In the study area, by law peasant communities generally hold land and natural resources as common pool resources. Whether they manage this common pool resource under a common property regime depends on different factors. This study shall contribute to clarifying the relevant ones.

Property Rights

The essay 'The Problem of Social Cost' by Coase, published in 1960, in which he pointed to the existence of external effects, is regarded as the basis for the property rights debate. A systematic development was undertaken by Alchian and Demsetz, as well as Furubotn and Pejovich (Döring 1998: 12). A property right is the authority to execute particular actions within a specific domain (Commons 1968). Property rights are a claim to future income from an asset (Heltberg 1999: 22). In this study communities dispose of common pools of resources, over which property rights are assigned. Schlager and Ostrom (1992) identified five property rights most relevant for the use of resources under a common property regime:

- Access: The right to enter a defined physical area and enjoy non-subtractive benefits.
- Withdrawal: The right to obtain resource units or products from a resource system.
- Management: The right to regulate internal use patterns and transform the resource by making improvements.

- Exclusion: The right to determine who has access and withdrawal rights, and how those rights may be transferred.
- Alienation: The right to sell or lease management and exclusion rights.

Collective Action

Collective action involves an investigation of the conditions under which (self-interested) individuals undertake actions that may benefit them collectively, or the manner in which they fail to do so. Originally, collective action theory focussed mainly on public or collective goods. Once a public good is provided individuals cannot be excluded, which leads to the problem of free-riders, a tendency towards inefficient collective outcomes, and the under-provision of public goods (see for example, Olson 1965). Over time the literature evolved assuming that cooperative outcomes can and are achieved in situations where the free-rider problem is overcome (Nabli and Nugent 1989: 1338). One focus stemming from this body of literature is the emergence of behavioural norms and rules. Success in collective action is explained by the nature of a group (for example, size, degree of homogeneity in different aspects) and the role of incentives for collective action. Apart from the group characteristics (Olson 1965; 1982), whether certain groups become organised or not depends on the availability of political entrepreneurs (Hardin 1982) and emotional attitudes towards, for example, the loss of power of certain group members (Brenner 1983), as well as communication, organisation and other skills of the group members and most especially the quality of the leadership (Nabli and Nugent 1989: 1338).

Apart from the problem of free-riders, there is also a further problem associated with collective action, namely that the common pool resources referred to in Hardin's 'Tragedy of the Commons' (1968) is prone to overexploitation. Recent studies (for example, Ostrom 2000) have shown that customs, social conventions and other institutional arrangements designed as cooperative solutions help achieve efficiency in resource use and strive to overcome these shortcomings of collective action. The intention behind this research study was to contribute insights into institutional arrangements and the performance of rural communities and their inhabitants situated in a decentralised setting, where collective action is required in order to manage common pool resources and improve rural livelihoods.

Asymmetries

Institutions never relate to a single individual, but to numerous people. A group of people share these institutions; people are affected by them, and possibly also want to change them. So within the group of people to which a certain institutional arrangement relates, there are different actors. In the real world, these actors do not all possess the same level of information, power, etc., as was assumed, for example, in neoclassical economics. Institutional theory takes into account the fact that there are asymmetries between actors with regard to the level and degree of access to information and power.

Institutional theory is used, for example, to investigate negotiations for a contractual agreement, taking into account any asymmetries in order to evaluate the outcome under the specific circumstances. If there are two parties in a contractual relationship and there are information asymmetries, adverse selection and moral hazard problems exist. Moreover, these asymmetries may lead to market failures and opportunistic behaviour, as well as to transaction costs (see next section). At this point the role of trust also comes into play, as a counterpart to opportunism. Institutional theory recognises a general 'agency' problem in contractual arrangements. The agency framework indicates that in situations where contractual arrangements are incomplete and/or information is asymmetric, the action of one individual, the 'agent', affects other individuals, the 'principals' (Nabli and Nugent 1989: 1336). A more powerful agent has, for example, the clout to regulate resource access. There are two main branches of investigation within the agency framework:

In the first, research endeavours to find the optimal form of contractual arrangement for the ideal type of principal-agent constellations, by means of complex mathematical models (Döring 1998). In the investigation of bargaining power during institutional design and change so-called game theories are applied in order to learn more in relation to the negotiation of pay-offs.

The second branch is orientated towards empiricism. It describes actual principal-agent relationships and investigates the respective characteristics, problems and the causes of problems. These aspects also relate to power asymmetries. In the context of this study this refers, for example, to the principal-agent relationship between community inhabitants and their elected representatives. So asymmetries extend beyond contractual arrangements. The impact of asymmetries can affect any process and influence the outcomes of institutional evolution and change.

<u>Transaction costs</u>

"Transaction costs represent expenditures of time and effort as participants search out one another, negotiate an exchange, monitor its execution, and enforce its terms" (Coomes and Barham 1994: 241). The transaction costs resulting from the preparation and execution, and the safeguarding of the resultant contracts and other institutional arrangements are likewise influenced by the basic institutional conditions. Heltberg (1999: 5) considered an institution as efficient if it minimises transaction costs under the specific circumstances. In this sense, institutions are transaction cost minimising arrangements. These may change and evolve with alterations to the nature and sources of transaction costs and the means of minimising them. Institutions demonstrate an ambivalent position in relation to transaction costs. Institutions can reduce transaction costs, but they can also cause or increase costs.

The concept of transaction costs is related to the analysis of organisational structures, the causes of market failures (for example, externalities caused by the lack of property rights or asymmetric information), institutional choices and policy choices (OECD undated: 2). The establishment of institutional arrangements, and their implementation and alteration are not without costs.

There is a growing volume of literature on institutional change, the related costs and rent-seeking and, in poor settings, economic survival aspects in transformation situations such as can be found in Eastern Europe. Informal networks, in particular, appear to buffer hardships and are stabilising elements in times of institutional uncertainty.

Transaction costs are important in the study setting, but were not the focus of this particular study. However, within the same project, in one community in the study area the establishment of a management plan for the common forest resource pool was investigated using the transaction costs approach (Hentschel 2002).

Path Dependency

Path dependency is a concept implying that change in society depends on the history of that particular society. Path dependency in the context of institutions means, for example, that institutional design, change and persistence depend on the antecedents, and are constrained or skewed by them. Previous circumstances are factors influencing the status quo, even though there also exist factors independent from the past. The combination determines the overall outcome. The author assumed that path dependency plays a role in the rural communities in the study region and investigated this aspect. In chapter 3 the theoretical concept of path dependency is explained in greater detail.

1.8 Data analysis

The data were analysed in different stages. After a process of familiarisation with the data through reviewing and reading, they were transcribed and a database created. Data were organised in the database and indexed, and then a process of theme identification started, re-indexing where applicable, and the development of provisional categories. Relationships were explored and pre-existing knowledge incorporated. The different parts required a different method of analysis. Depending on the issues discussed, qualitative, interpretative methods were used, but in parts also quantitative analysis. The basic data analysis methodology was deductive, as data were collected and analysed under a specific theoretical focus. However, the analysis procedures did not adhere exclusively to the theory-based agenda in order to allow for openness to further insights and the identification of relationships or the consideration of different theoretical assumptions.

2 DECENTRALISATION IN THE NORTHERN BOLIVIAN AMAZON – POLITICAL PARTICIPATION IN FOREST DEPENDENT RURAL COMMUNITIES

2.1 Introduction

A central topic in the current development debate is the link between local resource use and its potential role in poverty alleviation. More than a billion people live within the world's 19 forest biodiversity "hotspots" and among those who earn less than one dollar a day 90% depend on forest products for their livelihoods (Jenkings and Kaimowitz in Scherr, et. al 2003: II) The lack to adequately address this link partly explains the failure of efforts to improve rural livelihoods. Many Latin American countries have gone through democratisation and decentralisation in the last two decades partly caused by changes in legislation that affects land tenure and forestry. This new legislation and decentralisation is widely affecting rural, forests dependent populations.

Therefore, the leading research question for this chapter is: How do citizens in forest-dependent settlements perceive the new legal framework and decentralisation policies, and how do they participate at the local political level?

In this chapter is analysed how inhabitants of rural areas in northern Bolivia, who largely rely on forests for their livelihoods, perceive a process of legislative change and decentralisation that profoundly affects their main economic activities of non-timber forest products collection. The author examines how, as a result of this political transformation process, the people of rural areas re-organise themselves to safeguard their interests, records the perception of change in informal rules and social organisation in four different rural communities of the northern Bolivian Amazon. This chapter will examine and explain in what way the perceptions of the legal changes and its implications differ between the four settlements. Informal rules as well as social organisation play a crucial role in local forest use in rural villages in this region.

Section 2.2 provides the theoretical underpinning of this chapter. Subsequently follows necessary background information on the region and on the new legislation that is affecting forest resources use in villages in this region.After a short outline of the communities of the case studies (2.5), results are presented (2.6). Section 2.7 discusses the results of the fieldwork and draws some conclusions related to perception and participation of the target population of decentralisation in the rural area.

2.2 Decentralisation and the local institutional framework

Decentralisation is "the transfer of planning, decision-making, or administrative authority from the central government to its field organizations, local administrative units, semi-autonomous and parastatal organizations, local governments or non governmental organizations" (Cheema and Rondinelli 1983: 18). Under decentralisation, the state transfers regulatory and executive powers, responsibility and authority in decision making, institutional infrastructure and assets, and administrative capacity (Mandondo 2000). Decentralization can either occur through deconcentration, delegation or devolution (Mandondo 2000; Anonymous, n.d.). Under deconcentration or delegation, central governments reversibly transfer subsets of responsibility of their core attributes to branches of the government. Where devolution takes place, this transfer reaches local users.

Where the state has little resources or capacity to exercise control over the formal process of transfer of power, formal decentralisation may have little to do with where effective real control becomes allocated (Mandondo 2000). Localised groups, like economic elite, or those with connections that give them political power may co-opt the decentralisation process for their own benefits. This may have important implications for the allocation, and effective control of natural resources, including land and forests. In order to make decentralisation a democratic and democratization process, power transfer has to be appropriate and sufficient. This needs to include accountable representation where representatives of local constituencies need a domain of secure discretionary powers and rights, and the domain must be established and protected in order to count with security (Ribot 2002: 1).

Bolivia before decentralisation has been marked by a non-presence of the state in most rural areas. There was a concentration of financial resource distribution and inversion in infrastructure, health and education in the main axis La Paz-Cochabamba-Santa Cruz and an exclusion or disadvantage of the people living in remote areas. People in rural areas, in Bolivia and elsewhere, have always had forms of organisation. Communities are a form of collective expression that exists even without the linkage to the state. In the case of state-absence, an effective self-organisation can be even more required to deal with the problems of basic needs. This implies, that decentralisation, like the one that started in Bolivia in the 1990s, often has to meet the goal of reconciling the formal state with the reality of the nation (Ministerio de Desarrollo Humano 1996: 29). In such situations, there is no need to create something completely new at the local level, but to recognise the existence of organised communities and find a way to formally integrate them in the state in a participatory manner.

Current thinking of factors that lead to democratisation and decentralisation suggest the need that civil society takes actively part in the process and benefits itself from it. This chapter follows Linz & Stepan's definition of civil society as: The arena of the polity where self-organizing groups, movements, and individuals, relatively autonomous from the state, attempt to articulate values, create associations and solidarities, and advance their interests (Linz and Stepan 1996, cited in Bukes 2000: 25). By recognizing and assimilating organised communities, a civil society is made part of the pluralistic governance process and this enhances the likelihood of successful decentralization and democratization.

As a general principle, in a changing legal environment, as occurred in Bolivia in the last decade, forest users will have to define new priorities in their value sphere. New laws create a new framework in which some actions are excluded, new societal freedoms are opened, individual freedom is delimited, and power positions are newly fixed. Basically, new institutional structures resulting from legal change are influenced by the current institutional environment, and by the institutional history that shaped this institutional environment before the latest reforms. O'Brien and Patsiorkovski (2000: 3) have pointed that typically institutions that govern economic action of a society develop over a long period of time, because they are closely linked to, and co-evolve with social-cultural traditions. Part of the explanation of why institutional changes take place, or how fast they take place, relates to the route that previous institutional evolutions have followed. New institutional structures show a historical path dependency. In the Bolivian Amazon, some of the contemporary institutional outcomes of national legal changes are slowly making their way down to rural settlements. Their impacts partly need to be explained referring to the institutional evolution in the rural settlements. In the northern Bolivia case, there is currently an overlap of older private rules and new legislation. The institutional and organisational structures that had developed under previous conditions are now seeking new garments.

2.3 Background information

The economy in rural communities in northern Bolivia

The economy of northern Bolivian Amazonian rural areas is mainly based on the extraction of Brazil nuts, largely for export markets. Market-orientated agricultural production, cattle-ranching and gold extraction play a minor role in the regional economy, while the extraction of timber plays an increasingly important role (Bojanic 2000). Today, there are various independent communities that have Brazil nut gathering as their main cash activity. Private entrepreneurs may hold locally recognized property rights over forests (*barracas* or forest estates) as a result of the linkage to the former rubber elites, and employ seasonal workers to collect the nuts. In most cases, these entrepreneurs do not hold official titles for the forests they exploit. Remnants of private rules and social relationships from the past have been the factors regulating access to and managing the abundant forest resources.

The major role of forest product collection by inhabitants living in independent communities is quite recent. At the time when resource use started on a major scale during the first rubber boom at the end of the 19th century[28], the organisation of resource exploitation lay in the hands of *patrons*, people who controlled resource extraction in large areas of forests and used the work force of people whom they bound in a feudal relationship as collectors. Although the patron system has profoundly changed since then, traces of the old feudal system remain because of the previously mentioned structures and social relations. The appearance of *campesino* communities as a way of spatial appropriation coincides with the crisis of the traditional extractivist system. The ruling economic elite controlled rubber production by means of an absolute control of land, production, labour, markets, and internal supply. This organisation started to falter with the fall of rubber prices in the early 20th century, but was completed towards the 1940s. Smallholders installed themselves in previously unclaimed forest areas (Assies 1997: 44), and to a smaller extent on abandoned *barracas*.

The Agrarian reform law of 1953 granted the inhabitants of communities access to a forest plot with two *estradas* per family. Due to changes in legal authorities, non-registration of permits and exploitation based on traditional claims (DHV 1993e: 81), very few small holders managed to get legal title for their land. In earlier times, communities often tended to establish along rivers (Assies 1997: 45). At present, independent communities principally establish themselves along roads (see Stoian 2000: 188). This process has been going on for several decades and has increased as a result of road improvements in the late 1980s.

2.4 The new legislation affecting forest based economies in the north

The Agrarian Reform of 1953, that followed the revolution the year before, proposed the abolition of *latifundios* and the feudal relationships between patron and *campesinos*. The law also proposed a redistribution of land. To date, however, a just distribution and recognised ownership of land, water and forests has not been achieved (Urioste and Pacheco, undated). As recent as the beginning of the 1990s, chaos and corruption ruled the administration and distribution of land in Bolivia. Two bodies, the National Council for Agricultural Reform (*Consejo Nacional de Reforma Agraria*, CNRA) and the National Colonization Institute (*Instituto Nacional de Colonización*, INC), were in charge of land titling in rural areas. On the 18th October 1996 the president Sánchez de Lozada signed a new Law of the National Agricultural Reform Service (*Ley del Servicio Nacional de Reforma Agraria;* N° 1715), known as law INRA. This law is meant to resolve inadequate land tenure in the country by 2006. The law demands a comprehensive process of *saneamiento*, or all technical and juridical activities necessary for the regulation and consolidation of land rights. The law also demands a redistribution of land.

The law distinguishes six types of agrarian property. It recognises land held by *campesino* communities and indigenous communal territories or *tierras comunitarias de origen* (TCOs). The rights that peasants and indigenous people will have are severely limited, as they are not allowed to sell, rent, or mortgage their land. Urioste and Pacheco (undated) believe that these restrictions will not necessarily lead to a more transparent allocation of land, as this depends largely on extra-economical factors like political power, prestige and corruption. As of 2002, the land titling process is behind schedule.

[28] Extraction of quinine in this region preceded the exploitation of rubber, see Stoian and Henkemans (2000).

A new Forest Law, No 1700, was approved in July 1996, while the respective regulations were passed in December the same year. Except when on private property, in Bolivia forests belong to the state. Under the new law, natural forest concessions are made available to the private sector through a public auction process. Concessions are handed out for a 40 year period, renewable every five years. The annual payment for concessions by timber companies is based on the total area under concession, whereas previously it depended on the volume of timber extracted. Concessionaires must prepare management plans before they get authorization to start logging.

The new Forestry Law establishes additional types of concessions for local and indigenous communities. The new Forestry Law creates the so-called Local Community Groups (Agrupaciones Sociales del Lugar, or ASLs) and recognises their right to have forest areas under concession. Local groups can organise themselves, become recognised as ASLs and request forest concession rights. Indigenous groups can do the same inside their communal territories (TCOs). The Forestry Law also specifies that 20% of the state forest land within a given municipality can be converted into municipal forest reserves. These municipal forestry reserves can be given under concession to ASLs.

The new Forestry Law suggests a high commitment to sustainable forest management and development. Forest users include important local groups, and not only timber companies. In practice, however, the slow advance in the saneamiento process is a bottle-neck for the implementation of the forestry law. Without a finalised process of definition of property over forestland, municipalities cannot make forests available to ASLs. Local groups, like timber companies, have to prepare forest management plans, before timber can be harvested. In fact, currently much timber is sold from forests for which no management plan exists. Usually, communities either sell timber illegally or rely on management plans prepared by some NGO or timber company. In the latter case, the company will hold first right to buy the timber.

The Popular Participation Law[29] (*Ley de Participación Popular* LPP), approved in April 1994, introduces decentralisation to the municipal level. With the Administrative Decentralisation Law (Ley de Descentralización Administrativa), approved in July 1995, the administrative structures were complemented at the *Departamento* level. LPP has enabled the country's municipalisation, as it delegated important authority and responsibility to municipal governments. This change in authority and responsibilities was accompanied with a far-reaching redistribution of public funds to municipalities. Municipalities receive a financial budget in proportion to the number of inhabitants in the municipality. They also receive a portion of the money acquired through the taxation of natural resource use in their territory.

The LPP also institutionalised the participation of the people in local government decision-making. The LPP recognises the rural settlements and their role in local government in so far as they fulfil certain organisational requirements. It recognises different forms of "in situ" organisations as *Organizaciones Territoriales de Base* or OTBs; OTBs are the smallest

---

[29] For more details see annex 2

territorial representation units in the national government hierarchy. In the majority of cases, OTBs are formally acknowledged communities and settlements. According to the LPP, local citizens must have the ability to influence the decision making process concerning the allocation of the financial resources of the municipality and to have control over how decisions are implemented. The representatives of all OTBs within one municipal section elect the members of the Surveillance Committee (*Comite de Vigilancia*) within the municipality to which they belong. Each municipality proposes a municipality development plan (*Plan de Desarrollo Municipal, PDM*), which has a time horizon of five years. For each year an annual operational plan (*Plan Operativo Anual, POA*) is darfted. While each OTB has the chance to make proposals and demand the realisation of certain projects within a participatory process, the municipality has to enter these requests in its *PDM* firstly and then in its operational plan and prioritise the distribution of the budget. The Surveillance Committee supervises the realisation of the plan and budget spending of the municipality.

2.5 Research villages

A rough overview of the villages is sufficient for the issues touched on in this chapter. More details are provided in chapters 3 and 4.

El Sena

The community El Sena is located on the main road running through the northern Bolivian Amazon, at a point where river systems from the south and west connect to those from the north and the east. El Sena is situated within the homonymous municipality in the third section of the province *Madre de Dios* in the Pando Department. About ninety households constitute the community, which is the municipality capital. Once a *barraca,* it is now an independent community with access to forests and more importantly Brazil nuts. However, the *barraca* system is still important. The land titling process is ongoing, meaning that the extent of the community's land endowment is not yet clear.

Loma Velarde

The village of Loma Velarde is an extractive community with a village area of about 15,000[32] ha, located in the province *Manuripi* of the Pando Department on the River Orthon. Nine households (with a total of 13 families) form the community. It is located far from any urban centres and in the rainy season is only accessible by boat. In the dry season Loma Velarde can be reached by crossing a river and travelling a track using a motorbike, which shortens the journey time. The community was a *barraca* until the nineties, but is today independent and uses the forest as common property with exception of the areas hosting agricultural plots.

[32] At time of research land titling process had not been finished, so this data is based on unofficial sources

San Juan km 27

The village of San Juan km 27 is an agro-extractive community with a village area of 3400 ha and located in the province *Vaca Diez* of the Beni department. Located near the urban centre of Riberalta on the road from Riberalta to Cachuela Esperanza, the village had 27 households fduring the time of research. The communal land is divided into individual forest plots that are not only used for NTFP-extraction, but also for other forest use and agriculture. The first settlers arrived in the village since early 1970s.

Trinidadcito

Trinidadcito is an extractive community with a communal area of around 8500 ha, located in the *Madre de Dios* province of the department of Pando. It is far from any urban centre, and in the rainy season only accessible after travelling one or several days by boat. In the dry season, Trinidadcito can be accessed by motorbike. The village of 45 households carries out NTFP-extraction on land that is held under communal property. Only agricultural fields or *chacos* are worked individually. Trinidadcito used to be the centre of a *barraca* until it became an independent community in 1972.

2.6 Results

2.6.1 Knowledge of laws in rural communities

In order to benefit from opportunities created under new laws, it is necessary that people know about them. It cannot be taken for granted that, for example, information about the content of new state laws is easily transmitted to the citizens. This is especially true in remote areas, where the state has no real presence and people have few other means of accessing information. This may also imply that new legal obligations are sometimes not accepted, either because they are not known, or because they do not fit with local rules or conditions.

To identify how well informed they were about the new legislation, I asked the inhabitants to mention one or more laws they had heard of or knew about. In general, an average of about 50% of the respondents did not mention any law, or could not remember any at that time. El Sena and Trinidadcito had a higher percentage of informed respondents than Loma Velarde and San Juan km 27 (Figure 2-1). The respondents who stated not to know about laws were mostly female, while the better-informed inhabitants were mostly male.

The distribution of information to rural settlements is constrained by the channels available. No newspapers circulate rurally. In the absence of a telephone, long distance communication takes place by means of radio and then a messenger, as there is usually only one radio communication station per village, if at all. Under these circumstances, the transmission of information takes mainly place from person to person or via programmes in the radio. As batteries mean expenses poor families may only turn on the radio for one hour on Sunday. People travelling to town bring back the latest news, as do merchants and other people visiting the community. For legal information, people in town can address the state authorities, NGOs or lawyers[33]. The advice and information is then brought back to the village and transmitted orally and through booklets. Usually, the better informed people belong to the village authorities. One of their tasks should be to spread information in the village, but this does not always occur. The spread of information locally depends on the extent to which people can access seminars held, for example, by the municipality or a NGO. To learn more about the interviewees' in the respective villages sources of information in relation to legal issues see figures 4-3, 4-7, 4-11 and 4-15.

The educational background of the interviewees is also an influencing factor. One indicator of educational background is the rate of illiteracy; 17% of the interviewees in El Sena, 22% in Loma Velarde, 26% in San Juan km 27 and 13% in Trinidadcito are illiterate, according to the information provided by the interviewees themselves. It is possible that the level is higher but that people felt ashamed to openly admit their illiteracy. When compared to the data from the National Bolivian Institute for Statistics (*INE*), however, the data would appear to be realistic. The *INE* claimed in 2001 that the average illiteracy rate in Bolivia was 13.28%, with a lower average in Pando at 10.37%. For the rural area in Pando it oscillates between 9.59% and 28.39%. Therefore, the interviewees from Loma Velarde and San Juan reveal relatively high levels of illiteracy. These are also the villages with the highest ratios of interviewees claiming no access to legal knowledge. However, the values for all four villages were relatively low in this respect.

[33] Consultation with a lawyer requires cash and is only resorted to in the event of urgent problems, and not for general information.

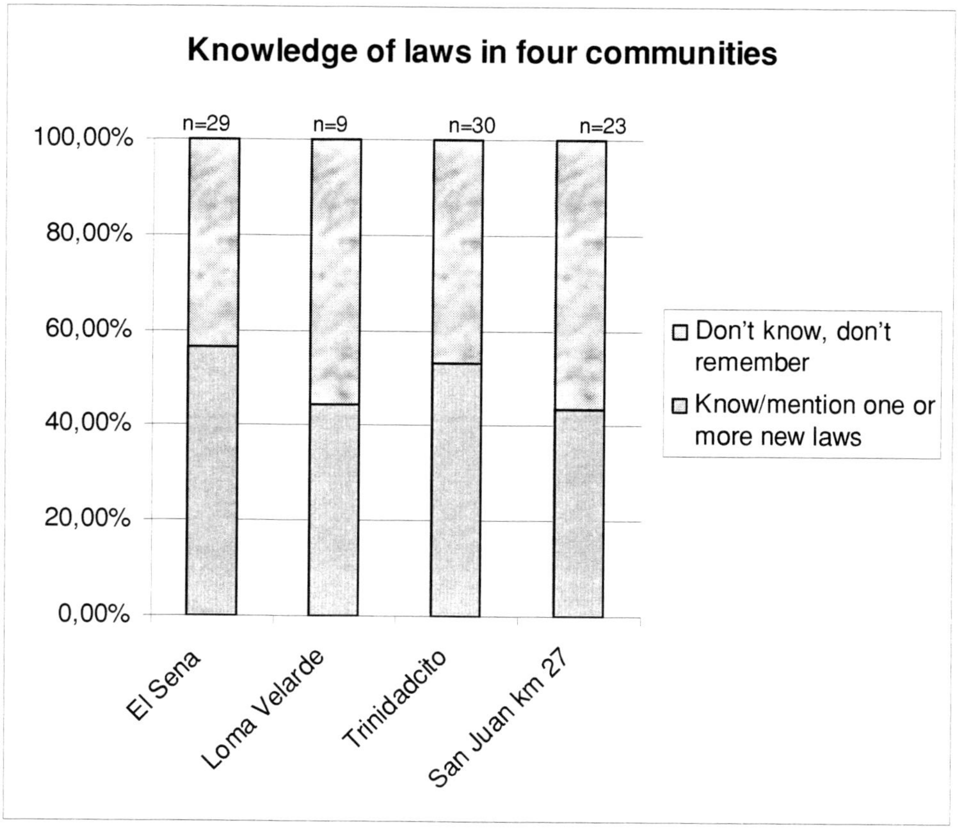

Figure 2-1: Knowledge of laws in four communities

2.6.2 Perception of laws

The researcher asked the respondents who could mention one or more laws after an open question to assess that particular law. The most frequently mentioned law was INRA. Not every interviewee who had mentioned a law was able to provide an assessment. In all villages, though, any direct evaluation related to INRA was positive. Statements such as "The INRA law is good because it fixes boundaries and secures property rights" and "The INRA law is good because land can not be sold" (personal communications to the author by interviewees) illustrate this. The Popular Participation Law was characterised as ineffective, because even the politicians did not adhere to it. Another respondent assessed the Popular Participation Law positively, because it brought money to the community. In many cases it was also perceived, however, that the village authorities largely misused that money. More details on other laws in footnote[34].

The author asked people if they had noticed any general changes within the community or their own lives as a result of new laws. If a respondent had mentioned a new law, then they were asked to mention changes associated with that particular law. If the respondent had not mentioned any law, then he or she was asked in general to note changes in the village over the last several years.

Table 2-1: Question on whether a change in the village was observed

	El Sena	Loma Velarde	San Juan km 27	Trinidadcito
Change	45%	33%	39%	63%
No change	38%	56%	9%	17%
No opinion expressed	17%	11%	52%	20%

The respondents who expressed no opinion were for the most part people who previously had not mentioned any law.

El Sena inhabitants associated change above all with the Popular Participation Law and the related money which authorities used for construction activities such as a new public square and the arrival of electric light. At the same time, many emphasised that there was little change because the money nourished a local elite. Only one interviewee spoke of land tenure and stressed that the former patron was obliged due to legal circumstances to cede a place for settlement and house constructions in 1996 in order to „free" the parts he wanted to claim as private territory. 70 ha were ceded and function today as a settlement "centre", with 25x50 metre lots for housing and important buildings of the municipality etc. The educational reform was mentioned in second place for the introduction of change. Despite implementation problems people consider it as a motor of change in a positive way.

Noticable were several comments on negative change. They all coincided that the situation to earn a living in El Sena got worse in the five years prior to the interview.

In Loma Velarde little change has been perceived by the interviewees. The positive changes which have been mentioned were improvements for drinking water and light. Apart from that there were only some improvements in housing due to private initiative of the respective inhabitants. Opinions as the following prevailed: "There was absolutely no change, neither at the economic level, nor at the political level. Everything stays the same" (personal communication by an inhabitant, translation by the author).

In San Juan km 27 respondents emphasised almost exclusively changes introduced by the INRA law, while in Trinidadcito, people mentioned changes brought about by the Popular

[34] Other laws were mentioned rarely. People held the perception that the Municipality Law caused quarrels. The Educational Reform law, which was also mentioned by respondents, received a mixed assessment. Two people responded positively to the law against intra-familiar violence (Law Nr. 1674), because it created a legal ground to act against any person who uses violence against children, women or men. Only one respondent from Trinidadcito and one from San Juan km 27 mentioned the Forestry Law and no comment was given on that particular law.

Participation Law. According to respondents in San Juan km 27, as a result of the *saneamiento* the boundaries of the community are now clear and community members can now be sure of the size of the communal territory after land conflicts with a neighbour over communal boundaries. This is important because San Juan km 27 is situated on uplands.[35] The soils in the community have lower productivity than those of other communities in the area, and are best suited for forest use. When the field work for the *saneamiento* process had been finished, the community decided to distribute land to newcomers.[36]. Within half a year the number of inhabitants increased by 50%. Many villagers regarded secure community boundaries as a positive outcome of the *saneamiento* and hence of the INRA law. At the same time, however, respondents complained that they had not experienced personal improvements with regard to resource use and benefit generation.

The distinction between community and personal welfare was not an issue in the responses of Trinidadcito villagers. This is explained by the fact that Trinidadcito manages its communal land as a common pool resource. Some improvements were made at the village level as a result of resources made available through the decentralisation process (i.e. Popular Participation Law and Municipality Law), but also through personal relationships with people who are member of the national parliament and in the district representative bodies. Respondents emphasised how much the quality of life had improved in the village because of the acquisition of a power generator, radio, telephone, public television and a new school building. In addition the community obtained a communal boat for the health post, such that it can provide services in other communities, and one additional communal boat used for purposes such as marketing of agricultural products.

2.6.3 Perceptions of political representation

Political culture can be defined as people's preference for one way of making decisions about how they should be governed. It is a people's views on who should make policy for the group and how the policy-makers should go about their task (unnamed, 2002). I studied the village political culture by inquiring how people perceive that their personal interests are considered at the village political level. The responses do not reflect the respondents' views on who should make policy, but the results do reflect who, in their opinion, is (and is not) making policy for them at the present. Following the principles of cognitive anthropology, the author tried to use interview techniques and analytical processes to bring out native categories of thought instead of imposing the analyst`s own cultural system on the data (compare Colby 1996: 211). At the same time it is clear that no researcher can be objective, and so the author favours a studied self-reflexivity, to be the 'positioned observer'[37]. I asked for the interviewees' perception with an open-ended question and gave no categories beforehand.

[35] Land not inundated during the rainy season, often identified as *terra firme*. In the villages it is called *altura*.

[36] All the better plots near a stream were already in the hands of the established inhabitants. Newcomers only could get less valuable plots..

In El Sena, Loma Velarde and San Juan 27 about one third of the respondents, and in Trinidadcito almost half of all interviewees, have the perception that no one represents their interests at the political level. Answers such as "Politicians, they all lie" or „I fight for myself" were commonly given to this question. The second most common response, however, was that a specific political party represented interests in village politics. This response was overwhelmingly more common in El Sena and Trinidadcito. In Trinidadcito, one member of parliament and a district politician, both belonging to one political party, helped to secure access rights to fishing grounds and other benefits for the community. Apart from Brazil nuts, fish is an important source of income in Trinidadcito. According to one villager these politicians "...buy our votes and we get what we want". In El Sena, the affiliation to the reigning party on national level has impact due to a close community connection to the prefecture. Inhabitants of San Juan km 27 cannot count on such political patronism, and neither do those of Loma Velarde.

The third most common response was that elected community representatives represented people's interests. Elected community members enjoy considerable legitimacy, especially in San Juan km 27 where the OTB operates as a labour union (*sindicato*). Membership in this union is obligatory for all adult community members. Participation in community meetings is also required for everyone over 18 and non-participation is sanctioned. The community representatives are elected in these meetings. Local community representatives were also mentioned in Trinidadcito, but here the role of OTB members is not considered so important[38]. This holds also true for Loma Velarde and El Sena, the former *barracas*. In change, in these two communities the former patron was mentioned sporadically. In the category other associations we have to think of the respective unions for teachers and health personnel on national level which are important for interviewees working in that field. Apart from that, in three of four communities, specific politicians were said to be important. The identified politicians usually had some personal link to the respondent, through kinship or a labour relation. Other, less mentioned categories show the wideness of the scope of the answers of the interviewees.

[37] This represents the ethnography approach common in interpretative anthropology. As Clifford Geertz put it "meaning is socially, historically and rhetorically constructed" (compare OLSON, 1991: 1)

[38] Rather, the inhabitants of Trinidadcito feel that the municipal agent better represents their interests. The municipal agent is the representative of the government at the community level.

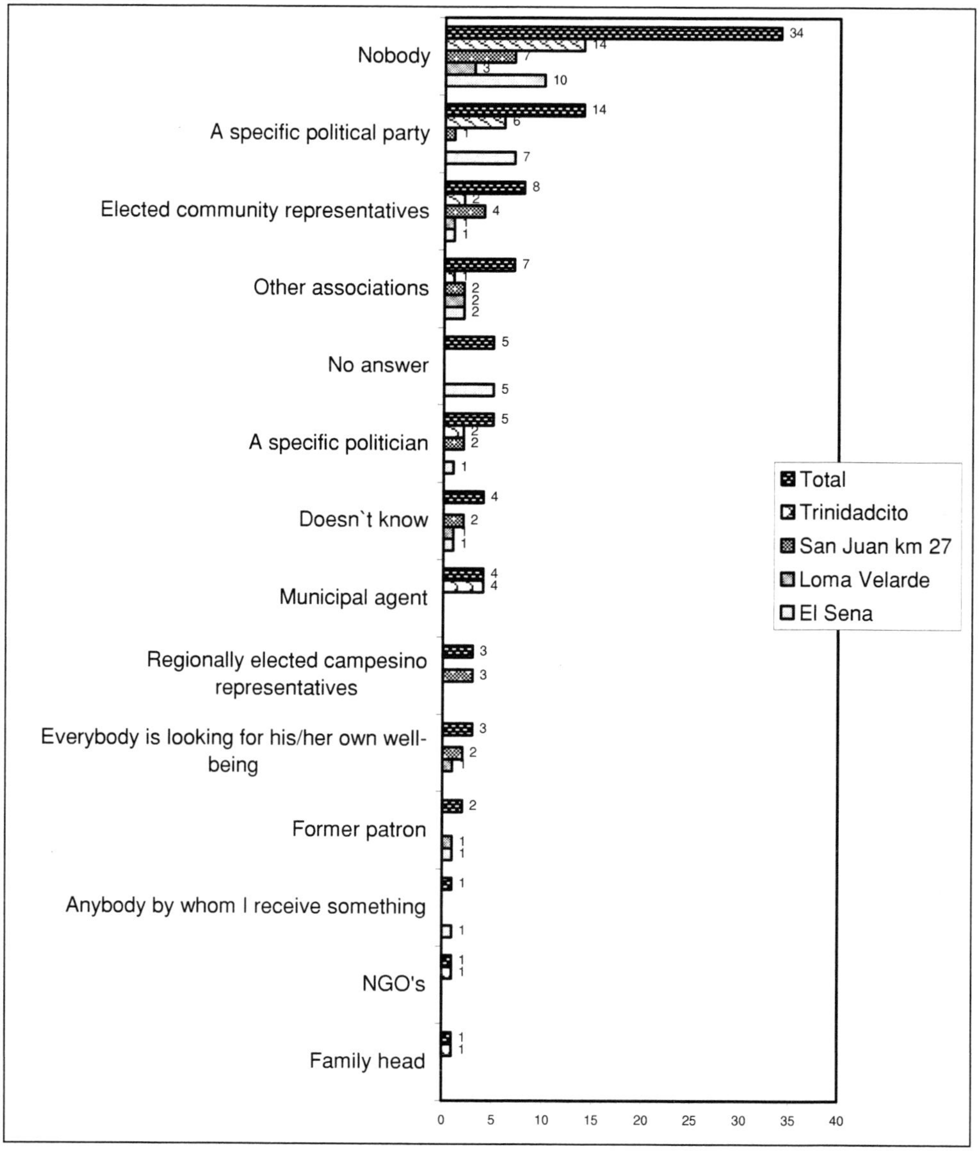

Figure 2-2: Representation of interests at the political level in four communities

2.6.4 Participation in elections

In Bolivia, it is required by law to vote in municipal and general elections. In the election of community representatives each adult in the community may vote, while in the municipal election only people who hold a valid identity card can participate. Turnout for elections in Trinidadcito is comparatively high (Table 4), which can partly be explained by the community's ties with the politicians in representative bodies. Many politicians with links to those communities buy community member's votes for re-lection, in exchange for providing them with ID cards.[39] Not all adults in the two villages posses such a valid identity card. A census conducted in 2001 by CIPCA Norte in 77 communities in the region showed that 44.8% of the population is not registered in any civil register, 56.2% of the rural settlers do not have a birth certificate (a requisite to get an identity card) and 82.3% do not own such an ID. There is little variation between men and women in these numbers.

Table 2-2: Rate of participation in last elections (rounded)

	El Sena	Loma Velarde	San Juan km 27	Trinidadcito
Election of community representatives	21%	67%	48%	55%
Municipal Election	66%	56%	52%	70%

Interviewees who voted in the last municipal elections were asked what criteria they used to decide which candidate to vote for. In San Juan km 27 a frequent answer was "I voted in blank, without making a cross". This is done in order to get the receipt showing that a vote was placed and thus fulfilling the duty of citizenship, but without really making a choice. In Trinidadcito the choice of who to vote for was heavily influenced by candidates offering cash payments to the village if they won. Some degree of coercion seems to go together with this practice. A respondent who at first did not go along with such practices eventually gave in because, as he personally stated: "nobody wants to have a lot of problems for a long time". It is also a common practice that political parties send trucks that take people to the polls. Meals and T-shirts entice people to vote for the party on whose truck they came. In El Sena the election reasons varied from friendship and capacity to statements such as " I vote always the same political party, no matter which candidate they present" .

For the election of community representatives the interviewees of all four communities mentioned that they focused more on the individual capacity of the candidates.

2.6.5 Elected office holders

The village leadership positions and a political representative body (today *OTB*) already existed before the Popular Participation Law was enacted. However, responsibilities of village leaders were enhanced through this law. In San Juan 61%, in Trinidadcito 57%, in Loma Velarde 56% and in El Sena 28% of the respondents to the survey had previously been elected to one of those positions. In general, however, nobody had volunteered as a candidate, except for two respondents in Trinidadcito. In most cases, other people usually put candidates for any of the positions on the ballot from the community. The reason to accept the office if

[39] Before the elections, political parties appear in villages and hold campaigns to provide people with IDs, in return for votes.

elected is not necessarily political interest or commitment, as the following comments in table 2-3 show.

Table 2-3: Comments by office holders on why they accept the job

If you don't want, they are annoyed
They oblige you, then you have to accept it
I never wanted to, but when they named me I had to accept. If I hadn't accepted they would have felt defensive. You have to please them.
I didn't like the idea, because I didn't understand about the tasks, but nobody else wanted to do it
They wanted me to be the responsible
I got the office by recommendation. First, I didn't want to do it, but my husband told me that I have to defend interests.

Only two respondents among 31 office holders (out of a total of 53 respondents) commented positively on their duty. One respondent commented that he: "... always had the luck to being elected for different offices. I like it because one is learning, can accumulate experience and has the opportunity to visit workshops in Riberalta". The other said that lately he had begun to see the positive aspects of this assignment. There is an interesting distinction of democratic election and politics in the statement of one interviewee: " I was elected by the democratic vote of the people and not by politics". Politics seems to be negatively assigned with undemocratic and corrupt practices which do not reflect the will of the people.

In San Juan km 27, each adult member of the community must pay a monthly fee to the community treasure. Part of this fee goes to the regional *campesino* federation, and the other part is used both by the community and for travel expenses for elected representatives. As payment is currently very low, the lack of money impedes the fulfilment of representation tasks. For example, as part of the *saneamiento* process, each community was given the chance to control and check their files in the INRA office in Riberalta. The representatives of San Juan km 27 could not go due to the lack of money. The elected representatives proposed to raise the fee, but most people were against this proposal. People feared a misuse of their money in addition to the fact that they could not afford a higher fee.

2.7 Discussion

Decentralisation in Bolivia responded to concerns of centrifugal tendencies within departmental capitals, and related federal tendencies (Grindle 2000, p.118; Sánchez de Lozada, personal communication 2001). The prime mechanism used by the Bolivian state is enactment of new legislation that redistributes power and resources to different levels of government and to civil society. People in remote regions who hardly counted before, become citizens with rights and obligations. They encounter themselves in a rule set and implementation mechanisms to which they are not used to and which they may distrust.

In order for a new legislation to be effective, the people to benefit or abide by it must first simply be informed of its existence, in such a way that they are able to understand the content. It is not enough to have just a vague comprehension of the law. Whether or not citizens comply with new legislation, and can benefit from it personally or for the community, depends on how politically aware a person is. Those individuals who are not well informed or who have incorrect information will benefit from new legislation only by chance. Lazarte (2000) in a study conducted in nine Bolivian departments showed low levels of information or mistaken information related to state organisations among 86% of the interviewees.

The results of the present survey show that the level of information among members of small communities regarding resource-related legislation or state agencies is low. The respondents that had some knowledge about the new laws usually judged them by assessing the direct impact they had on their life in the village. In the case of San Juan km 27, the INRA law was best known, while it was hardly ever mentioned in El Sena. In the case of Trinidadcito, the INRA law as well as the Popular Participation Laws were known. Loma Velarde inhabitants mainly thought of the Popular Participation Laws. The Forestry Law was scarcely mentioned at all, though all communities depend on forest resources for their livelihood. Possibly, its implementation has not arrived at the community level, or it is neglected because it does not affect current extraction practices. This fact warrants further study in order to assess the causes and dangers of this development with regard to the intended goals of the forestry law and legislative reforms in general. It has to be considered that a lot of "communities" in the Bolivian Amazon are quite young, and its inhabitants in many cases lived in dependency-relations with a *patrón* before. This situation has hardly changed in many locations (Pacheco, personal communication 2001). This situation contrasts with standards of effective citizen participation which requires: "... a form of political consciousness that is both critical of existing inequalities and injustice and yet, at the same time, aware of the promise of collective action in achieving progressive reform" (Souza 2001: p. 165).

In contrast to the respondents' perception that personal interests are poorly represented at the political level, the turnout of community members in elections is relatively high. However, many people participate formally in elections, but vote in blank. For this reason, the turnout does not tell much about actual political activity or personal conviction. In Trinidadcito, the collective vote of the population for a bribing candidate has been a successful strategy for the community to enhance its development. One such benefit, for example, is that inhabitants now have access to a boat to bring fish and Brazil nuts to markets in an urban centre. This confirms that: "At least corruption has been decentralised and money arrives where nothing arrived before – though it does not always end up where it should" (Sánchez de Lozada, personal communication 2001). There is evidence that the effect of decentralisation is felt in many rural settlements, but that it is taking place in very different modalities than initially intended when the respective legislation was enacted. A common phenomenon is that former political power and property structures remain basically the same, but only adopt a slightly new look.

The *saneamiento* process certainly appears to require a higher level of organisation within communities. This has not resulted in the creation of new leadership positions, but rather in an increase of tasks and their complexity of the current local leaders. Work done by the majority of these leaders is not remunerated, and only travel expenses are compensated. As the results presented here show, it cannot be assumed that all village leaders hold their post because of personal commitments, although this is certainly true for some individuals. Basically, village representatives must be regarded as people who fulfil a duty expected by the community. Similar conditions exist in, for instance, the Andes in Bolivia, where each community member has to fulfil communal leadership duties (Ticona, Rojas, Albó 1995: 82). These conditions alone cannot ensure an effective community representation, although they do meet standards of democracy.

There is certainly evidence that a political elite exists or may evolve in the communities discussed here. A selected group of community members has more knowledge of how the outside world works, and this information asymmetry may foster a political elite. This implies a danger that community interests are not represented and individual interests may be pursued without the awareness of the community. The fact that a municipality is located on community ground can make this effect worse or improve conditions, depending on the constellation of actors. Though people elect their representatives, there is not enough shared awareness and exchange of information between the representatives and the general population. This also complicates accountability of representatives.

In El Sena, political representation of community inhabitants was given only sporadically until a re-organisation before the arrival of the land reform. While there were individuals who wanted to be engaged as representatives, but circumstances impeded a real representation function, the situation in Loma Velarde indicated a lack of representation which grounded in little interest at the basis itself. The fact that each community member of San Juan km 27 must accept village representative tasks can be viewed as somewhat of a counterbalance to the danger of co-opting political changes. At the same time, information deficiencies become apparent when certain individuals take up responsibilities but cannot tap the full potential of their positions. In Trinidadcito, the representation of community interest is linked to a few certain individuals. Community members have only an indirect influence on the work of their representatives. Still, representatives seem to follow a successful strategy, which favours the community as a whole. Therefore legitimacy of representatives in Trinidadcito is high and the effect of information deficiencies at the community level can be regarded of minor importance in comparison to San Juan km 27.

The success of decentralisation, whether it aims at more effective and meaningful democratic governance, or at achieving some other socio-economic goal such as development, depends upon generating a particular set of responses from citizens and their representatives (Agrawal 1998: 8). This set of responses can be summarised as participation. While many scholars regard participation as purely positive, there are others who argue the risks of locally dominant actors who undermine broad democratic local governance, while strengthening their own position. The legislative changes in Bolivia that had the objective of decentralisation and equal distribution of natural resources showed different effects in the rural areas. In the northern Bolivian Amazon there is a notable advance in the area of legal rights. As a result, the great reliance on *de facto* rights is changing to *de jure* rights that do not only exist, but are beginning to be upheld by the state and create security for social agents.

However, progress is slow. Independent collectors that live in rural areas knew about the INRA law, and they assessed the impact of the INRA law generally as positive. Respondents mentioned the Decentralisation Laws to a lesser extent. This suggests that effective implementation and democratisation of processes of decentralisation and devolution first of all require improvements in the transfer of information of new legal change all the way down to the grass roots level. Not only, will this contribute to an awareness of new opportunities, responsibilities and rights, it is also one condition (but not the only one) to avoid co-optation of the decentralisation process by a local elite that will hold exclusive control over information flows.

In addition to information flows, the state needs to improve some minimal amount of services, to avoid co-optation by outside actors of the decentralisation and distribution process. Politicians who try to get into municipality or higher level political positions contemplate helping people in rural areas to obtain documentation, but only for the sake of gaining votes. Although this process does contribute to the conversion of the rural non-citizens into true citizens, it will not take place where there is little apparent political gain. As the proportion of the rural population is low in the municipality of Riberalta where San Juan km 27 lies, few politicians bother to help rural people to get, for instance, ID cards in return for votes. This may also lead to political neglect when it comes to policy-making for improvements in the areas that matter most for rural people: infrastructure, forest use by families in the communities, agriculture or agro-forestry. Trinidadcito is located within a rural municipality. Therefore, each vote is of comparatively higher strategic importance for politicians. This has had a positive influence on the opportunities to acquire support for community projects. Though Loma Velarde is located within a rural municipality as well, its inhabitants hardly received anything in their role as victims of a corruption scandal by the major and weak organisation in general. The inhabitants of El Sena are favoured when it comes to the improvement of infrastructure initiated by the municipality. As a community, however, there was at time of research little space to express needs and make demands.

All research communities are embedded in the same legal framework. However, circumstances and varieties at the village level lead to quite a different allocation of resources. They have in common that a majority of their inhabitants believe that nobody represents their interests at the political level. This suggests that they still do not feel as part of a state where they can exert rights that lead to democratic representation or participation. These people perceive the state as an external body. Those who see their interests represented, name either people with whom they have personal contact, or people who show physical presence in the local context. This result shows that the perception of the state includes only state institutions, organisations and politicians at higher administrative levels. The inhabitants of rural communities in northern Bolivia do not include themselves as actors in the political sphere. This contrasts bleakly with the influence of *campesino* and indigenous representatives at the regional and national level. Civil society in northern Bolivia still shows important asymmetries related to its interaction and impacts. While some organised groups with a rural mandate are bargaining in the political arena, most rural inhabitants themselves are not part of a real civil society yet. In the rural areas in northern Bolivia, as described here, participation in the decentralisation process is increasing.

3 SOCIO-HISTORICAL ASPECTS OF COMMUNITY FORMATION AND RESOURCE USE

3.1 Introduction

This chapter details an investigation into the socio-historical conditions in the northern Bolivian Amazon, and in particular whether institutions in place may be regarded as path-dependent, influencing the implementation of the reforms, organisation and resource use today and in the future.

Path dependency is important in institutional theory, but empirical research into this issue is scarce. Many transition studies, for example in relation to former communist countries such as the Ukraine, focussed on institution building for the future without taking into account the past institutional landscape. This resulted in unrealistic and inappropriate understanding of the restructuring of institutions due to the path dependent behaviour of the actors. Incomplete knowledge, uncertainty, high transaction costs and the reliance on customs and traditions resulted in the failure to assimilate the new rules. It would appear that path dependent processes create inert organisational tendencies, which have to be taken into consideration in policy-making and analysis.

The study aims to investigate empirically path dependency in a region where a profound legal and administrative reform process is taking place. Results shall provide insights into how this may affect the process.

3.2 Path dependency – theoretical aspects

The concept of path dependency is applied in different fields. In biology a process of adaptation is said to be path dependent due to particular genotype mixes. In social science the concept has a wider scope. Path dependency is an important element in theories related to institutions. In general, at a certain point in time society and its actors live within a given institutional framework. Institutions are subject to a constant process of change over time. The concept of path dependency implies that it is not merely chance or the free will of the actors involved, which determine the manner in which these institutions evolve or change. Social actors are constrained by rationales derived from limited information upon which decisions are made and organisational systems implemented. The imbalanced distribution of power and information results in unequal bargaining power for the respective actors.

In case of the northern Bolivian Amazon, path dependency exists if the changes to rural communities resulting from 'external' institutional change (a new legal framework for land tenure and forestry, among others) are linked to the previous institutional (and, as a consequence, organisational) setting. The new laws could not, therefore, have changed the institutional structure deliberately, but rather the local institutional setting determined the manner and the intensity of the path, the extent to which institutions were bent and changed in this evolutionary process. This bending and changing implies costs for the rural inhabitants.

There were costs associated with changing from a particular structure or state, summed up in transaction costs. If the costs are high in comparison to the expected benefits (given that the available information is less than perfect), or certain actors are more powerful than others and maintain the existing structure using force, then the system itself is locked in.

Evidence shows that it is important to take into consideration the rules of the specific society and the manner in which people act. In an investigation carried out in Russia one of the core principles of New Institutional Economics became apparent, namely "... that typically economic institutions develop over a long period of time and that they are deeply embedded in social-cultural traditions" (O'Brien and Patsiorkovski 2000: 3). One must not underestimate the capacity of institutions to change. When new structures emerge, however, they contain 'old' elements due to historical path dependencies. When the Russian government essentially privatised agriculture through various reform decrees in the 1990s and households could officially register as private farms, the majority didn't take this step, but remained linked to the collective (kolkhozy) or state (sovkhozy) farms which had previously had a monopoly on inputs, production, processing and sales (*ibid*: 4). In the Bolivian Amazon path dependency has not been investigated explicitly, but experts on the region assume that it exists (compare Molina 2001, and Pacheco 2001).

In this study the author adheres to Mohoney's (2000) definition of path dependent processes, assuming that they demonstrate three specific properties:

1. A largely contingent event shapes the probability of further events occurring.
2. The event must be related only stochastically to the 'initial conditions' of the system.
3. Once the contingent event has occurred, the subsequent policy becomes constrained and relatively deterministic.

The evolution and change of institutions in a rural community is neither isolated from the regional (and national) political, economic and social context, nor is a specific local institution necessarily a traditional one. The important questions are how and why an externally imposed institution becomes a local one, and "who succeeds in defining a set of issues or a course of action as the appropriate one" (Feierman 1990: 31) at the local level itself. In order to answer these questions we need to take into consideration the power relations and the exercise of power and authority (Blom 1998: 4). The search for path dependency is based on the assumption that path dependency plays a major role in the successful definition of the most appropriate set of issues or course of action in the context of institutional change. The indicators for path dependency in the local setting applied in this study are recounted under 3.4.3.

3.3 The problem addressed

This study focuses on rural communities dependent on forests, and required to stick to certain organisational norms in order to successfully claim a title to their land under the legal reforms, which includes access to forest resources. Subsequently, these resources are officially under their influence, yet must be managed as common property as intended under the law. Once the land entitlement process is complete, only regulations for resource use on a general level remain, such as the requirements for receipt of permission to use timber commercially or the procedure for the election of political representatives. The internal organisation of communities is determined by the respective communities, as is decision making in relation to resource distribution and use. This is the crucial point in determining the outcome of the reforms, which is not defined by law. It is at this point that investigating path dependency in the communal arena becomes important.

In this study, property no. 1 of path dependency is the implementation of the legal reforms governing land tenure, decentralisation and forestry, passed between 1994 and 1996. The implementation of the reforms and the requirement for rural peasant communities to organise according to the law in order to be entitled to claim land occurred later. The process started in different years in different parts of Bolivia. In northern Bolivia the *Participación Popular* (for further information see the annex) came first, followed by the process of *saneamiento*, which is advancing slowly. In two of the research communities the land measurement crew arrived as late as 2002.

For the stakeholders in the research area the reforms are a largely contingent event, with a high probability of further events occurring in its wake. At the same time, these reforms are not in any way directly linked to the initial conditions in the research area. The fact that there are rural *barraca* settlements and independent communities, which depend on forests for their livelihoods and are characterised by certain types of resource use organisation, is only stochastically linked to the reform program. Property no. 2 is also met, therefore.

The third property is the pertinent area from the point of view of this study. Are the processes in northern Bolivia path dependent upon the outcomes of the reforms being constrained (or expressed positively: formed) by the initial local conditions?

The processes in the independent communities are influenced by the community members themselves, but also by a variety of possible external factors: activities of state organisations, like the municipality and the forest and land reform agencies; of NGOs providing organisational, technical and financial assistance; also of peasant associations, the church, politicians, neighbouring settlements and powerful individuals from outside the community.

The behaviour of a community is a complex system. For the purposes of this study it has been reduced to the degree of organisation and common efforts to secure access to resources prior to the reform, and to internal power imbalances. There is an array of different community types in the research area. Some are organised with a strong communal identity and elected representatives who are accountable to the community, whereas others exhibit no collective action but are managed by influential individuals.

Such social aspects and the community's natural resource endowment are linked in order to estimate the future management potential. Another aspect of the micro-system community is the resource use culture demonstrated by the inhabitants. One area of investigation in this study was the size of agricultural plots and the conditions of land use. The results from questions on hypothetical resource use options reinforce the findings.

3.4 Background information

3.4.1 History of peasant organisation

Path dependency requires an understanding of the general historical setting in which institutional development takes place. Therefore, it is important to consider the general historical aspects of peasant organisation in Bolivia. The following is a rough outline of peasant organisation since the revolution in 1952.

As a result of the revolution, in 1953 the peasant organisations came under the influence of MNR, which lasted for eleven years. For six years after that they were managed under the military-peasant pact. The first free syndicates reportedly came into being in 1970 (C.S.U.T.C.B. 2003), and were ruled by the Kataristas for 15 years. Since 1985 the influence of left and rightwing parties has been changing. Up until now the peasant organisations have been organised into sindicatos, subcentrales, centrales, federaciones and finally the confederación. This pyramid system (which more-or-less coincides with the administrative divisions cantón, provincia, departamento and country) has been evident in many rural communities in the Andes and in the valley region. Each community or sindicato received its legitimacy from the respective level of the peasant organisation.

According to Blanes (1999: 19), the communities in the Oriente (the lowlands of Bolivia) were often excluded from this because the indigenous people there maintained structures reminiscent of the system that prevailed during the long period of Spanish rule and the influence of Jesuit missionaries, for example Capitanías, Asambleas or the Cabildo. Generally, large-scale property ownership changed little for the rural communities. However, taking the lowland indigenous point of view, Arnaldo Lijerón Casanovas (1998) provides an insight from a different perspective: The agrarian reform of the fifties, the aim of which was to campesinizar (~peasantise, ibid. 119), had negative repercussions in the lowlands because land and resource use were divided into small user units by law, which is contrary to the indigenous use of land as a vast common resource pool[40], and it ignored the socio-economic organisation of the tribes. Syndicates substituted the cabildo, a process only reversed by the concession of TCO's under the INRA law from 1996.

The area researched for the purposes of this study is the rubber and Brazil nut region located in the lowlands. The specific situation there was that the disintegration of the Casa Suarez had already begun in the first half of the century, prior to the agrarian reform in 1953, and so the biggest latifundio had already started to disappear. Under the agrarian reform law of 1953, rubber tappers received the property right for two estradas per capita – though a minimum of three is required for individual exploitation (compare Lijerón 1998: 118). In reality vast areas

[40] A fact which has been reversed due to social movement and the INRA law, 1996, which provides for *Territorios Comunitarios de Origen, TCOs.*

of land remained barracas, however, under the influence of a few patrones, several among them the former directors of the Suarez Company. There was little change, therefore. At that time a syndicate structure was only to be found in already independent communities. In Riberalta, the Federación Sindical Unica de Trabajadores Campesinos de la Provincia Vaca Diez (F.S.U.T.C.P.V.D.) was founded in 1953. The communities in the research region were not completely isolated from the process of sindicalismo, therefore. In independent communities people were free to organise as a syndicate, with a potential direct connection to the federation, whereas people in barracas learned of them through a liberation movement initiated in the region.

3.4.2 Community formation

The communities in the northern Bolivian Amazon are young in comparison to others in Bolivia, and when compared on an international level. The indigenous people of the region were originally semi-nomadic and had not been integrated into the Inca empire (Krempin 1997: 175). The establishment of more stable rural settlements began with the Jesuit missionaries who remained in Bolivia from 1689 until their expulsion from Latin America in 1767, which was followed by the appearance of the *barraca* system. However, a *barraca* of the end of the 19th century differed substantially from a community. The people who lived there were labourers, often caught in a feudal *patrón-zafrero* relationship and were not allowed to cultivate food to meet their own needs. Many of them only lived in the one place for a short period of time. Food was provided by the *patrón's pulpería*, where the workers paid with their work relatively high prices. The *patrón's* labourers had to work his *chaco*, with additional food in the *pulpería* usually coming from Santa Cruz and the trading companies in Brazil that exported NTFPs to Europe and the USA. Up until the present time, the whole region has been subject to an intense seasonal urban-rural migration, which is marked by the labour allocation of urban-based people in the forests for three months a year to collect Brazil nuts. There is also intraregional migration within rural communities and an overall process of urbanisation (Stoian 2000: 190).

The first 'communities' began to emerge during the rubber crises, when the *patrons* had difficulties drawing on credit, which they needed to support their businesses, and ultimately left the *barracas*. The workers remained, however, and this triggered community building. In the remaining *barracas* the people were allowed to possess a *chaco* of their own because it became more difficult for the *patrons* to import consumer goods (Assies 1997: 43). The first significant period of community establishment can be dated to the fall and disintegration of the *Casa Suárez* from 1940 to the beginning of the 1960s and the agrarian reform of 1953. The people who began living as a community were accustomed to another form of social organisation. The main work force in the *barracas* had not been from the region, because local labour was scarce. As Friedrich Umlauft put it as early as 1898, "What is it that one needs to establish a rubber industry? Three things: people, people and people." (Translation from German by the author) (p. 483). During the rubber boom they were hired from outside the region, mainly from Santa Cruz, by means of an enlistment system (*sistema de enganche*), by intermediaries and even by headhunters using armed force (especially among Indians of the *Chaco*[41] region and Moxos, with similar things happening on the Brazilian side of the border) (Stoian 2000: 64).

The communities started to evolve, but the inhabitants came from a dependency relationship, where agriculture was not allowed or only carried out to the extent required to nourish oneself. Therefore, having access to a parcel of land, which belonged *de facto* to them was new. The fact that there were neighbours with equal opportunities, and that everyone had a range of choices of where and how much to cultivate and to decide where it was better to collect rubber and where Brazil nuts was also new. A new form of social organisation and a new relationship between man and the earth began to emerge (CIDOB 1979: 36).

Krempin (1986: 221) reported that the social conscience of 'peasants' before the revolution in 1952 was restricted to life and solidarity within the family and the local community, exploitation and oppression by the *patrón*, and the rivalries and conflicts with neighbouring settlements. Following the revolution, and the resulting agrarian reform and universal suffrage, the peasants became more integrated into the economic and political life of the nation. This holds especially true for the communities in the Andes and the valley region. In the Amazon, as has been described above, community history shows that the influence of the *patrón* disappeared early in certain places, but remained until the nineties in many others, and still exists even today locally due to the organisation of the Brazil nut extraction economy. The *sindicatos* played an important role in a few communities of the Amazon in the late sixties and early seventies. Syndicate leaders initiated a liberation movement, which led to a breakaway from the patron (personal communication – Trinidadcito). The connection to the state developed rather slowly and was marked by the implementation of the reforms in the nineties, whereas previously in the north the local elite ruled.

3.4.3 Indicators for path dependency

How can path dependency shape the outcome of the reform? The indicators used in this study deemed appropriate for making a statement on the probability of a common property regime in the future are:

a) The degree of internal organisation prior to implementation of the land reform.
b) Efforts to secure resource access for the community (not individuals) in the past before the reform.
c) External organisational input for meeting requirements of the reform.
d) Power distribution/internal power asymmetries.
e) Resource endowment potential – land.
f) Resource endowment potential – Brazil nuts.
g) Resource endowment potential – fish.

[41] In this case not an agricultural field, but the name of a region.

Different variables were entered under each indicator, the definitions of which are given with the presentation of the results. Indicators a to d relate to the social aspects, which were the basis for the calculation of the communal resource management potential. Indicators a and b were positive, and c and d negative due to restrictions. Indicators e to g were used to calculate the natural resource potential. These two sums were combined to determine the implications for future common property use (section 3.5.1, table 3-4).

Though external organisational input into the communities for the purposes of reform may be considered positive, because occasionally a push factor and immediate action in relation to a certain event may be necessary, this author attributes a negative value to it on the basis of the following hypothesis: In the case of the communities observed in this study it is very unlikely that a system of community organisation and internal rules created mainly by external forces will be implemented by the local people. Therefore external influence on a community's internal rule setting was predefined as negative in the context of this study based on the assumption that it highlights of internal community deficiencies, which lead to authoritarian influence from outside. If a community is basically autonomous in its performance and seeks or receives external support for capacity-building or other benefits, it does not fall into the category of high 'negative' external influence.

3.4.4 Research villages

The most important features of El Sena, Loma Velarde, San Juan km 27 and Trinidadcito are detailed in table 3-1 below. The typology is based on the categorisation of Stoian and Henkemans who carried out their fieldwork until 1999. By the time the research discussed here had started, the only village selected from the barraca type, a barraca in transition, had already evolved into one of the independent community categories, namely extractive community. Therefore, all four communities are officially independent communities now, with differences as to when they became so.

In table 3-2 the migration background of the people in the respective villages is summarised. The data is based on all of the interviewees at the household level, not on the total of the village level. Nevertheless, the data provides insights into the formation of the village as well.

Table 3-1: Research Villages

	PANDO			BENI
Village	**Loma Velarde**	**El Sena**	**Trinidadcito**	**San Juán km 27**
Typology	Barraca in transition, then extractive independent community	Rural sub-centre (*barraca* in transition)	Extractive independent community	Agro-extractive independent com.
Households[1]	9	~90	45	27
Land use during fieldwork period:	**Common Property (CP)** for NTFP etc. Agriculture on certain plots	**NO CP,** NTFP extraction across the whole territory by various community members for the same person. Low incidence of households with plots for agriculture//	**CP** for NTFP etc. Agriculture on certain plots	actually **CP**, but resource use only on certain plots
Hectares: (unofficial total 2001)	495 ha +15,000 ha	not exactly known, private claims high	8,500 ha	3,260 ha (average plot size 50 ha)
Access	river (path in dry season)	road and river	river (path in dry season)	road
from Riberalta	remote	average	remote	good
Foundation	1942, then IC[2] ~1997	1940, then IC ~1996/2002	1908, then IC ~1972	1970s (always independent)
Province	Manuripi	Madre de Dios	Madre de Dios	Vaca Diez

Notes:
The number of households (not families) recorded is the value for October 2001

IC = Independent community. Date, when 'officially' no longer barraca, *but sometimes still without a working OTB*

MIGRATION BACKGROUND		EL SENA	LOMA VELARDE	SAN JUAN KM 27	TRINIDADCITO
PLACE OF BIRTH	**TOTAL**	**3**	**11**	**4**	**24**
FROM RURAL AREA	**TOTAL**	**27**	**56**	**70**	**47**
No division		-	-	-	-
Dependent employment	in barraca	13	34	49	20
	as peon	3	11	17	6
	on boat	8	-	-	-
Independent employment	in peasant community	3	11	4	6
	as merchant	-	-	-	-
Others	family obligations	-	-	-	14
FROM URBAN AREA	**TOTAL**	**40**	**11**	**22**	**26**
No division	only town indicated	18	-	-	10
Dependent employment	in shelling industry	3	-	14	3
	by the state	3	-	4	7
Independent employment	as merchant	10	11	4	3
	as craftsman	3	-	-	-
Others	family obligations	3	-	-	3
NOT SPECIFIED	**TOTAL**	**30**	**22**	**4**	**3**
Reason given for migration	business reasons	13	-	4	-
	family obligations	10	22	-	-
No reason for migration given		7	-	-	3
OVERALL	TOTAL	100% (n=30)	100% (n=9)	100% (n=23)	100% (n=30)

Table 3-2: Migration background: Peoples' location before they settled in the village

Note:
All numbers are percentages

The rural sub-centre El Sena (household coverage 33%) contains the highest number of inhabitants with a history of urban migration. There is a high proportion of people involved in trade, yet people with a history of rural migration also make up an ample part of the population. Of these, the majority were engaged in dependent work, as *zafreros*, *peones*, or serving on boats. In El Sena few among those with a history of rural migration have been in an independent community before.

The village closest to a large town – San Juan km 27 - with a household interview coverage of 85%, proved to have the highest number of community members with a history of migration from rural areas. Additionally, it has the highest percentage of people who used to work in dependent employment, as *zafreros* in *barracas* and as *peon*es, as well as in urban areas, in the shelling industry. The village was formed by a small number of people who left a *barraca*, settled where is now San Juan km 27 and then informed friends and relatives still working in the *barraca* that this was a place where they could settle and receive land.

In the remote villages Loma Velarde (household coverage 100%) and Trinidadcito (household coverage 67%) a substantial proportion of the people have a history of rural migration, and a great many others were born there and have never moved. Though remote, Trinidadcito also revealed a significant number of inhabitants with a history of urban migration. This is partly due to the high number of teachers needed in the relatively big school. In Trinidadcito teachers are excluded from natural resource use since they receive a monetary income from the state (albeit a low income), and newly arriving families only receive permission to collect Brazil nuts if they have children of school age. Women work important jobs in the village, (e.g. the vice-mayor for the area, as teachers etc.). Mention was also made of a kind of marriage policy, whereby men from the village married women from outside to balance the deficit of women in the village. In general it is noticeable that the women in Trinidadcito participate more, and there is a more emancipated atmosphere. This was observed by several individuals other than the author, and was even stressed with pride by some of the village inhabitants themselves.

3.5 Results

3.5.1 Internal rule setting

Usually all communities affiliated with the regional (and national) peasant organisation are governed by a charter. This written document sets out the rules for the community and *sindicato* members. It defines organisational structures, procedures, obligations and rights, such as land and forest use as well as sanctions in the event of the rules being broken. The communities in the research area are quite young. Whereas some have been independent from the date of their foundation onwards, other independent communities emerged from *barracas*.

To have a charter is a prerequisite for the *Personaría Jurídica* as a peasant community and for recognition as an *OTB* in order to participate within the new legal structure. Additionally, it is necessary to be organised in this way in order to claim communal peasant land under the *saneamiento* process.

As many rural settlements were in a process of transition from *barraca* to independent community, or did not yet possess a charter for other reasons, the regional *campesino* organisations started a campaign to incorporate them. They offered them incentives to organise according to the *sindicato* structure and create a charter. It has to be stressed that a OTB charter and the *sindicato* structure are different. The latter is in the interest of the peasant federations, whereas municipal administrations were not willing to accept OTBs termed *sindicatos* – despite a lack of any legal reasons for not doing so. This issue was settled in the region in 2001 as in problematic municipalities the communities merely avoided using the term *sindicato* in the charter, though organising as such.

In the following paragraphs the setting of rules in the form of a charter is discussed for the four case study villages. This does not mean that there were no rules before the creation of the charters, however. Where older charters had been developed in participation with the community members, such informal communal rules were officially recognised. In other cases something altogether new was created, requiring time to be assimilated by the population, if at all. If there was previously a patron, the author has assumed that there were no communal rules in the sense of local norms to which the actors deliberately chose to adhere, but instead rules which were accepted but set by an individual and not by the community.

El Sena

El Sena is a municipality made up of twelve communities, including the research community also called El Sena, where the municipality administration is located. The location of the research community is favourable in terms of the transport infrastructure. It lies on the main road within the *Departamento Pando*, along which all traffic must pass – whether it be to La Paz, Beni and Riberalta, or other parts of the country – eventually leading to Cobija and the bordering countries Peru and Brazil. El Sena is also situated at the meeting point of the river El Sena and the river Madre de Dios. Consequently, much important water traffic to the Departamento La Paz (e.g. timber from the Ixiamas province etc.) also passes through.

El Sena is designated a peasant community. However, the communal representation at the time of the study was not given and unclear until an outside initiative by NGOs and the regional peasant association in the run-up to the *saneamiento*. The community is divided into two geographic parts. The 'upper' part is where the majority of houses, municipal buildings, the school, a hotel owned by the mayor's family etc. are located. The harbour is located in the 'lower' part, which is home to many merchants, some small hotels and *galpones*, who live in houses or on boats. The policy of the 'upper' part of the community is to keep out merchants and other people from the community engaged in NTFP trade (which is in defiance of the near monopolistic position of the mayor's family shop). As a result they settled in the 'lower' part, under the goodwill of the Bolivian Navy, which owns the area.

Although something like an OTB existed in the 'upper' part, the president did not call any more meetings, because it was not accepted or recognised at the municipal level due to its demands etc. A number of committed people remained and continued to uphold the OTB and worked in the common interest, but without much feedback or support. At the same time there were attempts at the municipal level to create a *Junta Vecinal* as an alternative, which should in reality be the same. The main difference is that the OTB was by enlarge peasant-driven, whereas the *Junta Vecinal* is by definition urban; in El Sena the municipality itself was responsible for the top-down administration. Additionally, as only a limited number of people are either informed or involved, this alternative is prone to corruption. In the 'lower' part the inhabitants were better organised in their own *Junta Vecinal/OTB*, but without recognition at the municipality level and, consequently, they struggled to make themselves heard.

Due to the polity implemented many people were convinced that they had no right or opportunity to obtain access to land in the upcoming *saneamiento* process. One week prior to the announced arrival of the land measurement crews, several NGOs and the regional peasant association initiated a workshop in El Sena, inviting as many people as they could from both parts of El Sena in order to clarify the legal situation and the need for community representation involving everyone. Despite impediments placed in the way by the municipal administration, the workshop took place and was successful in the sense that people were made aware of the legal opportunities and challenges. This process developed a dynamic of its own and people began to organise themselves enthusiastically to prepare for the coming land measurement crew. On this occasion (27th April 2002) a majority of the inhabitants voted for an OTB.

The internal rule-making framework of the legitimate OTB was established initially under external influence and subsequently by the newly organised disparate parts of the community, which had previously lacked a platform to do so. Prior to this the mayor's family predominantly dictated the rules. They were the patrons before decentralization and continued to act as such after municipalisation. Although property rights relating to Brazil nut stands remained unclear officially, the collectors were obliged to sell to the mayor's family, and not to merchants. This is illustrated by the following quote from a woman, who has been a community inhabitant for thirty years and involved in the area's main economic activity, Brazil nut recollection (26th April 2002):

"Este año más vendimos al colla que a él. Don [the mayor's father, author's note] se enojò 'la barraca es mia , la almendra es mia. Los voy a meter preso a los que vendieron a otro lado'. Uno tiene que entrarse a pié no más y salir como puede. Entrar solo para castañear, la almendra se saca en tractor mientras nosotros tenemos que volver a pie."

"This year we sold more to a Colla[42] than to him. Don [the mayor's father] got angry. 'The barraca is mine. The Brazil nuts are mine. I will imprison those who have sold to others.' To enter the forest we have to come and go as we can. We just enter to collect Brazil nuts, which are brought out by tractor while we leave on foot."

She also added that the police collaborate with Don [...].

Apart from the income from Brazil nut collection, an important employment factor during the year is the improvement of infrastructure, the construction of administrative buildings etc. financed by the *Participacion Popular*. The following statement was made by a Colla, in which he refers to people employed for *obras públicas* in El Sena:

"Esclavitud moderna, hay patrones pero no se dan latigazos, pero hay presión psicológica. No se recibe salario sino víveres. Todos los recursos de la PP los manejan ellos como si fueron de ellos. Queremos que nos reconozcan como gremio sin descriminación. La mayoría de aca son collas (...). Conocemos nuestros derechos, no quieren que mejoremos la comunidad. Trataron de sacarnos, no nos quieren."

"It's modern slavery. There are patrons but they don't use the lash, they use psychological pressure. One does not receive cash but foodstuffs. They manage all of the Popular Participation funds as if they were their own. We want them to recognise us as a committee without discrimination. The majority here [in the 'lower' part, author's note] are Collas. We know our rights. They don't want us to improve the community. They tried to throw us out. They don't like us."

A political activist who initiated a campaign in the region for the upcoming election described El Sena as follows (2nd April 2002):

"Aqui es barraca. La gente está acostumbrada a trabajar 30 días del mes para tener a comer"

"This is a barraca. The people are used to working thirty days a month in order to have enough food."

<u>Loma Velarde</u>

The research community Loma Velarde is located on the river Orthon. The area is remote, which means many hours travel by boat (or boat and motorbike) from any urban centre. Until the mid 1990s the majority of the settlements were still *barracas*. Today some of these are independent communities. Loma Velarde became an OTB as late as the close of the nineties (although patronal structures partly continued). It did not have a charter of its own so the regional peasant organisation incorporated Loma Velarde into its campaign to provide them with one. Although this campaign took place in 2001, and resulted in a syndicate structure with some office holders, the charter was still incomplete at the beginning of 2002. Those

---

[42] Colla is the term for a person from the highlands, the Andes. The former rulers of El Sena practise a form of racism against Collas due to their strong presence as merchants.

responsible felt abandoned and did not know how to achieve their task. Some months later the initiative was taken up by an NGO, which had started to work in the community. Members of this NGO introduced a model charter, which was read out at a community meeting and each aspect was voted upon. In this case the formal rule setting received an external push, with the risk that the assimilation of the rules may take a long time or perhaps fail altogether.

San Juan km 27

The research community San Juan km 27 is located only one hour away from the urban centre Riberalta, with rapid transport means available. It was founded as a settlement of individual families and was an independent community right from the beginning. In San Juan km 27 the *sindicato* structure is an important trait of village organisation, and exists as long as there are various families. Accounts of the San Juan community go back to the seventies. Each family wishing to live in the community must become a member of the *sindicato*. The *sindicato* is formed by an elected body of office holders and all members. The communal *sindicato* meetings take place every two weeks and attendance is compulsory. Failure to attend without prior written notification explaining the reasons results in a fine, as does failure to attend following a repudiation of the reasons given. Each member (usually married couples, so they pay twice) has to pay a monthly monetary contribution to the *sindicato*. Half of the money goes to the regional federation and half to the community organisation to be used for various purposes.

Although the San Juan km 27 community observes a strict set of rules, they were not in written form until a NGO and the federation acted to have them set down in writing. In this case the rules have been in existence for a long time and were widely known by the community members. There is a high degree of acceptance of the rules, despite their original informal nature and the fact that they were merely transmitted orally. The setting down of the rules in writing following external influence was merely a formalisation of the rules. Interviewees indicated that they were informed that the community had a charter of its own from that point on, but in many cases they had not seen the document themselves. As a result they were not sure if that document contained 'new' rules of which they were unaware. Even if they had the opportunity to view the document, there is a considerably high level of illiteracy, especially among women.

Trinidadcito

The research community Trinidadcito is located on the river Madre de Dios. During the dry season it can be reached by motorbike travelling along a narrow path, a trip lasting several hours. During the rainy season access is only possible by boat. It has been classified as remote in the context of this study[43]. The most frequent transport means are boats, mainly carrying Brazil nuts. The duration of the trip from Trinidadcito to Riberalta by boat is ~10

[43] The construction of a road began in 2002, a number of months after the research presented here took place.

hours downstream and 20 hours upstream[44]. The history of the Trinidadcito settlement began in 1908. Initially it was a *barraca*, but there was a struggle for independence, the result of which was an independent community in 1972. It counts as a communal *sindicato* or OTB, and is at the same time a fishermen's *sindicato*. Fishing is an important source of monetary income for this community. The community has been successful in securing access to a lake rich in fish and claiming ownership against other possible users with the backing of the authorities, although it lacks a legal basis for these access rights.

The OTB's internal community rules were laid down by the communal syndicate, without interference from outside. However, these rules make only a part of the fixed rules due to the importance of the fishermen's association, to which many family heads also belong. In fact its economic importance meant a second level of communal rule setting was necessary. This community is set apart by the fact that internal rule making takes place without outside interference, whereas internally, there is a culture of active discussion of these rules.

The findings from the different research communities show a clear tendency. The shorter the period of time during which the community has been independent, the greater the external influence over the setting of rules, and the lower the degree of assimilation of these rules.

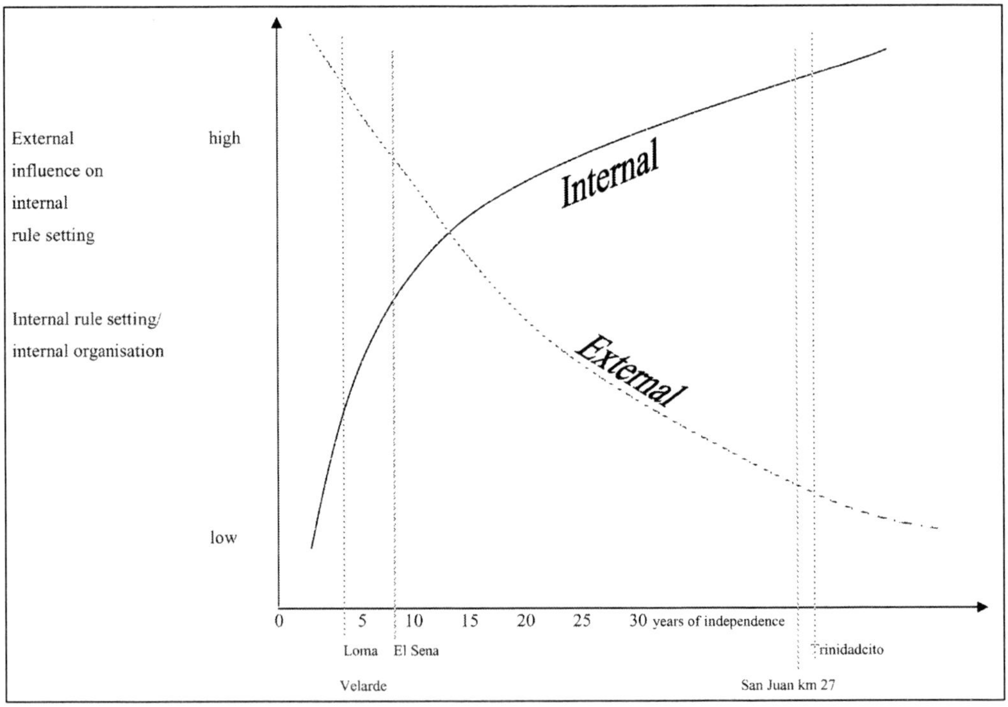

Figure 3-1: The Rule of Time

[44] A fast motorboat makes it in half the time, but is very expensive and only used by politicians or organisations with money. Another possibility is to use the Riberalta-El Sena road, and then a boat. This is also a long trip, however.

3.5.2 Communal resource management potential and resource endowment *or* what will become of common property?

The process of land (re)distribution under the reforms has not yet ended. Nevertheless, it is clear that the independent communities in the northern Bolivian Amazon account for a large piece of the cake. This does not only mean merely land, but also implies access to vast forest areas. In order to claim land these communities had to prove to the land administration authorities that they were organised. Whereas some communities accomplished this by themselves, others relied heavily on the assistance of external actors. By law, the common pool resources are regarded the 'common property' of the community. The intent behind the law is the management of the resource pool under a common property regime, but whether resources are actually managed as such depends on the inhabitants themselves.

Although under law the community owns a common pool of resources, the property regime has yet to be decided by the community members[45]. If this does not happen, or happens in a manner based more on individual user rights than common share contracts etc., there will not be a common property regime. The result will be a common pool of resources with a property regime that differs from common property, with economic, ecological and distributional consequences and, therefore, social effects. However, such a property regime is legitimate as long as the manner in which the decision is arrived at preserves the legal form.

In this section, a tool for the assessment of the community resource management potential and the possible implications for future common property use are presented, using mainly qualitative indicators. On the one hand, the communal management potential was calculated by means of qualitative factors (yellow part of the table). The resource endowment potential, on the other hand, was estimated using quantitative data (green part of the table). The outcomes of both for each village were placed in a cross-table. The result is the implication for future common property use (red results). In order to calculate the communal management potential, the yellow parts were valued positively, whereas the grey parts were considered negative. Each indicator and its variables, and the derived results, are explained after table 3-3:

[45] This distinction follows Ostrom (1997: 7). Ostrom pointed out the importance of distinguishing between the resource system and the property regime.

Table 3-3- Communal resource management potential

	El Sena	Loma Velarde	San Juan km 27	Trinidadcito
Degree of internal organisation prior to implementation of the land reform	XX	X	XXX	XXX
Efforts to secure community (NOT individual) access to resources in the past (before the reform)	X	(X)	XX	XXX
External organisational input for reform	II	II	I	I
Unequal power distribution	III	II	I	I
Communal resource management potential ⇒	low	low	medium	high
Resource endowment potential (hectares/family)	X(X)	XXX	X	XX
Resource endowment potential (Brazil nuts/family)	XX(X)	XXX	X	XXX
Resource endowment potential (fish/family)	(X)	XX	-	XXX
Natural resource potential ⇒	medium	high	low	high
Implications for future common property use	critical	critical	acceptable	positive

Timber potential *is not mentioned here because an estimate requires inventories (and it is not known how much timber has already been cut illegally). As all of these communities are surrounded by forests and dependent upon the forests, the greater the land potential, the greater the timber potential, generally speaking.*

Degree of internal organisation prior to implementation of the land reform

The more 'X', the better

X People regard themselves and their neighbours as members of the same settlement. However, no permanent and formal communal organisation with meetings taking place on a regular basis exists. There are no written rules, nor is membership fixed in a document. The exchange of information occurs in a casual, informal way, if at all.

XX A formalised communal organisation exists officially. Nevertheless, communal meetings only take place occasionally without the knowledge of all members. Decisions concerning all community members are taken without their participation or knowledge. Community organisation is incomplete and representation does not comply with democratic standards. There are other groups, which organise under the 'community' umbrella with competing interests and unequal access to power, resources and information.

XXX There is a formal institutionalised community organisation. Everyone knows about it and has the opportunity and/or obligation to participate. There are community meetings on a regular basis, leaders are accountable and the representation of community interests outside/at higher levels is partly secured (with certain risks and problems).

Efforts to secure community (not individual) access to resources in the past (before the reform)

The more 'X', the better

- No effort at all, or merely individuals acting solely out of personal interest.

X Initiatives by some individuals to secure access to resources for a majority of community members, but due to stumbling blocks within the settlement have had no success in doing so.

XX Initiatives at community level to secure access to resources, but success is only achieved with external NGO support.

XXX Initiatives at community level to secure access to resources have been successful, authorities satisfied with the outcome and provide the necessary backing.

External organisational input for reform

The less 'I', the better

I Community seeks external information and advice, but only a limited amount. The main tasks have been organised and accomplished by the community itself.

II External organisational input is high. Organisation required in order to meet reform requirements could not have been realised by the community alone, due to a very low degree of information and organisation within the community and/or only a small fraction of community members take the initiative, and face internal obstacles or lack of support.

Unequal power distribution/Internal power asymmetries

The less 'I', the better

I Community members have similar (bargaining) power. Power struggles occur, which lead to temporary advantages for each of them, but overall there is a balance.

II There is an imbalance of (bargaining) power rooted in the previous institutional structure, which is to the advantage of a minority. Other actors are strengthening their bargaining power by means of collective action. A more balanced situation is expected in the future.

III There is a severe power imbalance within the community, which leads to a monopoly situation in favour of a minority, on which the majority depends. The previous institutional mechanisms remain strong. The other actors face high costs if they are to change anything.

Communal resource management potential

LOW The degree of internal organisation is low to medium, with little effort made to secure access to resources before the reform. At the same time, external organisational input for reform has been high and significant imbalances of power are evident. The likelihood that resources will in the future be managed on a communal basis is low. If there is to be management, it will be the role of certain powerful individuals, at the cost of the other community members.

MEDIUM The degree of internal organisation is medium to high, with some effort made to secure access to resources before the reform. At the same time, there has been little external organisational input and there are no significant imbalances of power. It is likely that in the future all concerned will manage resources on a communal basis.

HIGH There is high degree of internal organisation, with a lot of effort made to secure access resources before the reform. At the same time, there has been little external organisational input and there are no significant imbalances of power. It is highly likely that in the future all concerned will manage resources on a communal basis.

Resource endowment potential – land

(hectares/family)

The entire communal area (as defined for the purposes of the reform) was taken into consideration in the calculation of the land endowment potential, discounting areas used for community purposes, and dividing by the number of families (in case of Trinidadcito the teachers' families are excluded from the calculation). The exact number must match the results of the reform process. In the case of El Sena the result of the land claims was relatively uncertain, therefore the evaluation is based on two options (without and with the X in brackets). As the quality of land can differ substantially, these numbers have to be regarded as a benchmark. For the calculation of land per family, the author did not distinguish between whether the entire area was used by all families, or if the area itself had already been divided in family parcels.

X	20 to 80 hectares
XX	80 to 250 hectares
XXX	250 to 1000 hectares

Resource endowment potential – Brazil nuts

(Brazil nuts/family)

X	42 *cajas* average, (with a range of 20 to 80 *cajas*)
XX	100 *cajas* average
XXX	150 *cajas* average (with a range of 50 to 300 *cajas*)

Resource endowment potential – fish

-	No fish at all.
X	Fishing is possible, but there are many potential competitors and the conditions for fishing are poor in any case. Catch is sold occasionally.
XX	Fishing is possible, with only a limited number of competitors. Depending on the season, there may be a relatively high number of fish, but there is a lack of marketing channels.
XXX	Fishing is possible and the number of competitors is very limited. There is very high quantity of fish. Processing and marketing structures are in place and generate substantial cash income.

Natural resource potential

LOW	Each of the three resource endowment potentials - land (and therefore forest), Brazil nuts and fish - is low.

MEDIUM Certain resource endowment potentials are stronger, some weaker, but taken together there is the potential to generate income.

HIGH Each of the three resource endowment potentials is relatively high, so the overall potential is high.

Table 3-4: Implications for Future Common Property Use

Communal resource management potential Natural resource potential	low	medium	high
Low	critical	acceptable	positive
Medium	critical	acceptable	positive
High	critical	acceptable	positive

CRITICAL Common property resource use is critical, if there are high risks of mismanagement by individuals and/or unequal benefit-sharing and/or poor performance.

ACCEPTABLE Common property resource use has potential, though there are some weaknesses.

POSITIVE Conditions are very likely to guarantee a good common property regime with income potentials and possible commitment to sustainable use in the long run. The risk of the manipulation of communal management may jeopardise this goal, but the democratic participation of the community could prevent such developments.

These diagnoses hold true as long as there is no significant change to the external conditions, such as another legal reform, in-migration from other regions or a change to the value of natural resources due to road construction, combined with short-term opportunities for deception by individuals, which the communal sanction mechanisms can not prevent in time.

3.5.3 Agri'Culture'

Subsistence agriculture is one important pillar of the communities, a bolster against risks to livelihoods in the rural area. Food is provided, even without the generation of financial incomes. Agricultural products can be consumed, bartered or sold (in case of emergencies or surplus production). In the northern Bolivian Amazon, a *Campesino* is forest dwelling NTFP collector, day labourer and even fisherman who has one mainstay, his or her agricultural plot, the *chaco*.

The case studies at hand revealed differing forms of agri'culture' in the four settlements. This can partly be explained by their geographical location as this defines the importance of agriculture geared to the market (as surplus production in addition to subsistence) and its relative importance in comparison to income derived from extractive activities (cp. Stoian 2000: 187). However, data indicate the extent of agriculture is also a result of the local 'culture' in respective settlements. This culture is influenced by community internal socio-political conditions which favour or interfere with agriculture.

El Sena

Seventeen interviewees were not in possession of a *chaco*. Thirteen were, but two of them were located in another area far away (20 km distant). The eleven people with a chaco within reach possessed an average of one hectare, with the majority possessing less. The majority of them sought a patch of land near the road, and having found one established their agricultural plot. This often implied relatively long walking distances.

The following quote refers to people without a *chaco*:

"El dueño es el dueño de todo. No se puede tener un chaco por acá."

A community member, 4th April 2002, in El Sena

"The owner is the owner of everything. It is not possible to have an agricultural field here."

Prior to the reform El Sena exhibited some urban traits, yet at the same time the people had little scope to develop an individual livelihood strategy due to their dependency upon the former patron's family and the sanctioning mechanisms in case of rule breaking. Apart from merchants, who are increasingly establishing themselves in El Sena, school staff and the municipality administration, the rural Brazil nut collectors predominate. Before the hurried organisation for the arrival of the land measurement crew, the proportion of independent collectors and *campesinos* was negligibly low, almost nil. Outside the Brazil nut season these people are mostly unemployed, and even lack food, as they have no agricultural plots. Therefore, they occasionally work as *peones* and craftsmen in public road improvement, or the nearby hacienda etc. As has been mentioned already, a frequent practice of the municipality is not to give them money, but rather more expensive food and other articles from the employer's shop. The people themselves say this has to be accepted, because it is a privilege to be given the opportunity to work. Any complaints would result in no work at all. In short, prior to the implementation of the reform El Sena was neither independent, nor was there agri'culture', but feudal 'culture'.

Loma Velarde

All interviewees, except one who had arrived recently, had a *chaco*. The mean size is one hectare, with a range from 0.5 (due to illness and the owners inability to work a larger plot) to 1.5 hectares. The people in this village live outside of a monetary economy due to the almost complete lack of any connection to the markets in Riberalta. They barter with merchants for sugar, soap, cooking oil and clothing. For work as *peones* they receive goods, too, instead of money. Although everyone practises agriculture, the choice of where is constrained by the presence of the former patron's cattle herd. The other community members lacked the power to force him to erect fencing, but had to react in order to protect their own production. As nobody had the money for fencing, people opted for plots far away from their homes, with the disadvantage of long walking distances. This nuisance was voiced mainly by the female interviewees:

"El ganado de [...the former patron] frega chaco, él es el único, 20 cabezas de ganado. No hay para proteger el chaco"

A female community member

"[...the former patron]'s cattle damage the chaco. He is the only one. He has twenty head of cattle. There is nothing to protect the chaco." (No money for fencing material etc., author's note)

"Nuestro chaco queda a 'media luna', 45 min - por los animales"

Another female community member

"Our chaco is a 'half moon' away. Forty five minutes – due to the animals."

"Por el ganado lo hicimos lejito"

Another female community member

"We made it (the chaco) further away because of the cattle."

In Loma Velarde agri'culture' certainly plays an important role for the people, but it is practised on a very small scale of only one hectare, and not more. The situation reflects that this community occupies a position in the transition phase from *barraca* to independent community.

<u>San Juan km 27</u>

In San Juan km 27 each family affiliated with the *sindicato* holds at least one lot, which includes forest used for non-timber, timber and/or agricultural purposes. The entire communal territory is located at *altura*. Of the interviewees, 87% hold one lot and 13% two. Everybody (100%) has a *chaco*. Of those with one lot, 55% have their lot, including the *chaco*, next to their house (equivalent of 48% of the total). The mean size of a *chaco* in San Juan is 2.5 hectares per family. The range is from 1 to 6 hectares. No one has less than 1 hectare.

In San Juan km 27 affiliation with the communal organisation and attendance at meetings is compulsory. The community is a member of the regional peasant organisation. There is a very strong peasant identity in the community, with a great emphasis on the importance of a free, self-determined life. The livelihood of the inhabitants outside the Brazil nut season is very closely linked to their agricultural plot and the eventual sale of surplus in nearby Riberalta. Agri'culture' is strong in San Juan km 27. The following statement made by a community member underlines this (18th October 2001):

"Prefiero la agricultura, tengo para comer continuamente. Con eso da para proveerse. Cosecho el arroz, lo guardo, y si se uno se enferma, entonces lo vendo a alguien que tiene su peladora. (...) Para nosostros que no tenemos profesión es lindo la agricultura. Tuvimos chanchos, pero no se puede, se quejaron vecinos, pero no tengo capital para comprar alambre, o hacerlo afuera."

"I prefer agriculture. I always have enough food. There is enough provision. I harvest the rice, store it and if somebody becomes ill, then I sell it to someone with a shelling machine. For those of us without a profession, agriculture is a good thing. I had pork as well, but it is not possible here. The neighbours complained, and I do not have the capital to buy fencing."

The community has always been independent and the majority of its inhabitants had experience of a dependency relationship before they arrived there. For many of them, their range of choice was very limited and they appreciate having their own agricultural plot and a patch of forest. There is great awareness of the importance of self-organisation, although there are some weak points of which they are aware themselves. The participation of all community members is set and follows solidarity principles. These aspects are cornerstones of a path dependency, which provides favourable conditions for the outcome of the reform.

<u>Trinidadcito</u>

Twenty six out of thirty people interviewed in Trinidadcito have a *chaco*. Twenty four interviewees practice agriculture on 42 ha, which means an average of 1.75 ha/interviewee and their family. Two people did not know the area of their plots. The area ranges from a minimum of one hectare to a maximum of four hectares.

In the community one finds certain entrepreneurial traits, especially in relation to the extraction of fish and its processing and marketing. At the same time, families engaged in the fishing activity also have their *chacos*, with sizes greater than the average of many other communities in the region. Furthermore, they are all engaged in the extraction of Brazil nuts to various degrees. There are many teachers in the community due to the existence of a large school, and its location in a big catchment area. All teachers, with few exceptions, are excluded from the use of natural resources. A future scenario exercise with a group of village members revealed that there are two fractions with different ideas concerning the shape of resource use in the future. One wants to enhance the fishing activities and invest in the construction of a fish farm to avoid resource depletion, and at the same time maintain agricultural activity as a complementary source of income. The other fraction believes the intensification of fishing activities will lead to a dangerous depletion of resources, will require investment and worry due to unclear access to this resource in the future (which they have secured for the moment, but in an informal, politician-dependent way). The latter regard the intensification of agriculture and surplus production as an opportunity to supply the regional market, using the communal boat and the road, construction of which was to begin at the time of writing. They were also considering a potential income from tourism.

Trinidadcito is a stronghold of agriculture and fishery, with a tradition of entrepreneurship. It is remarkable that this community practices risk-aversion by planting seedlings in the chaco, partly in *bajio* and partly in *altura*. Where the risk of flooding is higher, the output is higher as well. The NGOs recommend planting in the less productive *altura* in order to avoid total loss in the event of flooding. Nevertheless, many communities refrain from planting in the *altura* (where the harvest is smaller but secure) if they have an option. As a result the people in these places frequently lose everything and need emergency programmes to secure their survival.

Trinidadcito has a long history, which is marked by a liberation movement from a patron some thirty years ago. There are families with different priorities in relation to resource use and there is an active communal organisation catering for each different group. These groups hold discussions and compete to some extent, but there is also a strong communal identity. Due to the great initiative of certain individuals, and the subsequent collective action on the part of the community, they benefited from the *Participacion Popular* and secured advantages in other areas. The community members are very active, with a great entrepreneurial spirit. What is remarkable is that there are individual plots for agriculture, whereas forest use takes place in one single communal area. The conditions in Trinidadcito seem to represent a benchmark for the reform process.

In the left hand column of table 3-5 the main differences in relation to receipt of access to land for an agricultural plot are presented. The main features mentioned in the previous section are reiterated in the right hand column.

Table 3-5: Agri'Culture'

	Access to land for *chaco*	*Chaco* ownership
El Sena	Individual plots. No concession of land. Community members must find a plot themselves. No more than 1 ha permitted.	37% of interviewees Mean size: 1 ha/family min. 0.5 max. 2.5
Loma Velarde	Individual plots. On communal land wherever appropriate.	89% of interviewees Mean size: 1 ha/family min. 0.5 max. 1.5
San Juan km 27	Individual plots. On personal lot (granted by community).	100% of interviewees Mean size: 2.5 ha/family min. 1 max. 6
Trinidadcito	Individual plots. On communal land wherever appropriate.	87% of interviewees Mean size: 1.8 ha/family min. 1 max. 4

All of the interviewees whose migration background was presented in table 2 answered a hypothetical question put to them in relation to their preferences for the future, if they had the choice. They had to decide upon one of the two given alternatives;

Would you prefer to have a chaco, or a lot with Brazil nuts?

Would you prefer to have a criadero (animal farm) or employment?

In San Juan km 27, where many people stem from a dependency relationship related to Brazil nuts, 78% said the would prefer a *chaco* to a lot with Brazil nuts, and 90% would prefer their own animal farm to employment.

In El Sena Brazil nut activity is strong, but people do not have property rights over Brazil nut lots. Here 80% would prefer such a lot to a *chaco*. Two thirds prefer the animal farm to employment.

In Loma Velarde slightly over 50% would prefer the *chaco* to the Brazil nut lot and slightly more than 50% prefer the animal farm to employment.

In Trinidadcito 57% of the interviewees opted for the *chaco*, whereas 43% preferred the Brazil nut option. Two thirds preferred the animal farm to employment.

4 THE CAPACITY OF RURAL COMMUNITIES

4.1 Introduction

4.1.1 Chapter overview

The focus of the debate on rural development has shifted from number-orientated poverty measurement and respective policy actions to more integrated approaches. These approaches seek to imply important social factors and draw a more precise picture of inter-subjective reality. These factors are more difficult to grasp than numbers, but represent an important contribution to the understanding of well-being and performance of people in rural areas. Theoretical debate in relation to these social factors is in full blossom, while the empirical research lags behind.

The aim of this chapter is to contribute to the understanding of community internal processes. In the overall concept of the thesis, it addresses the research question pertaining to how resource users organise within the community and how they set rules in order to secure their livelihoods or achieve a certain degree of well-being. What are the critical determinants in this respect?

The author has determined certain factors[46] deemed important in this context:

(1) internal community organisations found in each of the respective cases,

(2) the institutions governing political representation and natural resource use.

These two aspects have been analysed based on community data. Three further factors referred directly to the interviewees in each respective community:

(1) personal networks which help to obtain information on legal issues, access money in case of emergencies and access medium/long-term credit;

(2) the interviewees' trust in their representatives, the former patron, NGOs and the corregidor (in the cases where there was no former patron; not intended as a substitute);

(3) community achievements and the related internal processes, analysed as 'performance elements'.

Factors (1) to (4) address the main 'tools' available to the community inhabitants, to be used for performance at community level. This represents the ideal case. These tools can also be abused; for example, when certain individual advantages are pursued at the expense of other community members, misusing community resources and decreasing overall performance.

Factor (5) exemplifies how a beneficial achievement for the community can be accomplished through 'performance elements'. What may be beneficial to one community member can be a disadvantage to another. However, the author regards as beneficial at community level the

[46] Factors in the sense of factors of production

creation and enhancement of any of the five types of capital contained in the approach of the normative concept 'Sustainable Livelihoods'. This approach was developed by DFID, and adopted by the FAO and UNDP with the aim of improving the lives of the poor and to enhance their sustainability (Carney 1998: 4, Henkemans 2001: 10). The five types of capital are human capital, social capital, natural capital, physical capital and financial capital. In the context of the capabilities and functioning approach proposed by Sen, any enhancement of capabilities, the creation of functioning and the amplification of the options from which the individual or the community can choose are beneficial. See section 4.1.3 for more information about the concept put forward by Sen.

The chapter is based on the empirical study of community capacity as an important basis of community well-being in rural communities in the northern Bolivian Amazon. Community capacity combines 'Social Capital' and 'Capability and Functioning'. These concepts will be explained in sections 4.1.2 to 4.1.4. The capability and functioning approach has been developed for individuals, but will be modified here to apply to communities. 4.2 contains the empirical results, to be discussed in point 3.

4.1.2 Social capital and social assets

The concept of social capital is used in various branches of the social sciences with different definitions. The differences do not lead to a de-integration of the concept, however; they correspond to different aspects of the same phenomenon and can bridge the gap between disciplines. All of these different argument styles share the fact that social capital guarantees some kind of advantage for the individuals or entities that participate in its generation, from which they usually benefit. While some authors directly assign social capital to individuals, others regard it as something that cannot be assigned directly.

Hanifan (1916), an early pioneer of social capital, stated that "social capital (...) refer[s] to (...) those tangible assets [that] count for most in the daily lives of people: namely goodwill, fellowship, sympathy, and social intercourse among the individuals and families who make up a social unit." Authors from the 1960s and '70s supported this view. For the purposes of this study, the focus will remain on later concepts of social capital that have a significant influence in the current theoretical debate.

Social capital is frequently referred to as "features of social organization, such as networks, norms and social trust that facilitate coordination and cooperation for mutual benefit" (Putnam 1995: 67). Using comparative political studies Putnam, a political scientist, revealed that the high levels of civic engagement and social connectedness gird the success of democratic societies[47]. Putnam and Helliwell (2000) investigated the role of social capital in economic development in different regions of Italy.

[47] He received both acclaim and criticism for his 'bowling alone' hypothesis, which suggested that the involvement of (North) Americans in community activities is decreasing with the increased potential to undermine democratic well-being.

The sociologist Coleman regarded the analytical concept of social capital as a tool to import the economists' principle of rational action to analyse social systems. His main point was not to discard social organisation in the process: "Social capital is defined by its function. It is not a single entity but a variety of different entities having two characteristics in common: They all consist of some aspect of social structure, and they facilitate certain actions of actors – whether persons or corporate actors – within the structure. Like other forms of capital, social capital is productive, making possible the achievement of certain ends that would not be attainable in its absence" (Coleman 1988, p.98). He focused on associations, which are characterised by hierarchical relationships and an unequal distribution of power.

The French sociologist Bourdieu regarded social capital as the resources that result from social structure: "Social capital is the sum of the resources, actual or virtual, that accrue to an individual or group by virtue of possessing a durable network of more or less institutionalised relationships of mutual acquaintance and recognition" (Bourdieu and Wacquant 1992: 119, expanded from Bourdieu 1980).

A sophisticated piece on social capital can be found in Woolcock (1998). He looked into social capital from different angles, showing the diversified themes of many authors on the subject and delivered a critical evaluation of these. Despite several critical remarks, his overall balance was positive (*ibid*: 188):

"Social capital provides sociologists in particular with a fruitful conceptual and policy device by which to get beyond exhausted modernization and world-system theories and make potentially important contributions to questions of economic development, contributions that complement orthodox economic approaches in some respects and challenge them in others. Social capital's greatest merit, however, is that it provides a credible point of entry for socio-political issues into a comprehensive multi- and interdisciplinary approach to some of the most pressing issues of our time. In social capital, historians, political scientists, anthropologists, economists, sociologists, and policy makers – and the various camps within each field – may once again begin to find a common language within which to engage one another in open, constructive debate, a language that disciplinary provincialisms have largely suppressed over the last one-hundred-and-fifty years. By the same token, it is important to concede that we still have much to learn about social capital, and that for the time being our empirical expectations of it should be correspondingly modest. Theoretical claims and policy recommendations made on the basis of the incremental accumulation of evidence constitute the surest and most responsible agenda for future research."

The advantages presented by Woolcock provided the main motivation for the application of the social capital theory as a research concept for this empirical study. Given the constraints on what or when something is social capital, the result of much ambiguous dialogue within this research field, a clear working definition of social assets in a concrete conceptualisation of social capital was desirable (see next section). A further aim of this study was to contribute to the development of the concept through the accumulation of data.

A concrete conceptualisation of social capital that bridges the gap between disciplines can be found in the work of von Twickel (2002). He re-differentiated, and in economic terms reformulated, the concept of social capital in order to apply it within an analytical institutional economics framework. Hence, he arrived at a common framework for the discussion among sociologists, political scientists and economists in order to find solutions and identify the role of normative steering. Von Twickel regarded social capital strictly as a good, a product requiring investment in order to realise cooperation benefits later on. The evaluation of social capital depends then on conditions such as whether organisational structure or norms can really contribute to the realisation of benefits. The mere existence of a structure or rules alone is not regarded as social capital. Relations, networks and institutions enter into the political process as invested goods or properties (von Twickel 2002: 110). The following formula expresses how institutional economics perceives the relationship between social capital and the performance of society:

Table 4-1 Formula of relation between social capital and performance of society

Performance of society =
f (social capital,...) = f (g (social assets, institutions,...),...)

Source: Von Twickel 2002: 111, translated by the author

In this formula the social assets stand for the required relationships and networks; institutions in this context adhere to the institutional economics definition, namely as rules and norms. The placeholder stands for other factors with similar functions, but not yet identified or specified (this is a logical deduction, whereas in the original document there was no explanation given). The distinction of social capital and social assets allows a more precise discussion, because the social assets usually need time to develop and achieve stability, which is a precondition in order to serve as capital for the realisation of benefits in a cooperation situation.

Granovetter (1985) criticised the "undersocialized concept of man"[48], and attacked new institutional economics as being crudely functionalist. The existence of an economic institution is often explained merely by the function it performs for the economic system. He emphasised the importance of personal relationships and networks of relationships, which he referred to as 'embeddedness'. This embeddedness is important for generating trust, establishing expectations, and creating and enforcing norms (Coleman 1988: 15).

Von Twickel's approach includes this aspect and, for the purposes of this thesis, has therefore been applied to serve as a working definition of social assets: 'Social assets' include organisations, institutions (as rules and norms), networks and trust. They usually require time to develop and are embedded in a conditioned setting. Social assets shall only be denominated

[48] He also criticised the over-socialisation of man as the other extreme.

as elements[49] of social capital when they generate benefits. So, in the context of this study social capital is to be identified *ex post*, after having generated benefits. Before any benefits have accrued, there are only social assets, which can be invested in, in order to generate social capital.

4.1.2 Capability and functioning

Commodity-based theories and utility theories do not cover an ample range of the concept of the standard of living and well-being (see Jasek-Rysdahl 2001: 315). Amartya Sen introduced his concept of capability and functioning as an alternative for understanding well-being in a broader scope. Sen did not agree with a focus on income (resources) or utilities, but preferred to argue in favour of the so-called 'space of functionings' (Klamer/Mante 2002: 6). "A functioning is the achievement of a person: what he or she manages to do or to be" (Sen 1985: 10). In this study functioning, as defined by Sen, shall be expressed in the term performance element. Capabilities, as opposed to functions, concern the ability of an individual to achieve different combinations of performance elements, and define the freedom to choose the life preferred[50]. Capabilities are real opportunities and alternatives, which may also be understood as yet unrealised performance elements (*ibid.*).

In Sen's (1979) seminal work, capabilities are the basis upon which equality can be evaluated. He approached the eternal problem of subjective indicators by dividing the evaluation into two parts: "(i) *specification* of the functioning achievements, and (ii) the *valuation* of the functioning achievements" (Sen 1985: 30).

Sen's approach is based on the idea that the standard of living is a measure of the life a person leads and the number of choices available to them for different life achievements. Sen concentrated on choice and opportunity, and according to him, capabilities represent the level of choice that individuals have. Sen defined capabilities as the "alternative combinations of functions the person can achieve, and from which he or she can choose one collection" (Sen 1993: 31).

The relationship between commodities and performance elements matters. Sen (1985) viewed commodities in terms of their characteristics: "The characteristics are the various desirable properties of the commodities in question. Securing amounts of these commodities gives the person command over the corresponding characteristics" (*ibid.* 9). For example, the possession of land provides the owner with access to the properties of the land, which can be used to build a house, practice agriculture, earn money, derive pleasure as a place to relax, provide support for conservation, etc. In relation to performance, Sen stated: "However, the

[49] There are more elements to social capital, but for the purposes of this study the author will focus on the four mentioned above.

[50] To investigate exactly these issues the so-called MISS (Measuring Sustainability in Sen's framework) Project was instigated by the University at Albany (State University of New York) at the beginning of January 2004. The aim of the project was to define a possible operative map of sustainable human development as intended in the capability approach, related to the concept proposed by the winner of the Nobel Prize for Economics Amartya Sen.

characteristics of the goods do not tell us what the person will be able to do with those properties." (*ibid.* 9). For example, if a person has no access to credit, then they may encounter problems due to limited performance choices[51], even though they may have the same area of land as another person in a superior financial situation[52].

"In judging the well-being of the person, it would be premature to limit the analysis to the characteristics of the goods possessed. We have to consider the 'functionings' [performance elements, author's note] of persons. While the ownership of commodities is a personal matter, and thus the command over the characteristics of goods owned is also a personal matter, the quantification of characteristics does not vary with the personal features of the individual possessing the goods" (*ibid.* 9). A motorbike has the characteristics of 'transportation', and this is the case whether or not the owner of the motorbike has a driving license, or enough money to pay for petrol, oil or repairs. "In getting an idea of the well-being of this person, we clearly have to move on to 'functionings' [performance elements, author's note], to wit, what the person succeeds in *doing* with the commodities and characteristics at his or her command" (*ibid.* 9). For example, we must assume that a badly organised or ill individual may not be able to do many of the things that an organised or healthy individual can do given the same bundle of commodities.

Capabilities are determined through utilisation functions (Sen, 1985, chapter 2). These personal utilisation functions each reflect one pattern of commodity use that this individual can actually make. There are sets of 'utilisation functions' from which one can chose. One of the main features in the literature on the subject of capabilities is that the utilisation functions are understood to be determined exogenously. However, Sen noted that utilisation functions depend upon time-dependent parameters like age, health, social conditions and education (chapter 12). Recently other scientists began to develop a relevant dynamic analysis (see for example D'Agata 2003). For the purposes of this study, the author adhered to this concept of dynamic human capabilities. The reasoning behind this was that individuals can change, deliberately or otherwise, due to both endogenous and exogenous factors, their utilisation functions (or their set of utilisation functions), or their characteristic functions over time.

Treatise on equality

Programmes for poverty alleviation and/or the improvement of well-being, be it regional, national or supranational, are aimed at people that are somehow disadvantaged or constrained in their activities, and worse off in comparison to others. Social capital and social assets are assumed to facilitate improved outcomes and are regarded by some authors to be an end in themselves. The existence of social assets and social capital is regarded a part of well-being

[51] No money to buy seedlings, tools for agriculture, etc.

[52] This is particularly relevant to the situation in Bolivia. A peasant family that possesses land within a community cannot use this land as security to obtain credit from the bank due to the legal regulations preventing the sale of communal land. It is possible, however, to sell the 'improvements' in the event that the family moves elsewhere. They can charge for the house they have constructed, the crops they have planted, etc. So the property 'earn money' is limited in the context of this study, at least in direct terms.

and a driving factor in poverty alleviation. Therefore, development research considers how these assets are created, and whether it is possible or useful to invest in their creation or maintenance. An underlying goal of many human development programmes is to smoothen inequalities and pursue a redistribution or improvement of opportunities, which is guided by some equality principle. But what is equality? Equality can be interpreted in many ways, which always distorts the outcome of the respective policy, as it seeks to decrease inequalities in compliance with the definition. Any kind of policy underlies some normative principles, which have to be made transparent.

Sen's approach to the problem concerning equality was to find a preliminary answer to the question of the right choice of variables. The focal variables are chosen according to the specific interpersonal inequality to be evaluated. When they are chosen, the resources should then be allocated in such a way as to ensure the equality of capabilities in the variable space (Sen 1992). However, Sen made it clear that equality in a variable space does not necessarily ensure equality in another variable space, because individuals differ in the ways in which they are able to convert characteristics into functionings. In the words of D'Agata (2003: 2): "As a matter of fact, equal allocation of resources (i.e. equality in the space of goods) can well imply, for example, a different distribution in agents' well-being (i.e. inequality in the space of well-being)". If people were exactly the same, this problem could not arise[53]. So, according to Sen, when pursuing egalitarian policies one has to separate the equality of well-being from the equality of resources used to attain a certain level of well-being.

Application of Sen's approach in this study

Whereas Sen's approach originally focussed on the individual, in this study the concept is applied to communities. The author justifies this on the basis of the following arguments:

- The distinction between functioning, having commodities and having utilities also applies perfectly to a community as a group of individuals.
- The focus on choice and opportunity is transferable to the entity 'community' as a juridical body, which is constituted by the population base and its representatives. It is clear that the choices and opportunities open to a community underlie different factors than those of an individual person. A community is a far more complex system comprised of various individuals. Taking into consideration the setting in the study region and the research object, the author determined that the possible level of choice at community level is mainly defined by the following elements: organisations, institutions, networks and trust. For more information on these elements see later in this section.

Figure 4-1 gives an overview of how features presented in the empirical section relate to the theoretical framework: Social assets in a community, as defined previously, can be termed social capital in the event of the generation of benefits. These social assets can be used to

[53] "Had all people been exactly similar, equality in one space (e.g. incomes) would tend to be congruent with equalities in others (e.g. health, well-being, happiness)" (Sen 1992: 20).

realise performance elements. There are both common and different traits in Sen's functioning of an individual and the performance elements of a community:

a) Decision-making

An individual makes his or her personal decisions on the choices he or she may have in relation to doing or being something. This person will act according to his or her priorities in relation to the given set of possibilities, under the assumption that the actions taken correspond to the best functioning. The resulting consequences may affect the individual in a positive or a negative way. In both cases, the individual bears the consequences with the certain knowledge that the outcome is the result of personal decisions (and the given exogenous factors). The individual has the option to try other functionings in the event of unsatisfactory outcomes in personal terms. In general, each person is the representative of his or her own personal interests and his or her own manager.

A community is a juridical body with all of its inhabitants as its base and their representatives, who are usually elected. The short-term choice is the same as for an individual. However, decisions made in relation to choices to do or be something are made by means of a communal selection process. How this selection process takes place, depends on the performance, for example, of the organisation and institutions that shape the respective communal body and on the power and information of each inhabitant. Whether or not the selection process is democratic, fair or equal (and this is independent of the detailed definition of a democratic setting), at least one and possibly many individuals will have to come to terms with a decision they did not support. Nevertheless, the consequences, be they negative or positive, will basically affect them just as much as those who favoured the respective decision. If there is a high degree of discontent due to unfavourable outcomes or an exclusion of community members in the selection process, abusive leadership, etc., this may lead to social uproar. Outcomes may be evaluated differently by the various inhabitants, and may result in advantages for one or the other. If an individual evaluates something as unsatisfactory, he or she will not view it as the outcome of a personal decision. Conflicts and struggles over interests and power are a vivid element in the communal sphere. What some inhabitants regard as unfavourable may still be favourable to the community as a whole.

In order to judge this, normative factors come into play. For example, given that all inhabitants had equal opportunity to participate in the selection process, were equally endowed with information and power; and given that leaders were democratically elected, endowed with skills, knowledge, means and information necessary to comply with their mandate, and were accountable to their base; then the selection process is a decision based on choices which have been made collectively. Though information etc. may be constrained, the constraints are distributed equally among individuals. This leads to the best option for the community (the aggregation of all individuals) within the given constraints. Unsatisfied individuals constitute a minority in the face of a working community structure, which will provide them with future opportunities to influence the decision-making process. If what is ultimately the community's best option causes discontent amongst a majority, then immediate collective action can take place.

This was an idiosyncratic example of democracy under normative aspects. In general, individual decision-making usually leads to a direct and personal responsibility. In the case of communal decision-making a chain of social action exists where in addition to structural aspects, socio-psychological factors also intervene. To illustrate: the decision made by each community inhabitant and their representatives' actions make up the communal bowl of soup from which everybody is fed. If the soup tastes good, everything is fine. If not, people can single out many factors, each of which may have led to the poor taste. The cooking is just one aspect; the most complicated part is to make the soup appetising. In any case, it is impossible to accommodate everyone's tastes. And who defines which flavour is best, or if it would not have been better to make steak instead of soup?

b) Age, health and education

A dynamic application of the Sen approach has been used, under which the functioning of an individual also depends on factors such as age, health, education, etc. The transfer of these factors to a community as a juridical body can be done in different ways. Each way highlights another part of the complex system that is a community. If we take into consideration the general age of a community and assume a positive effect of age on social assets and performance, then an older community may dispose of a higher community capacity. If we consider on the other hand the age of each community member, then a certain type of age stratification, for example many young people or many old people, provides different conclusions in relation to performance and community capacity. A third option in relation to 'age' is to base it on the number of years individuals have been community members, the length of time people have lived in the community. Is the community made up of a stable population, where migration in and out is low and some members reach a high 'community age', that is to say live there for a long time. Or is the average 'community age' relatively young due to high fluctuation rates. Depending on the situation, the establishment of a working communal system requires different strategies.

It is clear that a healthy person can accomplish more functionings than a sick one. If we look at a community, 'health' can be defined as a system that consists of the base and its representatives, and works without any major disturbances. So the example of democratic idiosyncrasy mentioned previously may be defined as a healthy community, which complies with its functions as a juridical body and serves its members.

It is assumed that in the case of individuals a high level of education endows them with one type of human capital. This human capital favours the individual because he or she has a greater degree of knowledge and more opportunities to shape livelihood strategies and create benefits. On a macro-economic level, it is assumed that an enhancement of human capital favours the performance of society in many aspects such as, for example, innovations and economic development, political participation and social peace. If we take into consideration the community level, we deal with a system of individuals. So education only can affect individuals, and the 'capacity building' of the individuals may occur in order to improve the system as a whole. It remains an aspect that is connected to the individuals, who interact amongst each other. In section 2.5 the author investigates an explorative means of connecting the individuals' levels of education and organisational membership based on empirical studies related to social capital, which assume a possible link.

Individuals act differently and have different preferences, as do communities. These actions and preferences depend on their internal system. Obviously there are differences in functioning and performance between an individual and a community, which has been indicated in some earlier examples. However, they have important features in common in relation to resource management, the generation of benefits and development. In the administrative and political sphere, communities (to be more precise, OTBs) make up the smallest territorial unit of a nation. Decisions and strategies have to take into consideration both individuals and communities. The means is different. A community is a conglomeration of individuals who establish internally their own forms of organisation, rules and decision-making. In any case, the quest for benefits, improvement, etc. is there in both.

Organisations, institutions, networks and trust are just some of the social assets of a community. However, the author considers them to be the most important ones in the context of this research study. The investigation will also address the performance element, but transferred to the community level. The performance element is an opportunity that has been realised[54]. The social assets provide a tool needed to achieve a performance element[55]. These five aspects have been investigated in each of the four communities selected. Based on the results, the relative community capacity of each of the communities is calculated and compared[56].

Kusel (1996) defined community capacity as "the collective ability of residents to respond (...) to external and internal stresses; to create and take advantage of opportunities; and to meet the needs of residents, diversely defined" (369). In other words, we deal with the attempt to assess the ability of the community inhabitants to collectively affect community opportunities (Kusel 2001: 374). It is beyond question that the particular socio-economic status affects well-being. There is a long history of well-being assessment on the basis of factors such as incomes, commodities, etc. However, communities with a high socio-economic status may not have a high community capacity (Doak and Kusel, 1996), in that the levels of wealth and social satisfaction do not inform us of the willingness of people to use that wealth, personal time and skills for the betterment of their community (Nadeau et al. 1999).

[54] Capabilities are opportunities and alternatives, which are not yet converted to a functioning/performance element.

[55] The social assets also define by their existence or absence a framework for capabilities (as unrealised performance elements and alternatives).

[56] For details of the calculation see 4.3.

In order to judge community well-being, the author holds the view that community capacity is one important factor, and socio-economic status another. The measurement of socio-economic indicators[57] is common in well-being assessments, but is not the focus of this study. There is no doubt, though, that a higher socio-economic status generally offers greater choice and the meeting of basic needs such as food and medical care. However, greater choice does not necessarily mean the realisation of opportunities benefiting the community. In general, the case study communities are poor in UN terms, so the overall socio-economic level can be described as low. Differences in socio-economic statuses between households may influence this investigation indirectly, resulting in power asymmetries and so on, but the focus of this study is community capacity and not a socio-economic inventory of the households of the case study areas.

As can be seen in the following figure, community well-being is intangible. It cannot be grasped definitively and is dependent on the definition one uses. Community capacity is the side of the coin that shows what choices and realised opportunities exist within the investigated aspects. The other side of the coin is the socio-economic status. The manner in which socio-economic endowment is used or enhanced, and whether it is transferred into community well-being, depends on community capacity.

In the greater part of the literature, social capital has been assigned to the interaction of individuals, which is to say to groups or a community. In this study, the author investigates social assets at community level. These social assets comprise the social capital base and serve as tools to generate economic and social benefits. This is complemented by performance elements, which have been derived from Sen's capability and functioning approach. Whereas Sen applied this approach to individuals, for the purposes of this study the author has transferred it to the community level. Therefore, this chapter shall yield relative community capacities, but also represents an experiment: The study shall show whether the application and transfer of the theoretical approach works and can be useful for the investigation of communities. In addition, section 4.2.5 also has an explorative character and shall shed light on how individual human capital may be linked to social capital.

[57] Measurement of individual socio-economic status is a hotly debated issue, especially the aggregation to a whole community. The frequent application merely of socio-economic indicators in poverty measurement has given way to more integrated approaches.

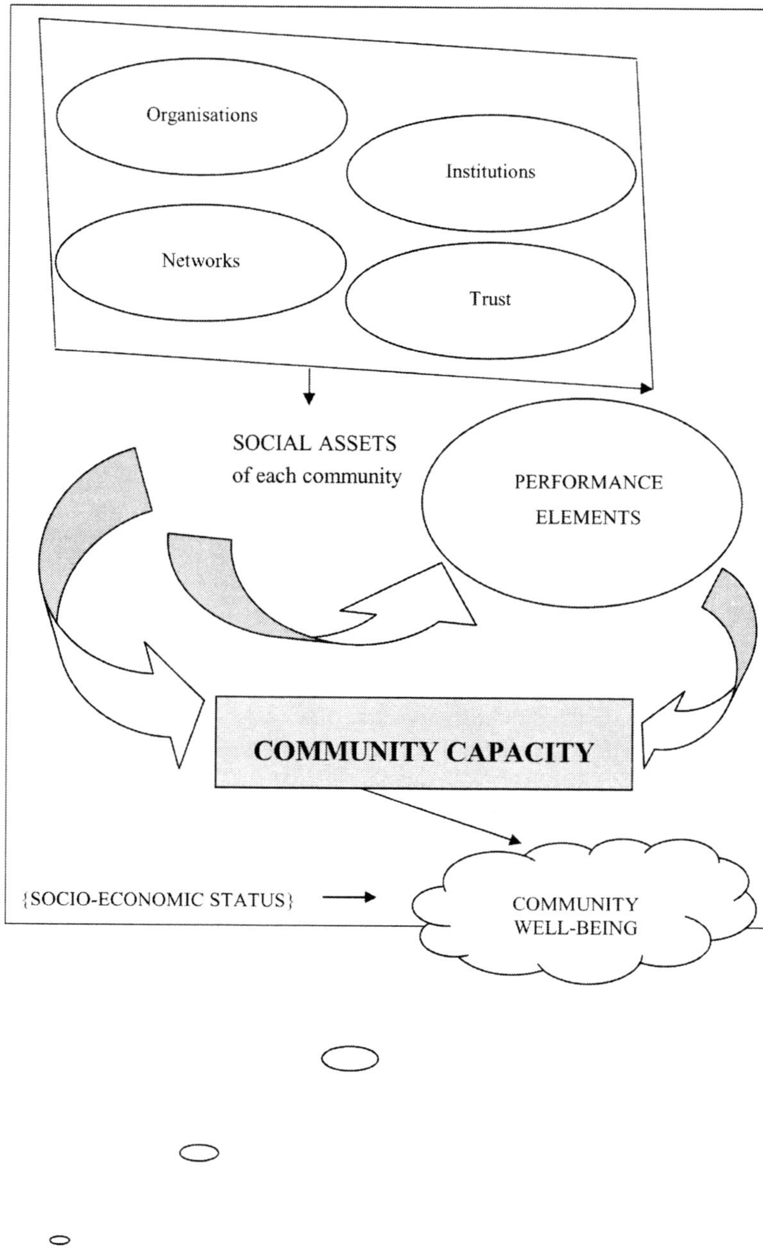

Figure 4-1: Community capacity as seen in this study

The following section explains the four selected social assets organisations, institutions, networks and trust within this study:

ORGANISATIONS: The development debate increasingly emphasises the strengthening of local organisations as a means of alleviating poverty. In view of the lack of a successful conceptual approach to poverty and the disagreement over the concept of 'local' (especially with regard to its new aspects in the era of globalisation), the scientific community widely acknowledges the need to analyse the context wherein 'the local' is constituted: What meaning is attached to it and what is its relevance to theory and practice in politics, economics, sociology etc. (Webster 1998:1). Organisations are social assets of local communities and form part of the structural social capital. The author uses the following definition of organisation for the presentation of empirical results in 4.2: An organisation is an entity consisting of people, a structure (which also implies institutions) and a basic common purpose. The focus lies on internal community organisations. These comply with the given definition and are rooted in the community itself. Organisations representing the state (such as the police, local forest administration authority office, etc.), and organisations based outside the community such as NGOs and the peasant federation are not included. Religious congregations are regarded as being internal because such local organisation only exists in the event of the activity of the local members. A health board or school are also related to the state, but pupils, for example, are themselves local inhabitants. Therefore, these organisations are considered internal.

INSTITUTIONS: To understand the distribution of benefits in the management of natural resources, especially in extractive economies based on NTFPs, and the respective capabilities they engender, an analysis and differentiation of the different forms of property rights is indispensable. In northern Bolivia, the system of property rights has been changed to some extent by the enforcement of the new laws since the mid 1990s. The established system of property rights implies a certain distribution of costs and benefits among those involved. Commons (1968, cited in Ostrom 2000) defined a property right as an "enforceable authority to undertake particular actions in a specific domain". This chapter will present two main domains of institutions in the local sphere:

a) Political representation

b) Access to natural resources (land and Brazil nuts).

With respect to a): Concerning the new legal framework and the attitude of citizens towards it, as well as the question of how they feel about their political representation, see chapter 2 of this document. The present chapter contains a short analysis of the legitimacy, sphere of influence and accountability of the community representative organisation and/or individuals filling that function for the case study communities.

With respect to b): At community level the access to agricultural land is considered just as important as access to Brazil nut resources due to the role it fulfils in the livelihood balance.

So this presents important institutions governing these issues for each community and how they are connected with distributional aspects in other fields.

NETWORKS: The problems of communities cannot be solved without taking into consideration the opportunities for action and cooperation offered by the existence of networks. This holds especially true for people who lack other opportunities to obtain information, jobs, credit, etc. Moreover, there is manifold empirical evidence of an increasing need for networks in times of transformation situations, as can be seen in former socialist countries in Eastern Europe. However, in welfare economics networks are generally not taken into consideration, or are in some cases even perceived as negative due to the possibility of distortion in respect of pricing and resource allocation (cf. Von Twickel 2002: 16). The notion of a perfect market with complete information, entirely rational individuals and no influence of individual preferences, etc. is obsolete, however.

For people in the rural northern Bolivian Amazon, information can be the determining factor for either good or bad livelihood performance in times of legal change and the upheaval of informal regulatory systems. Virtually nobody in the rural area disposes of social security in case of illness, etc. Therefore, cash is needed immediately in such situations, for example, to get medical attention and to pay for transport to get to the provider. Though families living in rural communities possess land, which is legally titled at community level under the Agrarian Reform Law, this land cannot serve as security against bank credit, it cannot be mortgaged. So if rural inhabitants need medium or long-term credit to improve their livelihoods, they have to find another source. These issues clearly constitute an aspect of well-being and give a picture of the options really open to people living in rural Bolivia. They are discussed further in 4.2, where data relating to the following topics are presented:

- Source of information on legal issues
- Access to money in emergencies
- Access to medium and long-term credit

Credit provided to the locals for participation in the Brazil nut harvest is excluded here, because it is usually short-term. In cases of medium-term credit supplied to facilitate the Brazil nut harvest, the interviewees indicated that it differs from normal forms of credit where one is free to decide how best to generate income in order to pay it back (e.g. investing in agriculture).

TRUST: Although there is general agreement about the fundamental role of trust in market and social relations, the debate has not yet arrived at a final result in relation to the definition of trust, or the conditions that determine its development. To measure 'trust' by means of processes and methodologies that satisfy the basic requirements of validity and reliability is more problematic still (Churchill 1979; Bayle 1995, cited in Raimondo undated: 2).

Generally, trust in someone or something can be defined as an attitude, characterised by the belief in the counterpart's reliability. More specifically, according to some authors, trust is the belief that the behaviour of the counterpart is predictable in terms of its direction and intensity, which means that future actions by the counterpart will conform to his or her obligations. The perception of reliability usually evolves with experience, in other words as a result of a sequence of satisfactory interactions. As evidence presented in a study performed by Castaldo (1995) showed, trust is defined by two constituent components: "the first one is predictability of the behaviour of the subject – or organization – in whom trust is placed, which comes from learning process based on experience; the second one is the certainty that the person concerned could not behave opportunistically and that his actions would be aimed to achieve joint" (Castaldo 1995, in Raimundo undated: 2).

The evaluation of trust is a delicate issue. In this research study the evaluation will be limited to a specific group, the interviewees, who either trust or have no trust in a specified organisation or person. The explanatory power of the evaluation is limited by the fact that collecting data on the issue of trust is complicated, and was not the main focus of the research. Nevertheless, the available data give a rough outline enabling a comparison of the level of trust in the different communities with respect to communal representatives, the former patron, NGOs and where there is no patron, the *corregidor*. The way in which this is done is explained in detail in the first case study presented in section 4.2.1.

PERFORMANCE ELEMENTS: As explained previously, according to Sen's approach performance elements are opportunities that have been realised.

4.1.4 Data used for analysis

The empirical section of this thesis will present a picture of the informal institutions in the communities with respect to a) political representation and b) the natural resources land and Brazil nuts, including the respective sanctioning mechanisms. One has to be aware of the fact that informal institutions are hard to grasp due to their nature as unwritten rules, which are applied, but cannot easily be recognised or understood by outsiders. The setting and application of informal rules often reflect the local power structure, which can make it even more difficult to investigate them. One also finds unwritten rules, which are not internalised as such or are only applied occasionally. In comparison, the data pertaining to the inventory of organisations are more easily accessed.

Networks hold a key position for facilitating transactions, be they information, goods etc. that create socio-economic opportunities or serve to smoothen hardships. The empirical section on networks will present data on selected aspects, which play an elementary role in widening bottlenecks for the inhabitants of a rural community in Bolivia. Conscious of the manifold characteristics of networks (which generally also imply institutions), the author focussed only on a few core aspects where the inhabitants possess a direct link upon which they rely. The results make it possible to determine whether within the same type of network the main emphases differ between the interviewees from different communities. This indicates the most commonly used 'channels'. However, a broader interpretation of networks is required in order to address the overall role of networks58.

The presence or absence of trust influences social actions in many ways. Confidence is necessary, especially in transformation situations where there are several options involving reliance upon different actors or systems. If confidence is rewarded, then trust is established, and this can help to establish security. In the case of different actors offering the same goods and services, trust may be the advantage that ultimately secures the transaction for one provider. In terms of a community, the inhabitants' trust in certain key actors is regarded here as a social asset. However, the extent of the data collection that took place was low and does not allow for the drawing of any major conclusions. Data collection on trust should be carried out by experts in this field. Nevertheless, the data collected are included here in order to underline the fact that the role of trust has to be taken into consideration.

This investigation presents some parts of a puzzle, based on the statements of the interviewees from the case study communities and other sources of information such as observation, informal talks and additional interviews with experts. This facilitated a certain triangulation of data and contributed to the validation of the same. To get a more complete picture, an in-depth study of these communities conducted over a long period of time is required. Still, the author believes to have identified some 'lines of conduct' that are important in these communities. For a more detailed reflection on the issue of data collection and analysis see the introduction chapter of the thesis.

4.2 The empirical findings of the four case studies

4.2.1 El Sena

Organisations in El Sena

see next page

[58] One study has already been carried out. In his book Bojanic (2001) incorporated network aspects specific to Brazil nut industry of the region in the nineties.

Figure 4-2: Organisations in El Sena community

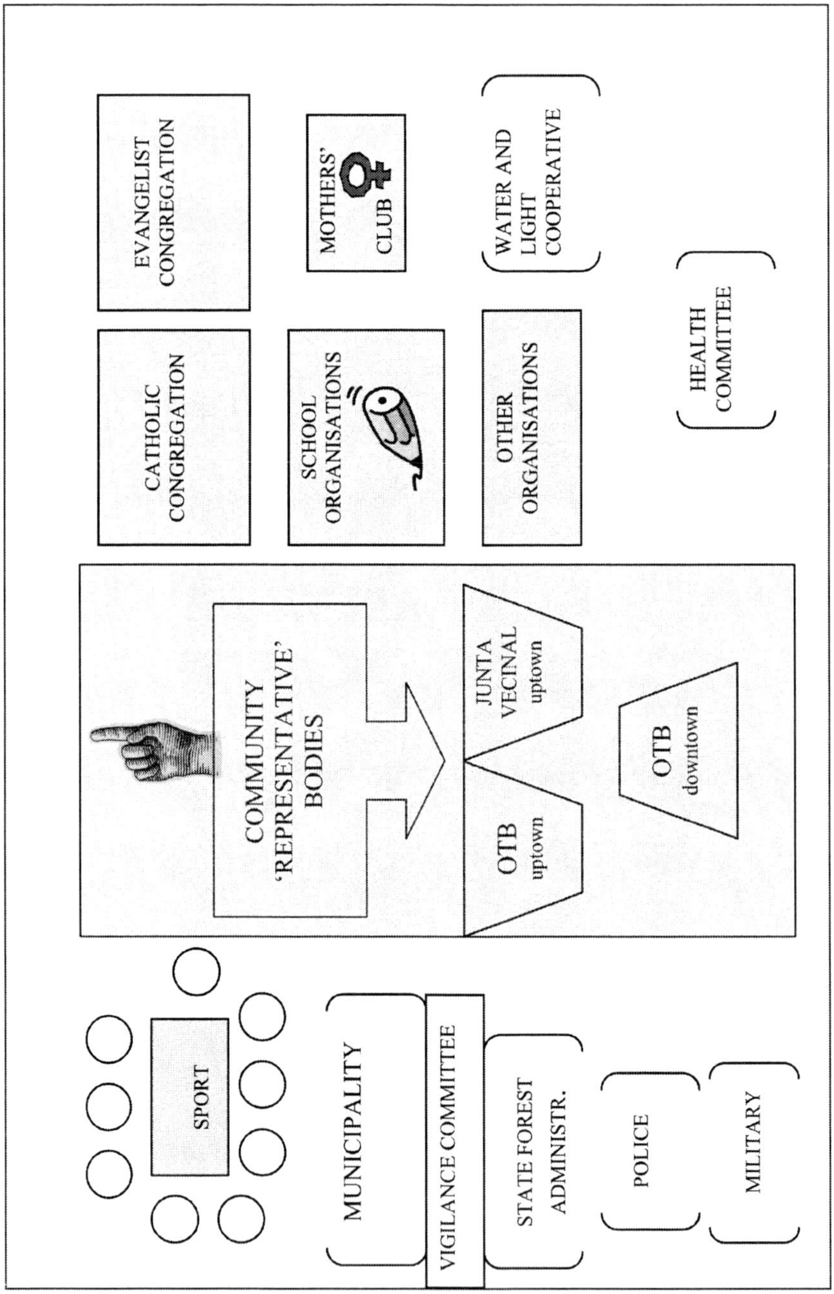

ITEMS in BRACKETS:

Municipality: The community of El Sena is situated in the same location as all of the important offices of the municipality of the same name. These offices are not incorporated into the internal organisational structure of the El Sena community, but as they are of importance when it comes to 'external' links and influences, they will be assumed as such in the context of this study.

The same is true for the control post of the national forest administration – *Superintendencia Forestal Nacional*, and the military. There are army barracks and military staff located at the margins of the El Sena community. The navy holds a control post at the harbour in order to control traffic on the water, and whether boats have the necessary permits and have paid their transport fees. One influence on the El Sena community itself is that people in the lower part –'downtown', live on territory belonging to the navy. The navy representatives accept this and protect these inhabitants – mostly merchants - from the intentions of an individual municipal authority representative to remove them from the area (as they compete with his own business). The police are also an external influence, mentioned merely due to their presence on community territory. Political parties are another external influence on the community, but in a more indirect manner, such as the support they provide certain individuals in power or opposition, the sponsoring of projects via the *prefectura*, etc.

The vigilance committee exists at municipal level. The committee is not accountable to the El Sena community, though (according to personal communications proffered by different interviewees). The committee is regarded as a kind of 'cosmetic' feature, which supplements the official structures.

Water and light cooperative: This association provides the El Sena community (including the municipality administration buildings) with water and electricity. There are manifold problems, however, such as a lack of diesel for the generator (sometimes due to infrastructure problems, sometimes due to lack of money), the failure to pay fees as a result of weak organisation and members' unwillingness to pay, partly due to frequent operational failures and the passive attitude of those responsible for repairs to the system. There is seldom any water pumped up to El Sena for the same reasons. To get water the population has to go to a nearby brook or the harbour, and some of the more fortunate have wells in their lots.[59]

The municipal health committee (*comité de salud*[60]) is important for the community, the municipality and beyond. The strategic location of the El Sena health post on the main road

[59] As one inhabitant of El Sena described the situation (personal communication): "*No hay agua, no hay luz. Es pueblo pobre no más. No tiene nada*". "There is no water, there is no light. It's nothing more than a poor village. It does not have anything." (author's translation)

[60] As the subject is organisations, the author has translated *comité de salud* as 'health committee' for all communities. In reality, these are health posts run by one or more people. While health assistants are paid, there is also somebody in the village to substitute for them in case of emergencies in their absence. This person works voluntarily, for example the designated midwife, and receives only voluntary contributions made by the families, or is an actor who has received instruction from the assistant on how to give injections.

from Riberalta and La Paz to Cobija and close to the connection of the river system from Ixiamas to the Madre de Dios means a high volume of patients, especially malaria sufferers. A building in El Sena with a number of rooms functions as a mini-hospital. An important fact that should be mentioned in the context of this investigation of the organisations in the region: the staff of the health post charge for medication which according to the state list of medication has to be distributed to the population free of charge. The community members were aware of this and, therefore, they greatly mistrusted the management of the health post.

Business organisations such as a sawmill, etc., are not taken into consideration for the purposes of this study.

ITEMS in BOXES:

COMMUNITY REPRESENTATIVE BODIES:

El Sena is a big community with 90 to 120 families. There is not one community representative body to represent legitimately the whole of the community, but (at the time of field research) three. Each of these three bodies represents a different section of the community.

OTB uptown: Uptown stands for the upper part of the settlement (in contrast to the part down at the harbour). Most houses are located in the upper part. The OTB president is opposed to the former patron and has links to the regional *campesino* federation. A small group of people gather on occasion, but to no great effect. The president says that the calls for meetings go unheard by many people because they fear that by attending they would create problems for themselves and so do not dare to go. There was not even enough interest to form a group to do voluntary work in order to improve the community. From the interviews it became evident that some inhabitants did not know about the existence of the OTB uptown. The *consejales* (members of the municipal council) did not recognise the OTB, because the OTB representatives provided the community members information in relation to their rights, and had informed them that they do not need a patron. The municipal council is influenced by the mayor, who is the patron's son.

Junta Vecinal uptown: This is the 'official' community representation. Whereas OTB is the name for formally acknowledged settlements in rural areas, Junta Vecinal is the denomination for the same in urban areas. The municipal authorities themselves initiated the Junta Vecinal, and termed it a Junta Vecinal instead of an OTB in line with the urbanisation policy they follow in El Sena. The organisation lacks the legitimacy of the population base, though. Meetings only take place if the authorities require that the community makes a decision in relation to a certain issue. Only selected people were called to attend the meetings; the others know nothing about them.

OTB downtown: The people who live in the harbour area are mostly merchants involved in the Brazil nut trade and owners of hotels or shops in the harbour. There are a total of 16 families. The inhabitants of the *zona negra,* the black zone, named thus by the powerful family in the upper part of the community, are protected by the navy, which ensures the persistence of their settlement. As it is strategically useful for businesses to settle in the harbour area, there is a demand for the territory. The occupants engage in trade of the territory, even though nobody has a legal title. As a result of the population of the harbour area's common desire for recognition as El Sena community members and their fight for rights, the inhabitants founded their own OTB with an elected executive, which is backed by the entire population of the lower part. They are well organised, meet frequently and collect donations from members to achieve projects beneficial to their quarter. However, at the time of the research the authorities at municipal level had not recognised them.

Mothers' Club: Some female interviewees mentioned the mothers' club. However, it engaged in little activity. The leading figure was a woman who was very ill at the time of research, and as she said personally, without her initiative nothing happens. The statements made by other women enforced this picture. They spoke only of earlier activities in a collective garden, and that there were never more than nine members. The head of the mothers' club mentioned that contact with the municipality existed, concerning the incorporation of a project for women in the municipal development plan. She wanted to be able to purchase a sewing machine or save money for other activities.

Catholic Congregation: The community has a tiny chapel. The former patron is affiliated to the Catholic Church and mass is held frequently. A plan existed to build a new church on municipal ground.

Evangelist Congregation: Unlike the Catholic congregation the Evangelist congregation does not have a site on which to worship. They meet privately in the houses of congregation members. Occasionally external preachers visit the community.

School Organisations: The school in El Sena is a *nucleo central*. This means that it is the central school in the region to which other schools from neighbouring communities belong. The school is located in an old building, but a new one was provided for in the municipal development plan a number of years ago. Like all schools, El Sena possesses a *Junta Escolar*. In order to comply with the rules of the educational reform law from 1994 and a respective *Decreto Supremo* No. 25273 from 8 January 1999, a parents organisation is required, the *Comité de Padres de Familia de la Unidad Educativa*, which is constituted by one representative of each grade. These parents' organisation members and two representatives of the respective OTB form the elective body of the *Junta Escolar*. At the time of research, the El Sena representatives came from the *Junta Vecinal* as one of the three 'representative' bodies. In an assembly involving the majority of the inhabitants, an executive director must be elected along with other positions on the board. The *Junta Escolar* representatives are responsible for the control and evaluation of school staff, participation in the development of the municipal educational plan and the administration of resources for infrastructure and equipment in the municipality[61]. Members of school staff are not allowed to become members of the *Junta Escolar*. They are organised in the *Junta de Núcleo*.

In El Sena one individual is a teacher, president of the *Junta Escolar* and president of the *Junta de Distrito* (for the district). Clearly this does not comply with the educational reform law. Apart from being a member of staff, the person is critical of what has been occurring. He outlined that the educational reform law has hardly arrived in El Sena. It is still commonplace for teachers to beat pupils, and the director[62] backs them against complaints by parents. Many of the other contents of the reform are barely known to the staff. Others pointed out that the municipality has neglected the issue of education and that there was no financial investment in that field for two years. At the time of research a committee evaluating the implementation of the educational reform arrived in El Sena and exerted pressure for change. If there were to be no changes, the director would lose his job (personal communication by evaluation committee member).

<u>Sport:</u> Football is a leisure activity in the whole research region, and in many rural communities football is an important factor for bringing together the inhabitants (many of whom live far apart) on a Saturday or Sunday in order to take part in or watch a game. Other families – men, women and children – usually meet at weekends on the communal playground, which can be found in almost all communities. On a neighbourhood and regional level, football matches are sometimes the only reason for social encounters between the widely separated communities. In some aspects El Sena already exhibits certain urban traits, which in sports terms is expressed by the existence of several more or less organised teams. The different teams correspond to certain social groups in the community. For example, the teachers form one team, the people from the harbour territory another, etc. Therefore, these groups provide the basis for and are an expression of social identity. At the same time this strengthens group formation, and results in the further distinction between groups and places. The matches are an opportunity to pit one's strength against the others in a playful way.

Twice a year El Sena is the venue for a big championship, in which many other communities from the region participate. For this occasion, each team seeks out sponsors in order to obtain clothing, transport fares for the outside communities, etc. The former patrons, members of the mayor's family, and politicians at prefectura (the political administration of the department of Pando) level perform a vital role in sponsoring such events.

<u>Other organisations:</u> Business organisations are not the focus of this study. At the time of research there was no NGO office on the community territory. However, NGOs have an effective external influence, and there have been reports of negotiations for their establishment directly in the municipality.

---

[61] "Velar por el mantenimiento y buen uso de la infraestructura y mobiliario existente en el Centro de Recursos Pedagógicos. Gestionar ante las autoridades del Gobierno Municipal los recursos para cubrir las necesidades de infraestructura y equipamiento del Centro de Recursos Pedagógicos."

[62] The school director is related to a municipal council member by marriage.

Institutions in El Sena

Political representation and public administration

As explained above, there is no body that fulfils the political representative function for the community inhabitants as a whole. There are currently three different bodies with the same mandate, and varying degrees of legitimacy. For any inhabitant seeking political representation as an El Sena community member, the informal rules can be summoned up as follows:

There is no system of democratically electing (such as a majority voting system involving all of the community's inhabitants) representatives who can then carry out their mandate publicly in an efficient way. Representatives who may have been elected democratically are hindered in their duties by ignorance at higher levels. As there is no common representative body for all community inhabitants at the moment, there is no democratic election system at community level. This is reinforced by the existence of the *Junta Vecinal* (uptown) initiated by the municipality, with occasional meetings to which only certain people are invited by the authorities. The *OTB* (uptown) is legitimised by its members, who attend meetings, and through the representation duties carried out by those holding positions. However, they represent only a small number of inhabitants from the upper part of the community. Therefore, the *OTB* (uptown) lacks the legitimacy of all the other community members. In terms of results, there is a weak executive with almost no impact on community life apart from providing a discussion base for community members in the upper part critical of the higher authorities. The *OTB* (downtown) as a representative body is limited geographically to the harbour area, where it enjoys complete support. However, it possesses no legitimacy at community level, nor does it count the support of the remaining community inhabitants. The inhabitants of the harbour area can democratically elect their representatives, they have the opportunity to themselves become representatives and they can take part in decision-making processes, as well as exert their rights and seek the fulfilment by the OTB members of their obligations for their own quarter. Yet, this executive has a small operative frame. Decisions and actions affecting the whole community and the municipal authorities remain unheard and are not implemented.

When it comes to public administration, the institutions follow the same pattern of logic as political representation. With no real political representation, the public administration in the community is deemed to be in illegitimate hands. If, for example, there is formal legitimacy given to the municipal authorities on the next higher level, the community lacks the control mechanisms and power to influence them. As there is no functioning *OTB*, the municipality's Surveillance Committee cannot have any member approved by the community. So the 'rule' is a non-exertion of representation, and the authorities lack the acceptance of the base.

Institutions pertaining to land and Brazil nuts

Land: There are three different zones in El Sena, each subject to different institutions; the harbour zone, the 'urban' upper part, and the 'rural' upper part.

a) The harbour zone: As mentioned previously, access to property in the harbour area is formally illegal, a fact ignored by navy authorities and the inhabitants already there. There are no sanctioning mechanisms on the part of the official owners. Illegal settling does not necessarily mean it is free. The housing area is traded, and previous 'owners' have to be paid. It is not known whether informal payments are made to the navy. Owners of *flotantes*, ships that lie in the harbour as floating hotels, pay a permission fee of up to 250 *Bolivianos* (about US$ 36 at the time of research) to the navy[63].

b) The 'urban' area: This area comprises about 70 hectares in the centre of the El Sena community, and consists of public municipality buildings, a *plaza*, some tiny streets where a pavement is planned, and where all of the cleared land is divided into lots of 25 x 50 meters. There are houses on many of these lots, and the others are construction sites. In order to obtain a lot the interested party has to make an application to the municipal authorities. When a lot is granted, the registration costs 60 *Bolivianos* (about US$ 8.6 at the time of research). Some interviewees in possession of a lot were not registered because of financial problems and they feared that they might lose it again. This is also true for the cases where people got their lot for free due to some personal connection to the mayor's family. For example, families that served them as *zafreros* for many years. Other lot owners mentioned that they had to buy the lot. The highest price paid among the interviewees for such a lot was one thousand dollars. The institution governing land acquisition in this area is not a general one upon which individuals can rely, but depends on their relationship to the authorities.

c) The 'rural' area: This zone comprises all territory that is not included in the two aforementioned zones. It is referred to as rural because, in contrast to the 'urban' centre, one can find forest, fields and housing not on areas divided into lots. The land is either public and/or private, because the Napo family has claimed some parts as private property and the titling process has been successful in places. In other parts, though, there is a lack of clarification and it is assumed that these areas are public, or state property. Under the scope of the land reforms the community families can now claim this territory for themselves. For more information in relation to this matter see 4.2.1.5. Access to land in this area did not follow a general rule, hence the lack of clarity.

[63] This fee has to be paid monthly. US$ 36 has been mentioned as the maximum, but the fee can also be lower according to the interviewees. In any case, the author considers this a relatively high amount of money in local terms, which prevents the fee payers making much profit. It is possible that the sum refers to periods greater than one month, or that the figure has been exaggerated.

Brazil nuts:

The institutions governing the extraction of Brazil nuts in the community of El Sena show similarities with institutions of the former *barraca* system. This is rooted in the history of the community as a *barraca* originally belonging to the company of the *Suarez Hermanos*, before falling into the hands of Don Napo senior. He held the position of administrator before the company broke up, and became the new ruler of the El Sena area. The *barraca* system was officially in place until quite recently, becoming more subtle and informal in El Sena with the arrival of the reform laws. However, some traits remained, and the family of Don Napo still holds power in the place due to the dependency relationship in which many of the inhabitants remained. The third generation of Don Napo (Don Napo jr.) holds the office of mayor in the municipality, and the first Don Napo describes himself as somebody who holds no official office but is "the machine that moves everything in El Sena"[64] (personal communication by Don Napo, author's translation). Many inhabitants accept that Don Napo regards himself and his family as the owners of the Brazil nut stands and the respective collection centres, even though they lack legal titles. Even people who do not accept this ownership claim deliver Brazil nuts to the Napo family because of dependence relationships and existing sanctioning mechanisms. The Napo family fulfils a function as job provider, for example in the construction of the municipal infrastructure, they provide credit to people loyal in case of emergencies (illness) and provide food from their shop.

For the Brazil nut harvest they give the collectors a *habilito*. The *habilito* usually consists mainly of stock from their shop, which is dearer than in Riberalta or the shops in the harbour area, and little or no cash. The person or family receiving this *habilito* must deliver all of the Brazil nuts collected to them. The first part of the harvest serves as a payback of the *habilito*, and the Napo family pays for the rest of the harvest in cash or in kind. Since they consider themselves the owners of the resource, the price they are willing to pay is lower than that which a trader/intermediary would pay. In cases where the collectors are paid in kind with expensive goods from the Napo family shop their income decreases substantially. As a result, many people collect Brazil nuts on their own and try to sell them directly to a trader instead of the Napo family. People who receive no *habilito* have no obligation to them. The sale to third parties happens only to a limited extent because there are precautions to avoid this and sanctioning mechanisms. First of all, the Napo family provides transport for the families to the collection centres in the forest. On the return trip the collectors have to travel on foot, whereas the Brazil nuts are collected by the Napo transportation. The fact that the collectors can not transport the Brazil nuts out of the forest prevents them from selling to others.

As these huge patches of forest cannot be controlled easily, some collectors sell Brazil nuts to other traders who enter the forest, or they manage to bring the harvest to the road and sell it there. In any case, this secures a higher price than with the Napo family, and it is more likely that cash will be paid. There are sanctioning mechanisms in place for the people who do so

[64] Originally in Spanish: "Soy la maquina que mueve todo aqui."

and are discovered, however. Interviewees claimed that sanctioning occurred in collaboration with the local police (staffed by two people) until 1996. The punishment was arrest and incarceration for an undefined period of time. This institution has since ended. In recent years, the sanctioning mechanism has been to take away any remaining Brazil nuts, and the individuals are placed on a 'black list'. In effect, this means that they are no longer counted as loyal and are not taken into consideration for jobs, nor do they receive aid in emergencies or if they need credit. Many people are not able to harvest Brazil nuts without prior receipt of credit, as they need to be able to pay for enough food to cover the period spent in the forest and provide for their families. Many people in El Sena do not have a *chaco* and occasionally need credit to secure their family's nutrition, when they lack all means of generating food or income. As a result, credit is necessary to survive, and this means a good relationship with the Napo family is a necessity for those who lack other networks or opportunities. Sometimes this also means the lack of an own initiative. Some interviewees argued that there are people so used to depending on a patron that they are incapable of taking their destiny in their own hands and actively doing anything for themselves. Don Napo himself said that he is sick of people who do not fulfil their part of the agreement in the Brazil nut harvest and said that each year the *habilito* declined[65].

Networks in El Sena

Information on legal issues in El Sena

Thirty percent of the interviewees in El Sena obtained information on legal issues from the media, the most frequent being the radio and booklets (printed versions of the laws themselves). Newspapers and television also served as a minor source of legal information, but newspapers can only be acquired in Cobija and Riberalta, and access to television is very limited in El Sena. The second most common source of legal information was the municipality. The third most common reply to the question was that nobody provided information (in other words, those who did not have access to media sources or actively went out and sought information basically remain uninformed). A small number of people obtained legal information by means of the OTB, certain authorities or lawyers living outside of the community. Single individuals obtained information from each of the following: a workshop, the police, a business associate, the forest authority/administration and one received his information from Don Napo.

[65] Bojanic (2001) provided a detailed description of the functioning and market relations in the Brazil nut economy up until the turn of the millennium.

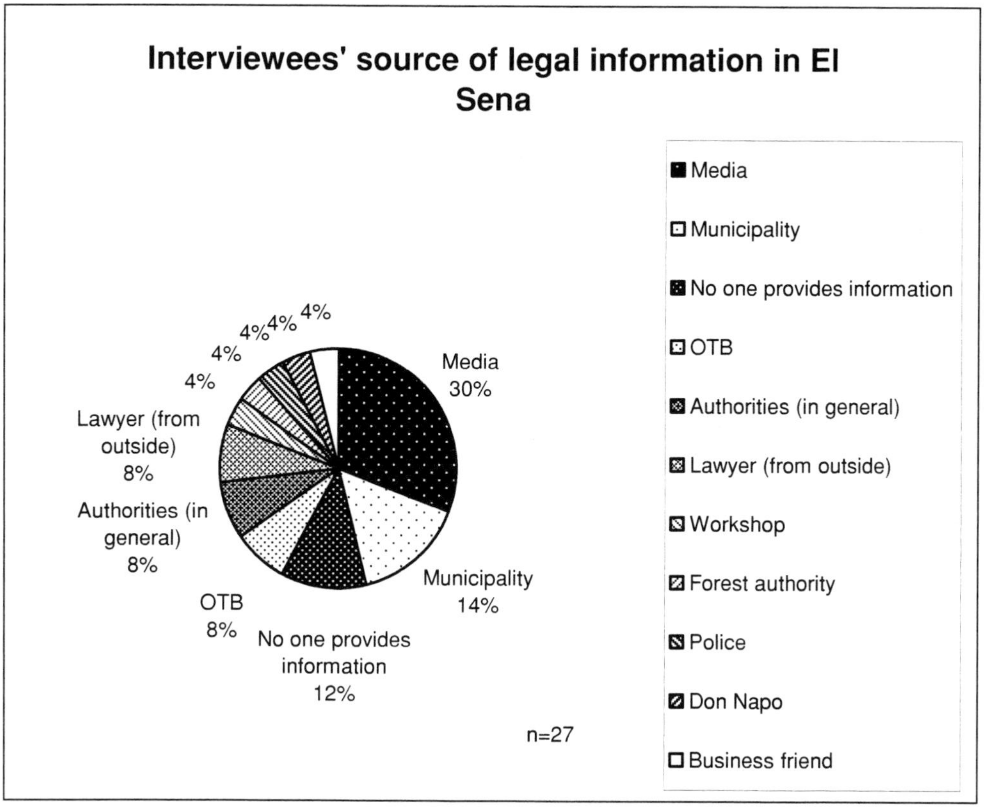

Figure 4-3: Sources of information on legal issues/El Sena

Overall, the village representation provided little information on legal issues. The municipality covered this shortcoming to a certain extent, but the main source serving the people was the media.

Access to money in emergencies in El Sena

In financial emergencies the interviewees relied above all on friends and relatives. A small number of people were able to help themselves by selling valuable possessions or animals. Whereas one individual claimed not to have any access to money in case of an emergency, each of the following sources were mentioned by one interviewee: communal campaign, their boss, Don Napo, a political party, the bank and their own savings.

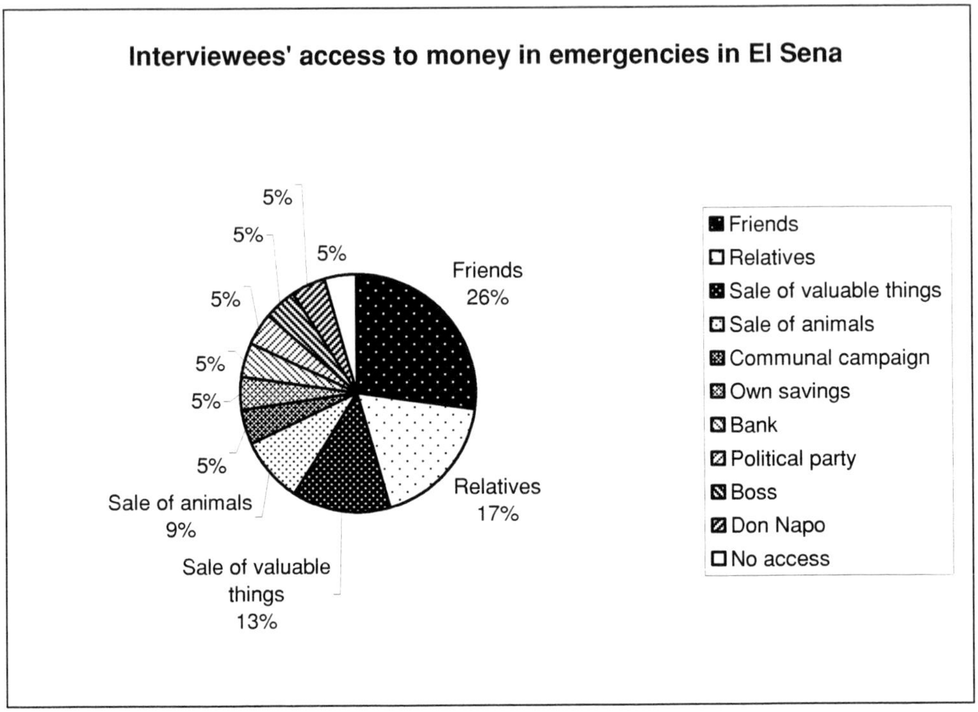

Figure 4-4: Access to money in emergencies / El Sena

Access to urgently needed short-term finance was treated separately from official access to money via banks, etc. Personal informal networks made up the main source of cash.

Access to medium and long-term credit in El Sena

More than three quarters of the interviewees from El Sena did not have any access to medium and long-term credit. Only 22% claimed this possibility. For the majority of them this was facilitated by their positions as teachers. The second most common source of medium and long-term credit was Don Napo.

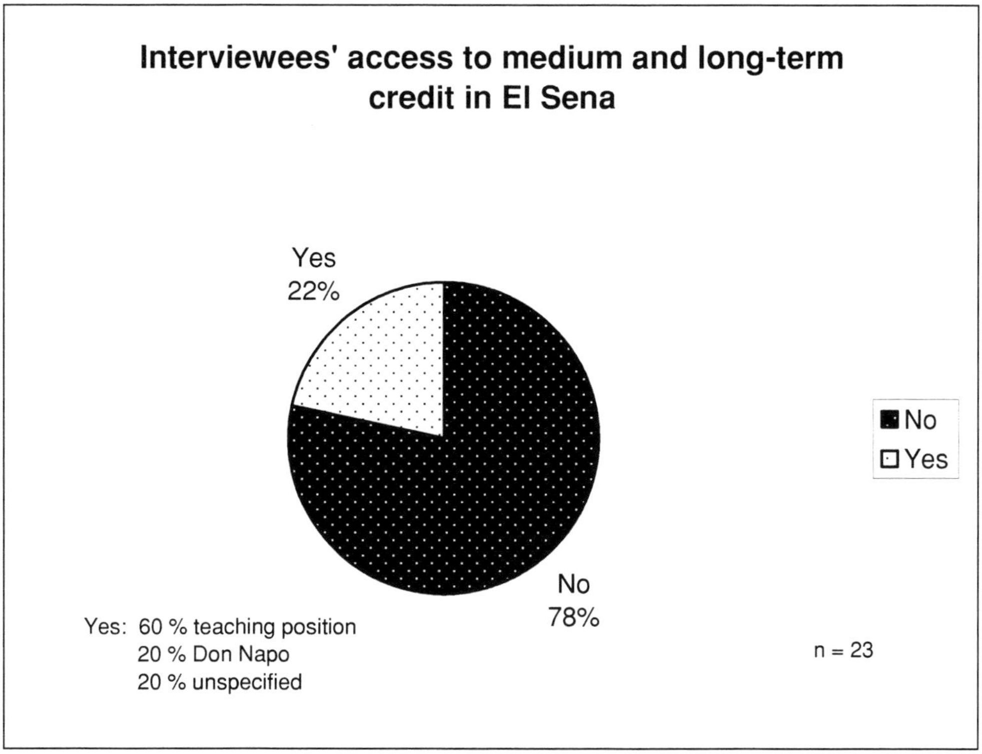

Figure 4-5: Availability of medium and long-term credit / El Sena

Trust in El Sena

The level of trust documented in the following results is comprised of the level of predictability of the behaviour of the subject or organisation in whom trust is placed. Trust means certainty that the person concerned would not behave opportunistically and that his actions are not solely motivated by self-interest. For both P (predictability) and C (certainty) the scope ranges from non-existing to very high, with the following scale:

very high (1), high (2), average (3), low (4), nil (5)

The P- and the C-level are added to give the level of trust. Therefore, a score of 2 represents the highest level of trust, while complete mistrust is represented by a score of 10. The level of trust will be calculated in each community based on the interviewees' trust in the communal representatives, the former patron and external NGOs, and the results can then be compared with those of the other communities.

Table 4-2: Level of trust in El Sena

Interviewees' trust in:	Predictability	Certainty	Level of trust
Community representatives	3	3	6
Former patron	2	4	6
NGOs	3	2	5
...			

The grading used for the scores has been accomplished using a contents analysis method. Qualitative judgements made by the interviewees were transformed into quantitative terms based on the deductive reasoning capabilities of the author.

Performance elements in El Sena

As defined at the beginning, community in the context of this thesis is regarded as the legal representative body and the population base that it represents. For the functioning of the community, one must be aware of what it manages to do or to be (cf. Sen 1985: 10). In the previous sections on El Sena the capability elements at the disposal of the inhabitants were discussed. To sum it up, there was no legal body that represented the whole community, which means that there cannot be any real functioning in the strict sense of the current definition. However, this situation underwent a sudden change during the very time that the author was present.

At that time the region was expecting the arrival of the INRA-surveying crew for the purposes of the saneamiento process. Though usually in competition, several NGOs united and sent a number of their staff to El Sena in order to push the organisation process in the community. At a first meeting on 26 April 2001 (to which all inhabitants who could be reached were invited) the NGO staff informed the community inhabitants of their right to claim land. It turned out that many thought they had no such right at all, as the former patron's family claimed that nearly all of the land was theirs. Moreover, they feared reprisals in the event that they partook in any unwelcome activities. As a result, no one in the community took the initiative to prepare for the arrival of the surveying crew. At the meeting the NGO representatives convinced them that they had legal rights and that they would lose the opportunity to lay claim to land forever if they did not act before the surveying crew arrived. The former patron's family tried to prevent more people from participating in the meeting by erecting a public television screen in the main street.

After a period of critical disbelief amongst the workshop participants the mood changed. They were convinced, and gradually became more enthusiastic about taking their fate in their own hands. At this meeting, which lasted several hours, the people began to organise themselves. A number of volunteers undertook to organise the community land committee. They managed to establish this committee on the same evening, with 25 people (all present at the meeting) signed up and prepared to do all the preparatory work (with marking of land boundaries etc.) in collaboration with all of the community members. Moreover, they began to list all of the families with personal identification numbers and those who needed people to attest to their existence in the absence of any documentation. Maps of El Sena were drawn up and the discussions over borders and possible claims began in conjunction with the neighbouring communities.

One day later a second meeting took place with a high degree of participation of community members. On this occasion, they elected the executive body for a new and united El Sena OTB. The people expressed their trust in a leading figure of the former 'downtown' OTB, from the harbour area. This person became president of the community. As it turned out the community managed to organise in time for the arrival of the surveying crew and the inhabitants received their entitlement to land and resources, also implying a high endowment with Brazil nuts. This election of an executive body had historical implications for the future well-being of the inhabitants of El Sena. As a result, the community became involved in the saneamiento process, which ultimately ends with land titling and legal access to forest resources for the families involved.

4.2.2 Loma Velarde

Organisations in Loma Velarde

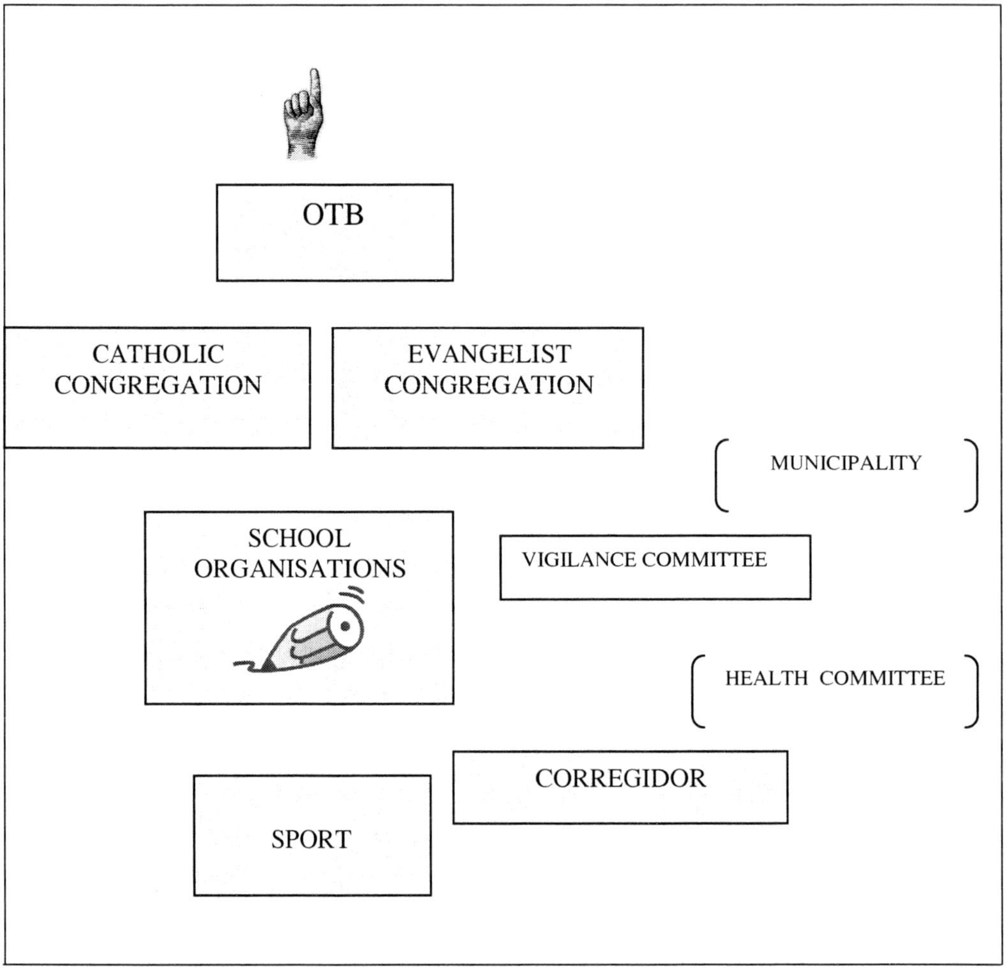

Figure 4-6: Organisations in Loma Velarde

ITEMS IN BRACKETS

Municipality: The Loma Velarde community consists of 13 families in nine households and is located in the Manuripi Province, which is in the municipality of San Pedro. The official seat of the municipality is located in the centre of the Loma Velarde community territory. At the time of research the one room office was closed due to problems between the mayor and the communities of the municipality. A revolt against the mayor and demands made by the communities resulted in temporary closure. The mayor fled to Riberalta, where he lives with his family. He only travelled to the community office occasionally when there were duties to be fulfilled. According to the law, one can only become mayor or a council member in one's main place of residence, and then only after at least one year. In this case the mayor was from Riberalta, as was the vice-president of the municipality council. This fact has never been put in to the *Corte tribunal* (tribunal court controlling the municipalities). Community members claim that all of the money sent to the municipality was stolen: they have never seen the realisation of any projects in which money was invested. Community representatives gathered and demanded access to the documents, but found nothing. If the information given in the informal talks is true, then there was no *Plan de desarrollo municipal*. The municipality was in effect a kind of 'ghost' government.

<u>Vigilance committee:</u> One person from Loma Velarde was elected member of the vigilance committee. As the municipality office was closed at the time of research, the vigilance committee did not execute its functions.

<u>Health committee:</u> Loma Velarde has a health post; it is only one room in size and the building in a poor condition. At the time of research a new health post was under construction, a solid building with two separate rooms and an entrance corridor. The health post is the only one in the area and serves about 12 communities. The community had to wait six years from the time of petitioning until the construction was initiated. There was one health assistant and one woman employed on a voluntary basis who specialises in midwifery.

ITEMS IN BOXES:

<u>OTB:</u> The OTB of the community functions as an agrarian syndicate, officially founded on 3 May 2001. The syndicate is affiliated to the regional peasant organisation, *Federación Madre de Dios*. The executive body consists of six people, who hold nine offices, meaning that some individuals fulfil two functions. There are no regular community meetings. On the one hand, the community members are not interested (personal communication, secretary general); on the other, the executive body is poorly coordinated. Meetings only take place in the event of emergency – for example, when there is a visit by an external actor or when the community has to decide something, etc. The OTB organisation was still very weak. In line with the requirements of the *saneamiento* process, a community charter was presented in Cobija, but the community did not have a copy of the document. During the research, the secretary general was drawing up another community charter on his own. As he admitted to a lack of knowledge of the best way to do this, a NGO advising the community at the time was asked to help. The text was presented to the community who decided unanimously to accept it as the community charter. There is a community meeting of the OTB on average less than once a month.

Corregidor: The former patron, Orlando Suárez, who became a community member, now holds this office[66]. This individual also holds the office of *Consejal Titular*, which means he is the leading council member at municipality level. In a personal communication he stated that a conflict exists between himself and the mayor.

Catholic Congregation: There is no church building in Loma Velarde, but there are two catholic *animadores*. The *animadores* are a kind of religious leaders and are responsible for preparing mass. Although all of interviewees with only one exception regarded themselves members of a religious organisation, there is little activity in this respect at community level. The catholic members said that mass is seldom said, only happening occasionally when the *animadores* arrange something and then in the community centre (a building that consists of one big room usable for all kinds of purposes).

Evangelist Congregation: There is no Evangelist church building either. Members of the (external) Evangelist congregation from Maranata visit the community sometimes and organise a service.

School Organisations: The school in Loma Velarde is a *nucleo central*. To this central school belong schools from nine other communities. A director and two teachers who are responsible for all eight grades with a total of 31 pupils run it. Additionally, an *asesor pedagógico* has the duty to advise and facilitate staff (and parents) in all nine schools. The main goal is to achieve better implementation of the educational reform law and make sure that the new form of teaching is understood and applied. As the school building is old, the community has made a petition for a new one. Like all schools, the one in Loma Velarde possesses a *Junta escolar*. The situation in Loma Velarde does not exactly comply with the law, however. There is no parents' organisation. One member of the OTB, the Land Secretary, is at the same time president of the *Junta Escolar*. Teaching has been reported to start weeks after the official date, but the people have not complained to the higher authorities[67].

Sport: There is one sports club each for females and males in Loma Velarde, where people play football and volleyball. Some interviewees mentioned that community inhabitants do not play amongst one another or meet regularly. The teams only become active when there is a championship involving other communities, or when they themselves visit other communities. The former patron said with pride that he trained 'his' community football team in the past. There was only occasional sporting activity taking place at community level at time of the research. In comparison to other communities in the region, sporting activities in Loma Velarde are below the average.

---

[66] In post-independence Bolivia, a *corregidor* was an official (usually white or *cholo*) charged with administering local Indian affairs. Today *corregidor* refers to the lowest authority in the hierarchy of the national executive, which is structured as follows: president, prefect (*departmento*), subprefect (province), mayor (municipality) and *corregidor* (canton).

[67] One reason for this may be that all school staff is related by blood or marriage to the family of the former patron. He is a member of the municipal council, and his son is the local health assistant, an important function not only for the health of the people, but also for credit and transport.

Institutions in Loma Velarde

Political representation

The situation of the syndicate/OTB as the representative body of the village is described in section 2.3.1. The institution(s) governing political representation at community level can be described succinctly. There are two alternative views possible:

a) As the population base hardly ever meets and the OTB does not work regularly, there is no such institution yet, if an institution is understood as a rule that has been internalised by the people. Since they seem to show no interest, and as neither the locals nor the executive level exhibit any fixed behaviour patterns, these representative institutions have still to be developed.

b) The prevailing institution with respect to political representation is spontaneous action and reaction to urgent needs that require a community decision. The basis can count on an elected and legitimate representation in emergencies. However, the lack of human capital and other interests does not allow the development of a more powerful or efficient institution.

Due to the political conditions in the community, it can be assumed that the former patron, current *corregidor* and *consejal titular* fulfils some representative functions in the event that communal interests in general and his personal priorities converge. For example, he is equally as interested in the implementation of projects in Loma Velarde as the other inhabitants. Though not elected by them, he is able to represent their interests at municipal level. The institution behind this is that the inhabitants cannot influence the representation of their interests through this channel – if, then only in an indirect way. Still, there is a chance for improvement where there is a convergence of interests. Their 'representative' lacks accountability and legitimacy, however.

The public administration practiced by the community representatives is limited to urgent matters. At municipal level, public administration cannot be effectively influenced or controlled by the community inhabitants (except the council member) for the reasons outlined earlier. As there is no working democratic institution, other institutions are applied: demonstrations, protests, and demands are made, and if they are not heeded the members of Loma Velarde and other communities resort to threats, as happened to the mayor. These actions led to the closure of the municipal office in the area. Though the representative organisation of the community is weak, there is spontaneous direct collective action by the inhabitants. There are records of sanctioning mechanisms at community level. For example, one community particular inhabitant was presented the opportunity to become a municipal council member. However, when he voiced an opinion contrary to that of the more powerful *consejal titular* there were reprisals, including the cutting off of the electricity to his family's home. This information was provided by the victim himself and was confirmed in statements made by other inhabitants.

Institutions pertaining to land and Brazil nuts

Land: At the time of research the surveying crew of the *saneamiento* process had not yet arrived in the community, which belongs to *polígono*[68] number nine of the Pando Department.

The territory of the community consists of 495 ha in the community centre where nearly all of the buildings like the school, health post and residential dwellings can be found. Outside of the centre is an additional area of about 15 000 ha of forest with Brazil nut stands, brooks and a lagoon. At the time of research the whole area was treated as common property, except the housing area and the agricultural plots. There were no conflicts with the neighbouring communities over land at the time of research. The land in the community available for housing is limited by natural conditions, though. Many parts of the area are inundated in the rainy season. Basically, when choosing a site for the establishment of a new dwelling agreement must be reached with the other inhabitants of the community. In reality, though, there is little demand in this respect, and in addition, the most favourable patches of land for housing in the central area have been occupied for a long time.

There are only two places along the river from which the community can be accessed in the rainy season. The house of the former patron is situated at one of the community's two 'harbours'.

Brazil nuts: At the time of research, every family living in Loma Velarde had the right to collect Brazil nuts on the community territory. Contrary to the situation in other villages, in Loma Velarde only the men harvest the nuts, and only on occasion take their older children or wives to the camp to cook. There are no individual land parcels on which collection takes place. The entire territory is handled as common property. Basically everybody can collect where he wants. The majority of the Brazil nut stands are in an area that is difficult to access.

In order to reach them, the collector has to cross the River Orthon in a canoe and enter the inundated rain forest, crossing a brook and passing through a lagoon. The trip to the first camp requires two hours of paddling. In much of the inundated area poles or trees in the water, and the need to search for a pathway often hinder progress. From the first collection centre, the *Centro Pacahuara*, it takes an hour and a half to get to the other centre on the main path by foot. From this centre a lot of collection trails branch off into the forest, with walking times of several hours. The Brazil nuts have to be transported to the centres in a bag carried on the back of the gatherer. Full bags weigh between 72 and 86 kg, depending on whether the Brazil nuts are dry or wet. Another centre on the other side of the lagoon, the *Centro Las Cortinas*, can be reached by boat. The advantage of this centre is that the relief is lower and the forest is flooded to an even greater extent, which means the gatherers can travel there by boat, requiring less time.

[68] *Polígono* is the unit of territorial subdivision under the *saneamiento* process

This is especially important for the transport of the Brazil nut harvest. It is hard work to transport the nuts in canoes. As not all of the inhabitants own a canoe arrangements are made with others to transport the gatherers and the harvest. In general there are no conflicts during collection, neither between local gatherers, nor with neighbouring communities, due to the huge area. The difficulty is the issue of the transport of the harvest back to the main part of the River Orthon and to the community. Those able to organise a boat with an engine (instead of a canoe) and greater loading space are better off. Usually people without access to a boat sell their harvest to them directly at the collection point for a lower price. Where access to a boat is available, larger quantities can be extracted and sold for a better price. With a boat it is easier to clear a channel in the waterway using a machete or saw, transport is much faster and it does not require great physical strain. Canoes are more versatile in overgrown pathways, though. The researcher took part in such a trip to the collection centre in a canoe. It turned out that at that time no other inhabitant possessed a larger boat. The only boat owner was a visitor, a *colla* resident in Riberalta. He is a merchant who offers transport services and wanted to negotiate his acceptance as a new inhabitant. His planned next step is to construct a fish farm in Loma Velarde to provide a possible source of income outside the Brazil nut season.

The interviewees outlined that nobody receives a cash income for the nuts harvested in Loma Velarde. They are all paid in kind as they lack a means of transport. Each family sells individually. They mentioned the existence of a plan to tackle this problem; they wanted to organise a common group of gatherers sharing a boat and selling their harvest together in the next season.

The former patron is only marginally involved in the Brazil nut business. He says that he has got nothing to do with Brazil nuts, and that he has not bought any for years. However, he is the only one in the community with a store of food, oil, sugar, soap, matches, etc. Therefore, people exchange Brazil nuts for these products. The author also observed the patron's daughter pay a female inhabitant for her work with second hand clothes. The former patron's family members all have a job with a regular income (teacher, health assistant) and do not take part in the harvesting of the nuts.

One inhabitant mentioned that he had personal connections and was therefore able to become involved in the Brazil nut harvest of a neighbouring community for one season. This offered him the chance to use their contacts with the cooperative in Riberalta, which sells Brazil nuts on the international fair trade market. They had a contract requiring them to deliver a certain quantity, so it was to their mutual benefit incorporate him as a member. As a result the price he received for his harvest was higher than that of his community colleagues.

The institutions of Brazil nut collection in Loma Velarde are established and adhered to without any major conflicts. Transport is a determinant and stimulating force for the development of agreements between individuals in order to overcome hindrances. Brazil nut collection in that remote area is characterised by payment in kind and barter to a greater extent than in other areas.

Networks in Loma Velarde

Information on legal issues in Loma Velarde

The Loma Velarde interviewees' main source of information on legal issues was the media. In most cases this meant radio and books (on laws). There was no access to television or newspapers in the community, and there was seldom contact with these media outside of the village. The Loma Velarde school authority served as the second most important provider of legal information. A few interviewees claimed to obtain information from the municipality, a neighbour and the former patron.

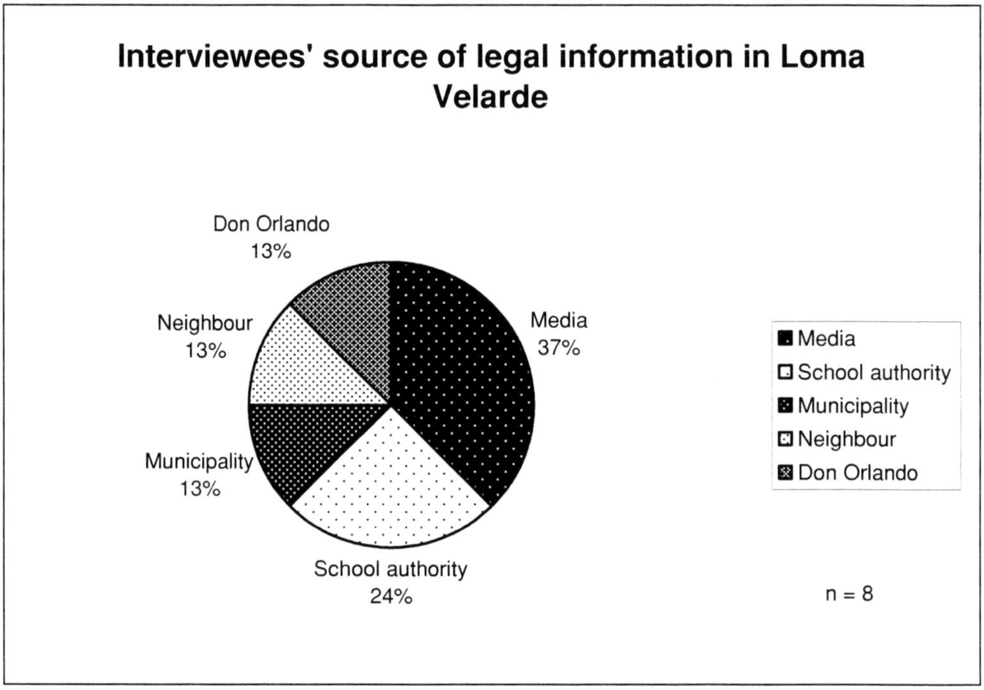

Figure 4-7: Sources of information on legal issues/ Loma Velarde

To sum up, interviewees in Loma Velarde relied mainly on radio and the school authority for information on legal issues.

Access to money in emergencies in Loma Velarde

There were several options used more or less equally by the Loma Velarde interviewees to access money in emergencies. They accessed short-term cash with the help of a friend, a relative, the health assistant, a clergyman from outside the community, by communal campaign and through the sale of animals or agricultural products. Only one individual claimed to have no access to money in emergencies at all.

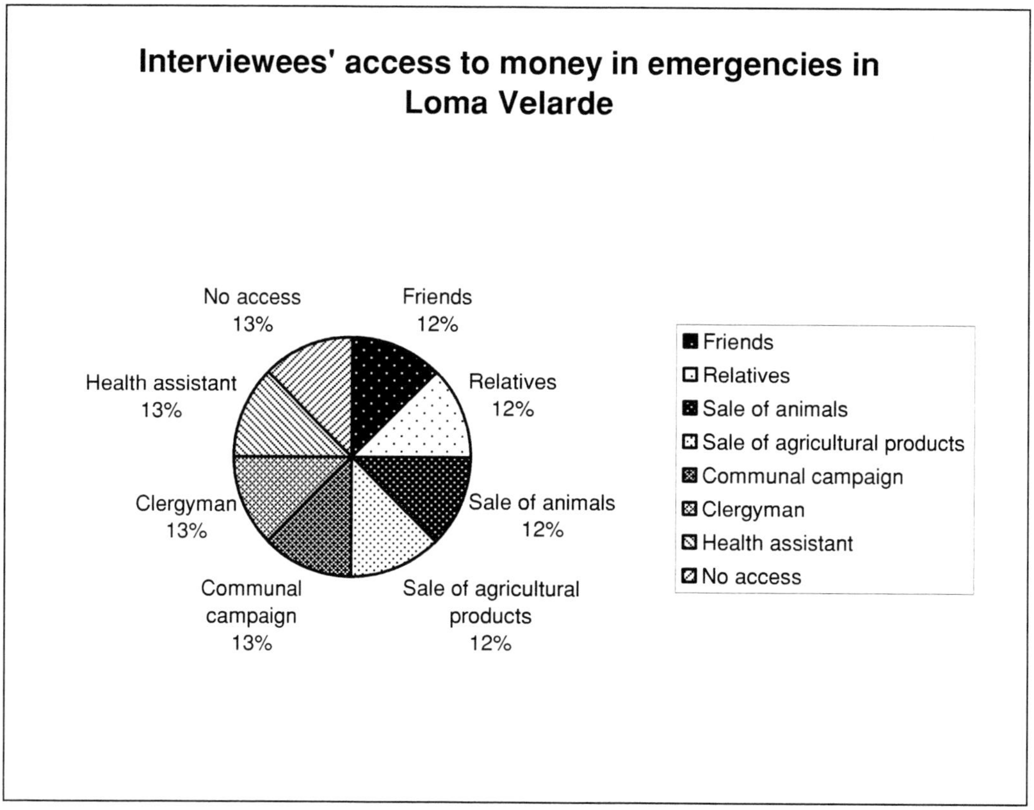

Figure 4-8: Access to money in emergencies / Loma Velarde

In short, each interviewee from Loma Velarde had (or had not in one case) a different source from which to obtain money in case of an emergency.

Access to medium and long-term credit in Loma Velarde

About two thirds of the interviewees did not have any access to medium or long-term credit. One third answered positively, but did not specify the credit source.

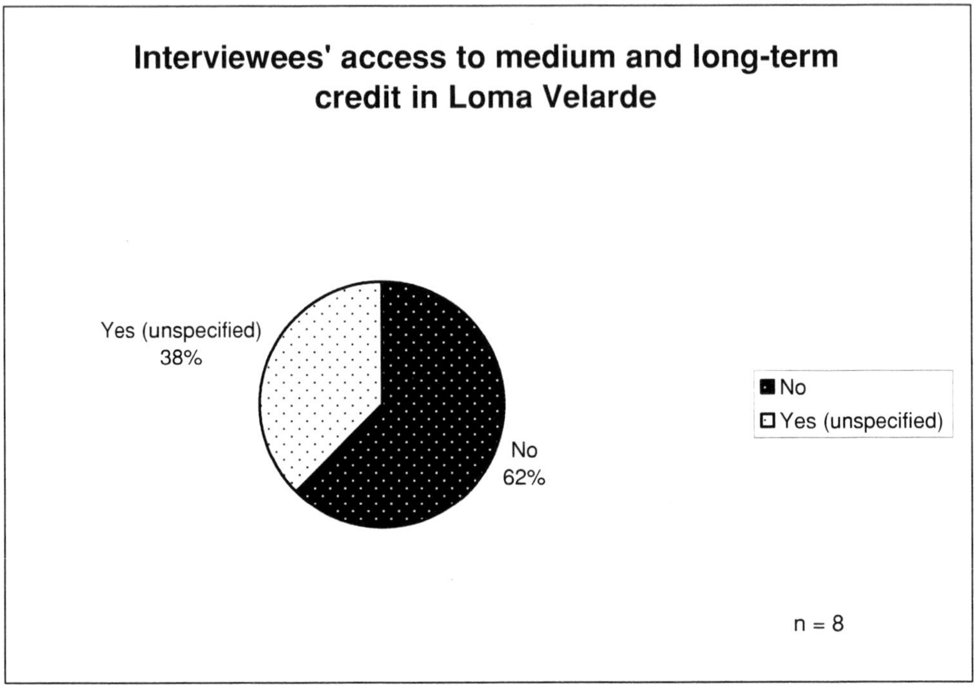

Figure 4-9: Access to medium and long-term credit / Loma Velarde

Trust in Loma Velarde

Table 4-3: Level of trust in Loma Velarde

Interviewees' trust in:	Predictability	Certainty	Level of trust
Community representatives	3	3	6
Former patron	3	3	6
NGOs	2	1	3
...			

The grading used for the scores has been accomplished using a contents analysis method. Qualitative judgements made by the interviewees were transformed into quantitative terms based on the deductive reasoning capabilities of the author.

Performance elements in Loma Velarde

What has the community (the executive and the base) managed to do or to be at the time of the research? Little functioning was observed. An important fact, however, is that no conflicts exist with their neighbours over the community borders and access to Brazil nuts. The community participated in the removal of the mayor as a sanctioning mechanism following the embezzlement of community money. In cooperation with a NGO, the executive started to function for the well-being of the community whereas in the past it merely 'muddled through'.

4.2.3. San Juan km 27

Organisations in San Juan km 27

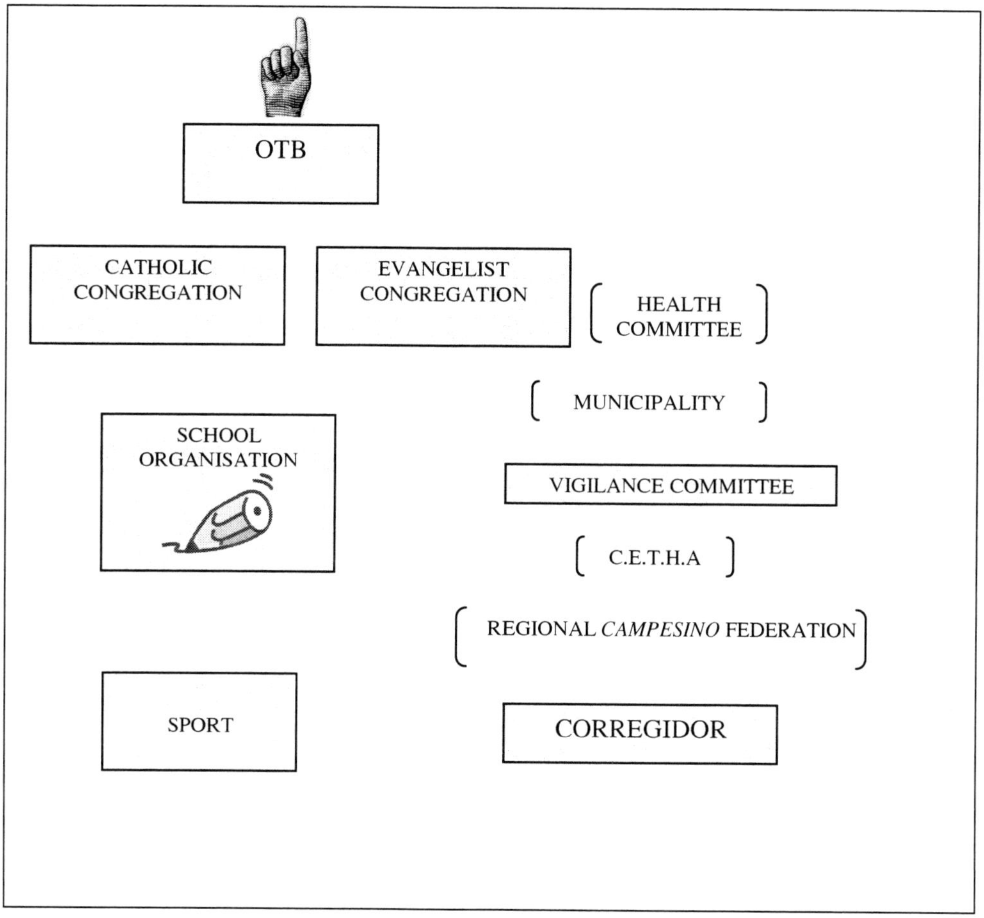

Figure 4-10: Organisations in San Juan km 27

ITEMS in BRACKETS

Municipality: The community of San Juan km 27 belongs to the municipality of Riberalta. There are no municipal offices located in the community, and municipal representatives are seldom seen in San Juan, which is located 27 km from Riberalta. The distance in terms of time travelling is three hours due to the poor road conditions. The relationship between the community members and the municipality is non-existent in the minds of some inhabitants, with only occasional contact concerning the drawing up of documents and other administrative matters.

Vigilance Committee: The OTB of San Juan participated in the election of the municipal vigilance committee members, to which no community member was elected.

C.E.T.H.A: The organisation *Centro Educativo Técnico Humanístico Agropecuario* has its regional seat in Riberalta, with other *centros* located throughout the country. The organisation's aim is to improve education in rural areas by offering basic and higher education courses for adults, especially promoting literacy campaigns and the greater participation of women. Teachers come to the community once a week, and participants have to pay a small fee. In San Juan the course began with the participation of several interested couples, but at the time of research the number of men was greater than women. Some local women who had attended previously mentioned that there was little money available in the family at that time, only enough to cover the fee for one person. In these cases the men tended to prioritise their own educational requirements.

Health Committee: The community possesses a health assistant and a tiny room, which serves as a clinic. The health assistant lives in a big house quite close to the room and to the main road, which connects the community with its surroundings. The assistant has a motorbike, which he uses to attend to twelve communities. His wife underwent tuition on the giving of injections, etc., and substitutes for him in his absence.

Regional *Campesino* Federation: The agrarian syndicate of San Juan is affiliated to the federation. The relationship is good and involves frequent communication.

ITEMS in BOXES

OTB: The OTB in San Juan km 27 is organised in the form of an agrarian syndicate or labour union. All of the families in the community are compulsory members. San Juan km 27 possesses strict, democratic and egalitarian rules for community organisation. Family participation is expected; at least one adult has to attend meetings[69]. Regular meetings of the elected executive and the members take place every two weeks; in case of important issues extraordinary meetings are held. If attendance is not possible, prior notification including a legitimate excuse is necessary. If a petition is not submitted, or if the petition is rejected, non-attendance is punished with work or a fine. In general, each member family has to pay a monthly fee to the syndicate.

Corregidor: The *corregidor* of the canton, which is located in San Juan km 27 does not carry out his task of conflict resolution successfully. A number of inhabitants do not credit him with any authority and mistrust him as a result of past incidents. To a certain fraction of the community he is merely a source of amusement, and he is no longer called upon when conflicts do emerge. The loss of trust in the *corregidor* stems from negotiations he entered into with a company (*Bolital*) in an attempt to sell community timber illegally. Eleven

[69] If obligation to participation or elections can be called democratic depends on normative concepts.

families in the community participated in this activity initially, but then the company delayed payment, and after much persistence the families eventually received sums lower than originally agreed.

Catholic Congregation: A tiny chapel was erected in San Juan km 27 in 1992. The community is divided between catholic and evangelist. The catholic community has a youth group, which meets each Saturday to prepare mass, held every Sunday. There is also a liturgical group comprised of women and youths from the community who look after the chapel in turns.

Evangelist Congregation: San Juan km 27 has a growing Evangelist community, which includes a number of influential elders. Their services take place each Wednesday and Sunday. At the time of research the service was held in the Catholic chapel with the permission of the Catholic congregation. Occasionally a congregation member prepares the service, and there are frequent visits by a brother and sister from the Evangelist congregation seated in Brazil, which also has a headquarters in Riberalta. A new building for the Evangelist congregation was in preparation at the time of research. Community members said that the representatives of the Evangelist mission demanded a new building at the side of the road. Congregation members were asked to make significant financial and labour contributions to the construction, as well as contributions towards the transport costs of the couple visiting the community. These religious authorities told the congregation members to refrain from involvement in politics.

School Organisations: The school has two teachers and one school director (located in Riberalta), as well as the parents' organisation and a community member elected president of the *Junta Escolar*. The school offers classes up to the eighth grade, with a total of 63 pupils at the time of research. The community provides the teachers with an agricultural plot of 1 ha, which they cultivate together.

Sport: There is a well organised sports club in San Juan. They play football every Sunday, and every second week the elected executive meets with all members. A tiny monthly monetary contribution is required from the members in order to buy T-shirts and footballs. If a member donates more money in the event of an urgent need, the other members each spend a day and a half working his fields in return. According to the interviewees the sport club was doing well.

Institutions in San Juan km 27

Political representation and public administration

The situation of the syndicate has been described already. All inhabitants of the community elect the executive democratically. Inhabitants have the opportunity and indeed the obligation to participate in the choosing of legitimate political representation by means of election. The OTB representatives in San Juan km 27 are recognised at higher level and can contribute to the achievement of interests at community level. Their legitimacy is reinforced by the formal acceptance of office in the presence of a federation representative who transfers power to the executive after the communal election.

The executive can use its influence in the drawing up of the *PDM* and its *POA* in order to realise projects that are beneficial to the community. In this sense, public administration is guaranteed due to the presence of legitimate and accountable representatives. However, these representatives face difficulties at municipality level. At the time of research there were problems in the municipality of Riberalta because an elected mayor was turned down by the opposition, who favoured another candidate. This opposition candidate tried to take office, which aroused more protests and lacked any legitimacy. Then a third person came into play and chaos ruled in the municipality. The police tried to keep peace on the streets, but in such circumstances public administration is obviously greatly impeded.

OTB representatives can secure control over project realisation via the election of the vigilance committee. The vigilance committee in Riberalta faces similar problems to committees elsewhere. The officeholders lack information necessary for efficient control. This is partly because the municipality does not let them access all the information they need, and partly because they do not possess enough legal and administrative knowledge. Moreover, they are not sufficiently rewarded for their work, which can lead to frustration and the neglect of duties. Within the existing frame, however, due to the institutions applied in San Juan, the administration takes account of the interests of the inhabitants.

Land: The territory of San Juan km 27 is quite small (which makes it even more remarkable that they are very willing to redistribute land. The number of families expecting entitlement to land rose by about 30% during the research period). Though many communities used the immigration of families as a strategy in order to demand more land under the reforms, this was not the case in San Juan. The surveying crew had already passed through by the time the new families arrived. Besides, there are bordering neighbours with whom land disputes had been settled before.

Though the territory of San Juan km 27 as a whole is community land, it is divided internally into a communal area for the school, health post, football ground, meeting place etc. There is also a communal patch of forest set aside for a future reserve, and individual parcels for housing, agriculture and forest use. Whereas in many villages only agricultural plots are conceded individually, in San Juan forest plots may also be conceded.

The borders of the community were fixed at the time of research. Nevertheless, the community is open to newcomers and welcomes especially people in need, e.g. elderly and single women with children. There is a strong religious influence and San Juan disposes of a spirit of solidarity. At the time of preparation of the *chaco*, this results in mutual help if someone is not able to complete all of his or her tasks in time due to illness, etc. When a new inhabitant arrives he or she must first pass a probation period in the community, during which time they may only live there provisionally. After the probation period, all of the inhabitants decide at a communal meeting whether they are accepted as community members. With acceptance comes the formal incorporation into the syndicate.

Legally, communal land cannot be traded. Internally, though, there is a market for housing and land. The calculation of the price depends on the investment that was necessary for the construction of the house, the work invested in the agricultural plot and the cost of seedlings, and the condition of the forest patch as a whole. If newcomers do not buy an existing house with a respective plot, they need to select a new area. The OTB's Land Secretary is the governing institution in this respect. He is informed about all free patches of land that the community is willing to make available for settling, agriculture and/or forest use. The Land Secretary offers the buyers one, two or three of these patches from which to chose. Though this institution is transparent, one has to keep in mind that good patches of land have already been occupied for many years and are rarely transferred or sold to newcomers. In San Juan the soils are relatively poor and dry, and there are only few parcels that include a brook. Newcomers have to be content with what they get.

Brazil nuts: The institution pertaining to the access to and usufruct rights over Brazil nuts is basically the same as applies to land. In order to access the Brazil nuts, the individual has to obtain access to an individual plot (see previous section on land). Apart from the natural circumstances, the small size of the parcels (between 30 and 50 ha) only allows for a modest number of Brazil nut stands. Therefore, the Brazil nut harvest is limited. Benefits depend on the specific natural resource endowment and the collection habits of the family. It is not possible to enhance the derived benefits by supplementary collection on communal territory. However, the access to this specific resource is assured. Many community members also work as *zafreros* in a *barraca* outside the community after having harvested their own plot[70]. There are also records of community members who enter the bordering military territory illegally to harvest Brazil nuts, as yet unnoticed. Each family sells their nuts individually. Sometimes merchants pass by, but many people prefer to take their own harvest to Riberalta personally in order to receive a better price and cash in hand. This is only possible if they can organise transport. Apart from the health post's motorbike the community owns no means of transport. As San Juan is located on a connection road to Cachuela Esperanza, trucks pass through, occasionally offering lifts.

Networks in San Juan km 27

Information on legal issues in San Juan

Interviewees obtained information on legal issues mainly from their OTB representatives. The second most important providers of legal information were the peasant federation, the NGOs and lawyers. A small number of interviewees got information from the INRA office, and a single interviewee cited each of the following: a school authority, the *corregidor*, someone from the municipality and a policeman.

[70] The later part of the Brazil nut season coincides with the beginning of the rice harvest. Therefore, people must prioritise the occupation that is more important to them, or invest in a work force to support the harvest of both the rice and the Brazil nuts. All of the rice must be harvested within two weeks, otherwise there are substantial losses.

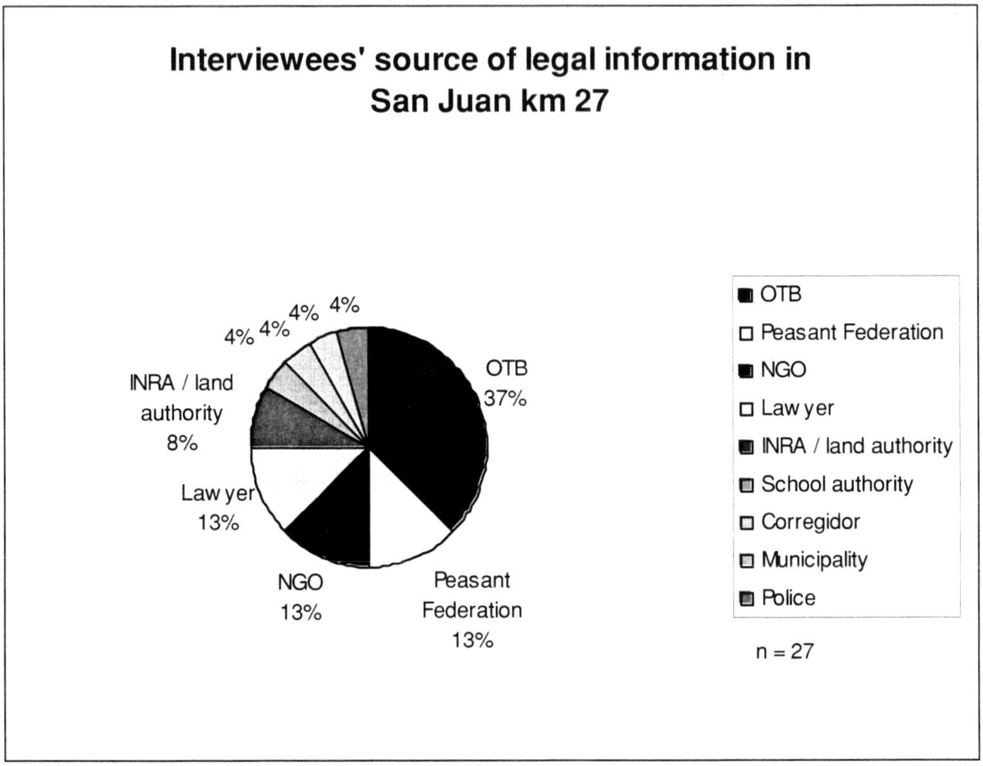

Figure 4-11: Source of information on legal issues/ San Juan km 27

The central source of information on legal issues for the interviewees from San Juan km 27 was their local village organisation, as well as organisations that generally represented their interests from outside.

Access to money in emergencies in San Juan km 27

Most interviewees in San Juan could count on the solidarity of their neighbours in emergencies. Their main source of cash was by means of a communal campaign. The second most frequent source was the sale of agricultural products. The help of relatives and the sale of animals provided some interviewees with urgent cash, and one person turned to a friend for cash. One person had no access at all, and another interviewee's only option is the bank, with the help of a prayer.

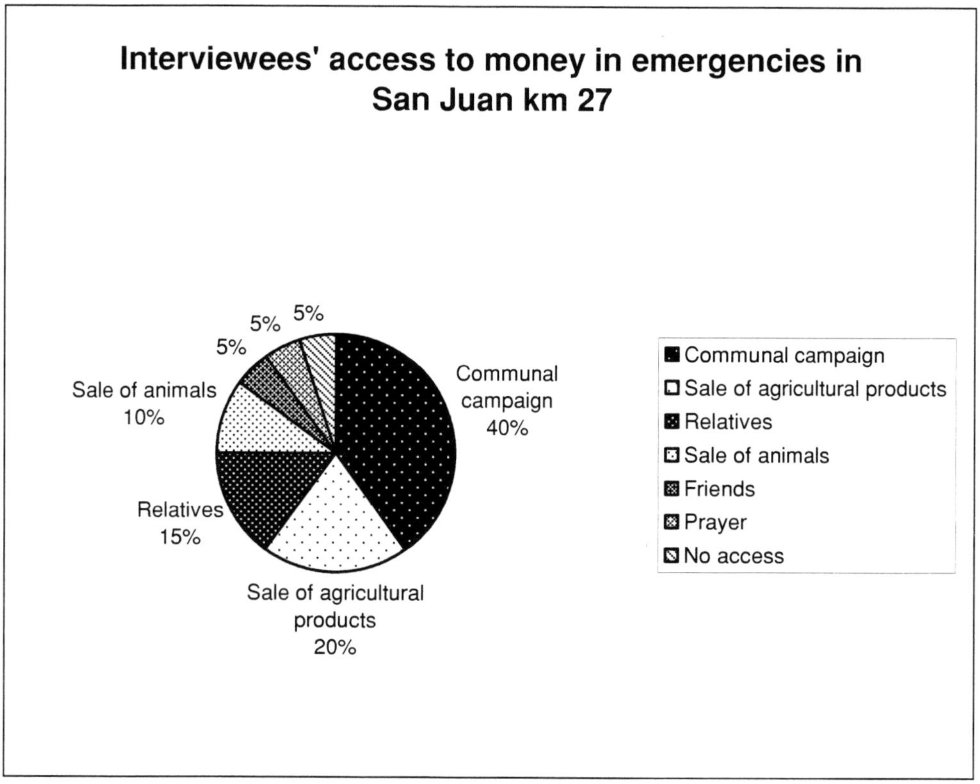

Figure 4-12: Access to money in emergencies/ San Juan km

In summary, interviewees in San Juan km 27 were likely to receive financial help in emergencies, and in the event that they did not have the option of selling their products through the solidarity of their fellow community members.

Access to medium and long-term credit in San Juan km 27

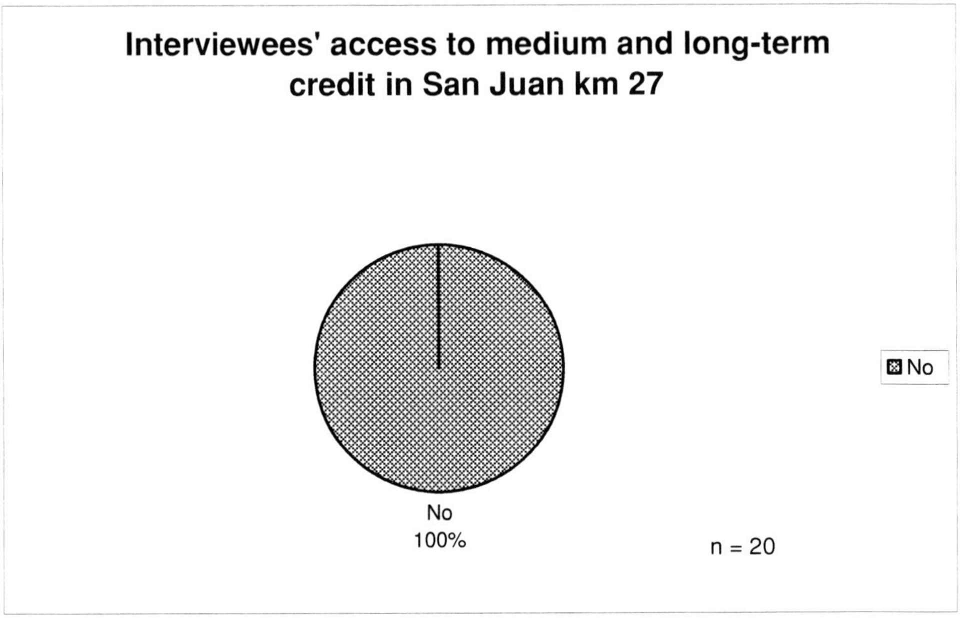

Figure 4-13: Access to medium and long-term credit / San Juan km 27

None of the interviewees in San Juan km 27 had access to medium or long-term credit.

Trust in San Juan km 27

Table 4-4: Level of trust in San Juan km 27

Interviewees' trust in:	Predictability	Certainty	Level of trust
Community representatives	1	2	3
Former patron	not applicable	not applicable	not applicable
NGOs	2	1	3
Corregidor	4	5	9

The grading used for the scores has been accomplished using a contents analysis method. Qualitative judgements made by the interviewees were transformed into quantitative terms based on the deductive reasoning capabilities of the author.

Performance elements in San Juan km 27

The performance elements of the community's executive and its population base exhibit various traits. In general, there is a well organised framework, within which the base and its representatives operate. They have managed to establish clear and transparent rules, which have to be followed or sanctions are incurred. At the same time, inhabitants are forced to participate in community matters regardless of their desire to or not. Moreover, in emergencies community inhabitants can count on the solidarity of their community and are helped. So, all members participate and are treated relatively equally. This is also rooted in the link between the self-administration of the community and two meaningful religious congregations. On this basis, the community managed to progress in many aspects despite quite a modest endowment with natural resources. They cultivate close connections to the regional peasant federation, NGOs and the individuals who can provide them with useful help and information. In this way they managed to solve a border conflict with a private owner in their favour. The executive was also aware of possible opportunities at the community's disposal and arranged participation in a project for the construction of wells in order to access drinking water. The community's insistence at municipal level combined with the influence of the health assistant also resulted in the acceptance of a bid for the construction of a mini-hospital in San Juan, for which 12 communities had been competing.

4.2.4 Trinidadcito

Organisations in Trinidadcito

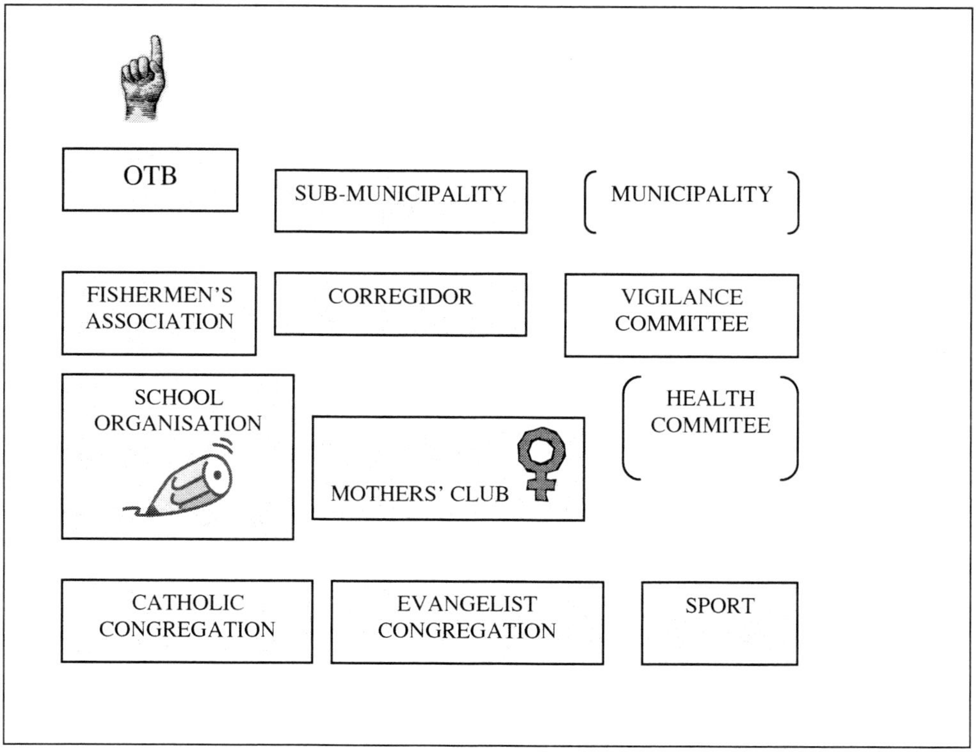

Figure 4-14: Organisations in Trinidadcito

ITEMS IN BRACKETS

Municipality: Essentially the community is part of the municipality of San Lorenzo/Blanca Flor. In educational matters, however, Trinidadcito belongs to the municipality of Gonzalo Moreno. This split is not necessarily a disadvantage, as will be outlined under functioning. Together the municipalities of Blanca Flor, Gonzalo Moreno and El Sena form a *Mancomunidad*.

Vigilance Committee: The OTB took part in the election of the respective representatives. No information in relation to vigilance committee's work was made public; there is no community member on the municipal vigilance committee.

Health Committee: One health assistant works in Trinidadcito. The health post consists of a tiny room for attending to the ill, and a larger room in which the family of the health assistant lives. The post is equipped with a freezer that is fed by electricity from a solar panel, which means vaccines requiring cooling can be stored. The health assistant has to attend nine communities, which he visits by boat. There is also a telephone in the health post that serves the communication needs of all community inhabitants, together with a radio, located in the sub-municipality.

ITEMS IN BOXES

Sub-municipality: In Trinidadcito a sub-mayor/ municipal agent (female) holds office. This *agente municipal* is responsible for a territory that comprises the municipal district of the rural area in which Trinidadcito lies. The municipal agent is situated below the mayor in the municipal hierarchy. The woman in office is the daughter of one of the most established community inhabitants (resident for 65 years), has lived there most of her life (having spent some time in Japan), and is a teacher at the local school. Therefore, she is very keen to do something for Trinidadcito. There are no records of whether or not the other communities in the district are content with her work. The municipal agent describes her work as crucial to the "progress of the community".

OTB: The Trinidadcito OTB executive was democratically elected by the community inhabitants. In fact, the OTB representatives work closely with the municipal agent. The meetings are not usually designated OTB meetings, but communal meetings at which the municipal agent attends. At the time of research the charter was still being drawn up. According to the OTB president, the sub-municipality has existed since 1996, with the OTB founded two years later.

Fishermen's Association:

Trinidadcito has access to a lake rich in fish. Fishing is an important source of financial income; many families earn more from fishing than Brazil nuts. Many inhabitants regard the fishermen's association as the most important organisation in the village because it generates income. The association holds a regular meeting once a month. Each member has to pay a monthly fee of 10 *Bolivianos*. Membership is only open to male village members, and currently numbers 23. Non-members are not allowed to fish in the 'communal' lake. If they live in the village or are recognised as accepted visitors, they can accompany an association member as a fishing assistant. The assistant receives, depending on the agreement, a minor part of the catch, or a certain amount of cash.

School Organisation: Trinidadcito has two school buildings, an old one and a new one that was built recently. It covers all three educational levels and is the *nucleo* for several other schools in the region. There is one director and 17 teachers to accommodate about 100 pupils. The school is considered "the best school in the region" (personal communication by various persons) in every respect. The *asesor pedagógico* lives in the village for the majority of the school year. There is an active parents' group and a *Junta Escolar,* which meets frequently. The *Junta del nucleo* has a high number of members. As a result of the large number of teachers in Trinidadcito there was a shortage of housing. Many of them come for just one school year, and do not settle in the village. The community organises buildings with a number of individual rooms, so that various teachers can live under the one roof.

Corregidor: The person holding the office of *corregidor* is located in Trinidadcito and is perceived as important and his authority is recognised. He takes his task seriously and regards himself as the "representative of the government" (personal communication). He meets with all of the organisations in the community, and works in the resolution and mediation of conflicts between community members and/or outsiders. There are several records of penalties being incurred, usually in the form of cash payments. In more serious cases the culprits have been transferred to the next municipality that possesses a jail cell.

Catholic Congregation: The community has a tiny chapel located centrally. Mass takes place once a week on Sundays. A catholic youth club with 18 members meets on Thursdays. They engage in activities such as reading the bible, fundraising for the purchase of religious books by playing bingo, and they also constructed a toilet near the church.

Evangelist Congregation: There is an active and growing Evangelist community. They meet in different private houses three to four times a week and have a strong group identity. Their religious rules prohibit the drinking of alcohol and dancing. This leads to problems each year around the time of the community anniversary party. Each community member has to contribute in cash or kind, but some Evangelists are not willing to contribute to the festivities in any way.

Sport: The community has good sporting facilities. Not only the casual football pitch, but there are also facilities for basketball and volleyball next to the new school. There are sport groups for both women and men. Football remains the central sporting activity, though. In 1989, together with four other communities, Trindadcito initiated a 'regional world championship' – *el Mundialito*. The organisation of this tournament is so successful that each year more communities participate. There are currently four regional divisions and around thirty communities, which compete for qualification to the finals. The husband of the municipal agent is the trainer of the local team. He is responsible for the organisation of the main team, as well as a second team to provide opposition in training. The team is sponsored by politicians, contributions made by community inhabitants, etc. On Saturdays many community inhabitants come to the sports ground to watch the match. Through the contest with other communities, the team helps to construct group identity on a community level.

Mothers' Club: The activities of the mothers' club and the woman who holds office as submajor are closely connected. The club planned to establish a common agricultural plot with vegetables. The members vary, depending on their interest in certain activities.

Institutions in Trinidadcito

Political representation and public administration

The village OTB representative body is described in section 2.5.1. It fulfils its task mainly in cooperation with the municipal agent. The fishermen's association and the *Junta Escolar* are influential in decisions made at community level, and in many cases the inhabitants form part of all three organisations. As the OTB representatives who coordinate with the municipal agent are elected democratically, the inhabitants can claim real political representation. As a result, the preconditions for legitimate and successful public administration in Trinidadcito are good. Given the good cooperation between the OTB and the municipal agent, who has a strong interest in the community, public administration at municipal level often benefits the community.

Land: The territory of Trinidadcito is treated as common property. Only the agricultural plots, are handled individually. To establish a new agricultural plot, the community must first be asked for permission. In general, teachers who only live in the community temporarily are not allowed to have a *chaco*. Exceptions are possible for long-term visitors or residents, however. Newcomers wishing to be accepted as community members have to present themselves at a communal meeting and remain in Trinidadcito for at least one year. After this probation period, all of the local organisations (*OTB*, *Subalcaldia*, *Junta Escolar*, etc.) meet to agree upon the candidate's acceptance as a community member.

The status of the communal territory of Trinidadcito is ambiguous. It shares a boundary with an indigenous territory, and along the river it is bordered by two private properties. The *saneamiento* process started in the indigenous territory. The indigenous representative organisation offered the community the chance to integrate its territory into the indigenous community, representing a substantial gain for the population of Trindadcito, because the 'indigenous' title would have strengthened any claims made by their representative organisation. For the inhabitants of Trinidadcito this might also have meant a larger territory (depending on the agreements with the neighbouring indigenous community Galilea), improved forest property rights, and a faster titling process, but no individual title for their community. There were two fractions in Trinidadcito. One favoured integration and was in the majority initially, until the inspection committee of the Ministry of Indigenous Affairs found that there was only one inhabitant in Trinidadcito with an indigenous surname. However, there are records that Trinidadcito was incorporated in the TCO-titling process. In the end, the outcome of a discussion held at community level revealed that none of the community members wished to lose their *campesino* identity, which they then maintained.

Trinidadcito has been formally incorporated as a member of the regional *campesino* federation and is regarded as a normal *campesino* community. However, according to the new land register the title was for an indigenous territory, and not a *campesino* community. The municipal agent and the OTB initiated negotiations with neighbouring communities, as a result of which the community bought a patch of their land in order to enhance the community territory. All of the inhabitants had to contribute to the purchase with part of their Brazil nut harvest. Only a few people were willing to talk about that particular issue, which seems to have been a source of conflict in the community, with no consideration taken of the opposition.

<u>Brazil nuts:</u> The Brazil nut stands are treated as common property, as is the land on which they stand. The Brazil nut resource is plentiful[71]. Nevertheless, the permission for Brazil nut collection and the derivation of its direct benefits is limited to certain community members on the basis of the following criteria:

- Only 'traditional' families or inhabitants have the right to collect Brazil nuts. Traditional in this context means that the individual or family has been resident in the community 'a long time', or is descendant from somebody who is considered 'traditional'. The meaning of traditional is not strictly defined and depends on the will of the community.
- All families with children in the local school are granted the same access and usufruct rights as those deemed 'traditional'.

Another limitation in relation to the Brazil nut harvest is the agreement upon an official opening day for the collection season. Though the Brazil nuts are available from December, collection usually doesn't begin until the middle of January. The reason for this is that the fishing season does not end until December, when the spawning season starts. Due to the ensuing Christmas and New Year festivities, the community members had agreed at the time of research on a starting date of the 15 January. If anyone is found collecting Brazil nuts before this date, the Brazil nuts are taken away and the persons' status in the community is damaged.

Among those in the community with access rights, the smaller families and those with young children often complained that they were at a disadvantage, as larger families with a greater 'work force' were able to harvest more in a shorter period of time. However, from a redistribution point of view one may argue this is a social institution, as the larger families need a greater income. People with no access rights usually seek to generate income through the collecting of Brazil nuts in the neighbouring *barraca*. At least 120 individuals take part in

---

[71] 'Plentiful' in this context refers to the total quantity of Brazil nuts harvested divided by the number of families, and then compared against the same average harvest per family for the other communities. For more specific information see chapter 3.

the collection of the nuts in the community, and collect an average of 120 *cajas* per season. At the high point of the season it is possible to collect 9 to 12 *cajas* per day.

As some collection centres (like *Barbechon*) are too far away to transport the nuts to the village, merchants with motorbikes buy the nuts directly from the collection centre. Nuts from closer centres are transported to the community. To the extent possible, the community then transports the nuts to Riberalta using the communal boat, where higher prices can be attained[72]. However, nuts are also sold to external merchants from within Trinidadcito, one of whom has a storage house in the community. The inhabitants plan to put the Brazil nut harvests together and sell them for a higher price as a cooperative (a price even higher than is paid in Riberalta), but at the time of research this had not yet happened.

Networks in Trinidadcito

Source of information on legal issues in Trinidadcito

One quarter of the interviewees in Trinidadcito obtained legal information from their OTB, and almost as many received this information from the municipal agent. The third most important source of legal information was the corregidor. The school authorities were asked occasionally, and in individual cases the media, a workshop, a NGO and a lawyer. One individual claimed that he/she has no source of legal information.

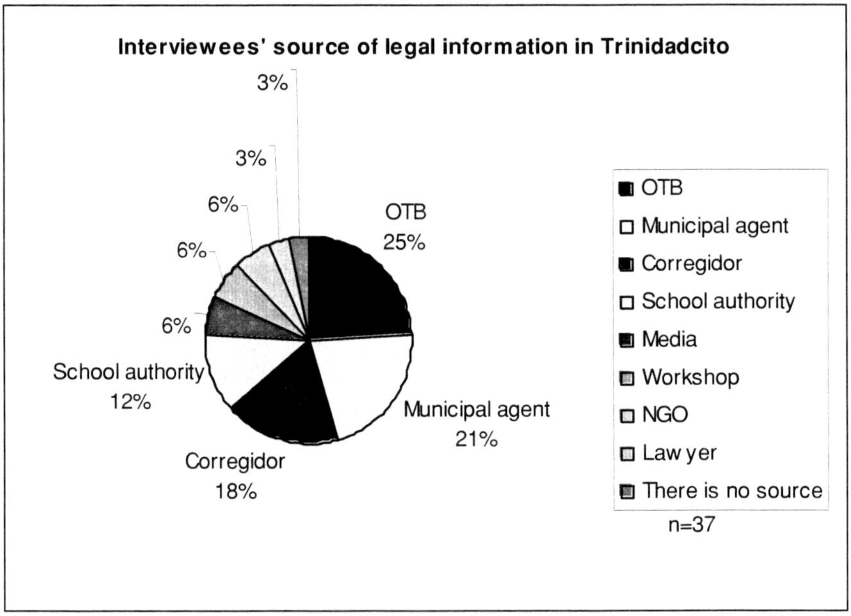

Figure 4-15: Sources of information on legal issues/ Trinidadcito

[72] In the 2002 harvest season the difference was 8 Bolivianos per *caja*. Nuts were sold for 25 Bolivianos/*caja* in Barbechon, and for 33 Bolivianos/*caja* in Riberalta.

The interviewees received their information almost exclusively from their administrative and political representation and the authorities.

Access to money in emergencies in Trinidadcito

In the event of emergencies the interviewees from Trinidadcito solved money problems primarily through the sale of animals (one third). The second most common means was the sale of agricultural products or with the financial help of relatives. About one eighth of the interviewees relied on the solidarity of the community and communal campaign, and another one eighth raised money through the help of friends[73]. One individual sold valuable items, one had no access to cash in urgent situations, and one individual claimed that his/her only means of access to money urgently was probably through prayer.

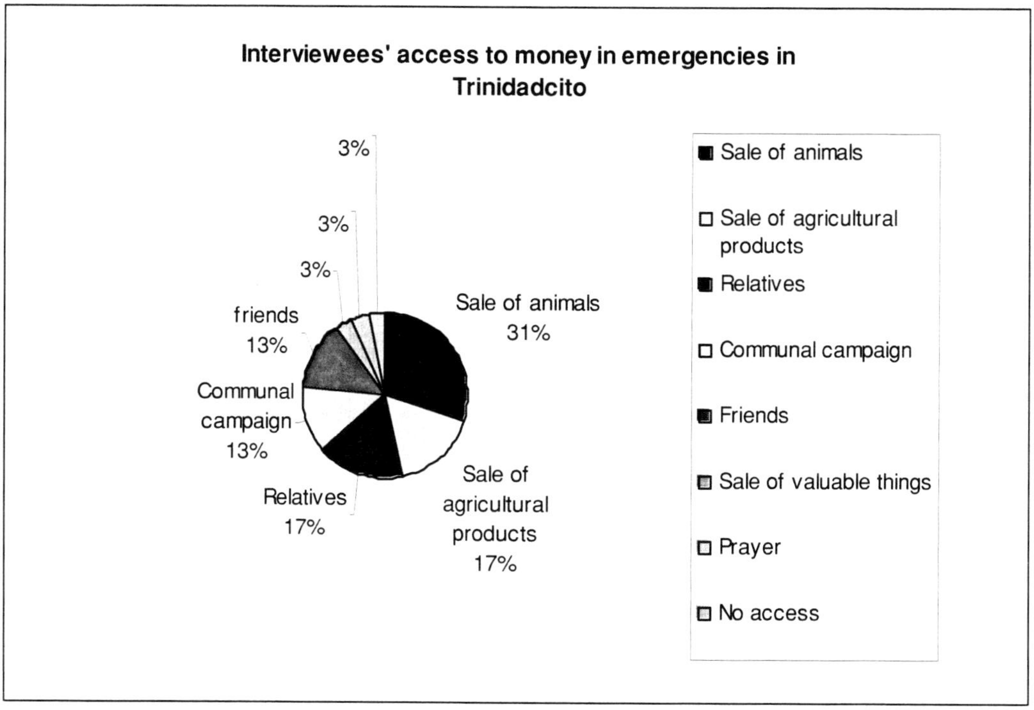

Figure 4-16: Access to money in emergencies/ Trinidadcito

So the overall picture in Trinidadcito is: About half of the interviewees had products at their disposal that they could sell to generate cash in case of emergencies. Nearly as many again relied on relatives, friends and other community members.

[73] However, these two categories ('communal campaign' and 'friends') are not necessarily mutually exclusive. A friend can be a neighbour, and vice versa. It depends in which 'category' the interviewee places the person.

Access to medium and long-term credit in Trinidadcito

Three quarters of all interviewees in Trinidadcito did not have access to any medium or long-term credit. One quarter answered in the positive. Many of them did not specify from where they could get the money, however. Some individuals did give details, namely through their position as a teacher, through the fishermen's association, a bank and a powerful individual known to them.

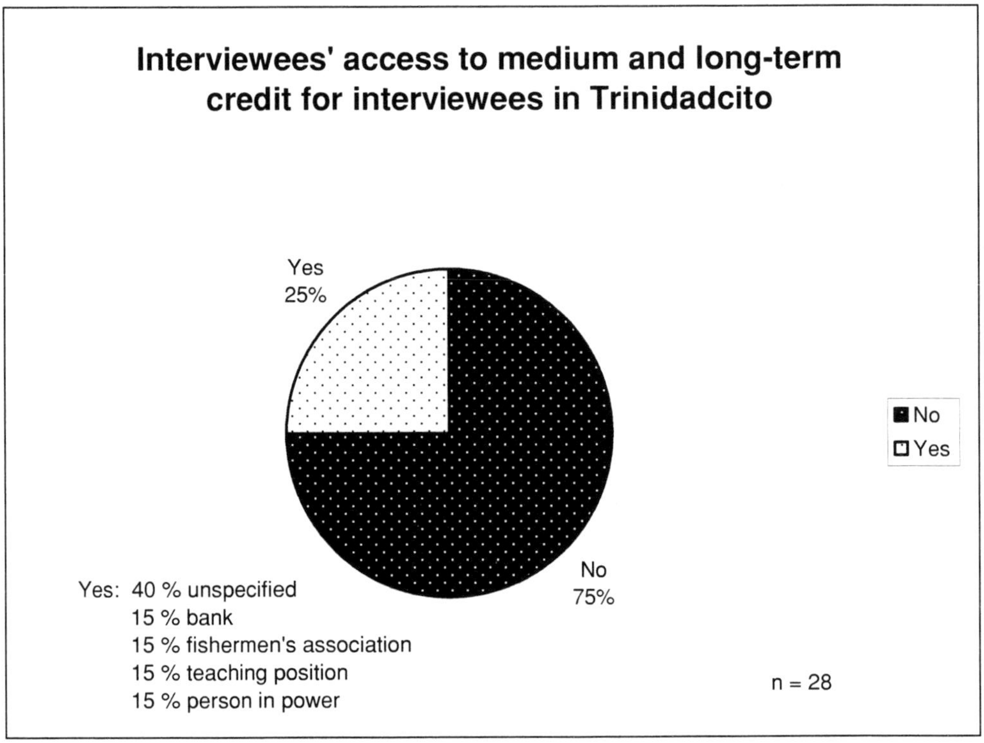

Figure 4-17: Access to medium and long-term credit / Trinidadcito

Trust in Trinidadcito

Table 4-5: Level of trust in Trinidadcito

Interviewees' trust in:	Predictability	Certainty	Level of trust
Community representatives[74]	1	2	3
Former patron	not applicable, too long ago	not applicable, too long ago	not applicable, too long ago
NGOs	2	2	4
Corregidor	2	1	3

The grading used for the scores has been accomplished using a contents analysis method. Qualitative judgements made by the interviewees were transformed into quantitative terms based on the deductive reasoning capabilities of the author.

Performance elements in Trinidadcito

The performance elements of the Trinidadcito community were manifold at the time of research:

- The municipal agent and the OTB negotiated the construction of a road to their community for the following dry season. For the relatively cut off community, which has had to rely on boats and muddy motorbike trails this is a crucial step towards better transport conditions. The strategy of negotiating with two municipalities proved the key to success. These competing municipalities belong to a single *mancomunidad*[75], Trinidadcito being one important community in terms of population. The Trinidadcito representatives threatened to change over to the other one if they did not get what they wanted.
- A similar strategy was applied for the building of a new school (educational matters are the responsibility of Gonzalo Moreno, while the money for construction came from San Lorenzo). In the end, the representatives from Gonzalo Moreno were annoyed by the sign at the school building naming those responsible for its construction.
- The electorate in Trindidadcito is quite loyal to the representative of one political party who perceives the community as his "cradle". In turn, together with a politician responsible at department level, he uses his influence to fulfil petitions in the community's favour. Upon application for a boat for the health assistant, allowing him to carry out his work in other communities along the river, the community was also granted a second for general community purposes, which they plan to use for

[74] Due to the specific constellation in Trinidadcito, this point implies both OTB and municipal agent at the same time.

[75] According to the Municipality Law, *mancomunidad* refers to 2 or more municipalities that are spontaneously associated with the aim to jointly develop projects, plans, programs or other activities which have a common purpose. The municipalities of Gonzalo Moreno, El Sena and San Lorenzo (Blanca Flor) are associated to one *mancomunidad*.

the sale of fish[76], agricultural products, Brazil nuts, etc. The community is relatively rich in comparison to other communities in the region. Apart from the two boats, the freezer in the health post, the radio and the telephone, there are several solar panels and motorbikes, as well as one communal television and video recorder.

- Their political connections also made it possible for the community to claim ownership of the lake from which all their fish comes, although geographically it is situated in the next province and does not belong to the community territory. Trespassers[77] are prohibited and the community holds exclusive fishing rights. As they formally committed themselves to compliance with regulations for the protection of this area (including keeping the lake clean and respecting the close-season for fishing between January and May, etc.) the authorities granted them exclusive property rights to the lake. The protection status of the lake means that they are freed from paying taxes on the catch to the department. However, the permission for access to the lake has to be renewed each year, which means future access is not guaranteed.
- Another facet of functioning is the vivid culture of discussion in Trinidadcito. For example on the community's annual anniversary a theatre play openly critical of the *subprefecto* was performed, in the presence of the *subprefecto*.
- The Trinidadcito community members were considering strategies for the community's future. The outcome of a 'future scenario workshop' instigated by the author indicated that community members had already been contemplating this issue for a long time, and that two different trends prevail amongst the community members. They are unanimous in their plans for future Brazil nut harvests, but not in relation to other issues. While one group favours a prioritisation of fishing and proposes the establishment of a fish farm to secure the resource, the other group

[76] The 'Paiche' catch can be sold fresh, primarily to intermediaries who have cooling facilities and can provide immediate transport to Riberalta. The intermediaries pay 5 Bolivianos per kilo. At the time of research, most fish was sold salted and dried for 4 Bolivianos per kilo. This requires minimal investment in materials and labour. Salt and foil is needed, in which the fish is stored for three days. Then it has to dry in the sun for several days. With the new boat, the community could sell their fish fresh in Riberalta, for a better price than is received from the intermediary. However, this would require an investment in cooling facilities. Not all association members favour this plan. There is also a general risk of over fishing in the future, which would require the establishment of a fish farm. Nevertheless, under the given conditions, fish is generating a high income. It provides a higher income than the Brazil nut harvest and the season is longer, lasting from June to December. Fishing is also less labour intensive than the collection of Brazil nuts (personal communication to Stahl (2002) by a man who fishes and collects nuts). The average catch made by a fisherman and his assistant is a 150 kg Paiche per week.

[77] An example: On 18 April 2002, six fishermen from Riberalta were fishing in the lake. As soon as this was noticed in Trinidadcito, 11 community members formed a delegation and went to the lake. They declared the activity of the fishermen illegal, took half of the catch away and forced them to leave the lake immediately. The people of Trinidadcito say that there are few conflicts because they are located closest to the lake, and the other communities (have to) accept their 'ownership'. This example was provided by Johannes Stahl, a student of ethnology, who worked in another community, but participated in the fishing activities of the Trinidadcito fishermen association as part of his research. The author of this study was unable to participate in this activity without impinging certain gender-related boundaries, which may have had negative repercussions for her further work in the community.

wants to enhance agriculture and produce greater surpluses for sale outside of the community through the foundation of a cooperative. This group fears the loss of access to the lake and would prefer to focus on other alternative sources of income.

In summary, the performance elements observed in Trinidadcito show that the community operates much as an enterprise that knows its own value, and is able to use that to negotiate successfully. The main cash income activities, Brazil nut recollection and fishing, complement each other perfectly in the annual calendar, and also combine well with the time of the rice harvest, an important source of food for the communities.

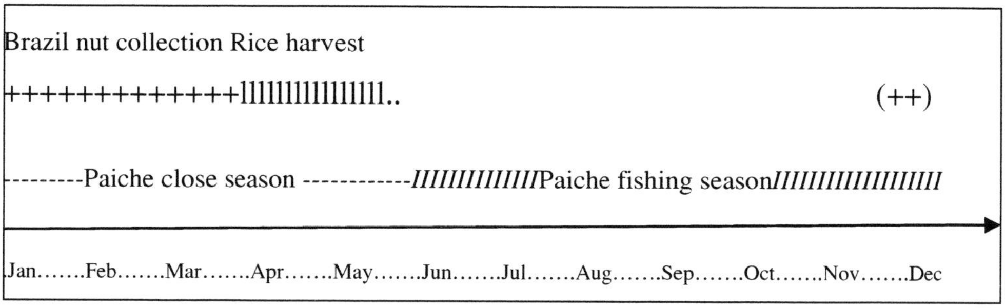

Figure 4-18: Calendar of activities[78] for Trinidadcito

4.2.5 The individual education-organisation link in all four communities

Flap (2002: 52) referred to shortcomings of the social capital research programme and called for serious consideration of "the analogy with human capital, minding the commonalities as well as the differences" as a major provision for the further development of research in this field. The following data relates "education" to "organisation". The hypothesis for this link assumes that the human capital factor education (measured in years of schooling) corresponds with high participation in organisations[79] in adult life. Such participation is a social asset, and in certain circumstances can become or is social capital.

The data from the four study communities show the following:

[78] The activities graphed are not complete, but this figure highlights how the timing of an important agricultural activity (rice harvest) goes with the timing of important extractive activities.

[79] Organisations in this instance included OTBs (syndicates), other political organisations, *Junta Escolar*, parents' organisations, professional associations, as well as sport clubs and religious groups.

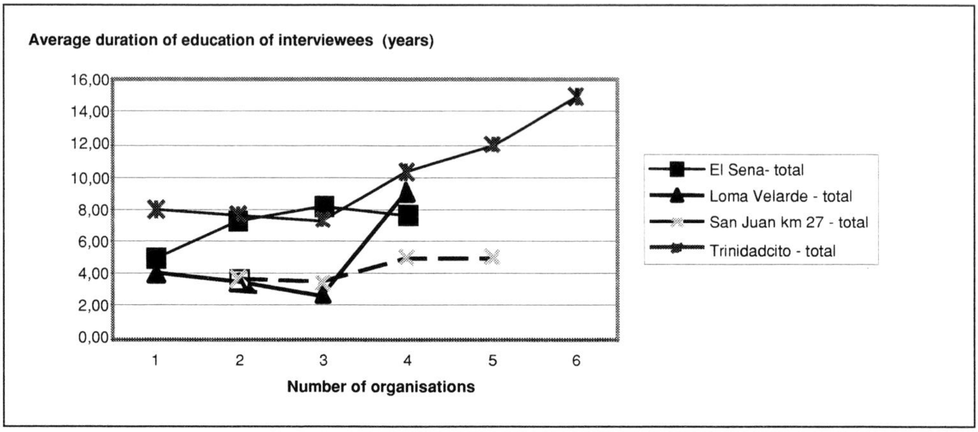

Figure 4-19: Frequency of organisation membership in relation to education in years (average total)

El Sena:	n=26
LomaVelarde:	n=8
San Juan km 27:	n=23
Trinidadcito:	n=28
Total:	n=85 interviewees

The symbols in the graph do not represent individuals, but the average years of education attained by interviewees in the same category of membership frequency. That means for example people who are members in three organisations, had an average of eight years of education in El Sena, and about three in Loma Velarde. If each individual were plotted on the graph, there would be dots above and below the symbols. Although the graphs are not always continuous, overall there is a clear trend evident from the case studies: The more years of education, the greater a person's engagement in organisations, which confirms the hypothesis.

If a distinction is made between the sexes, the data provide a different picture:

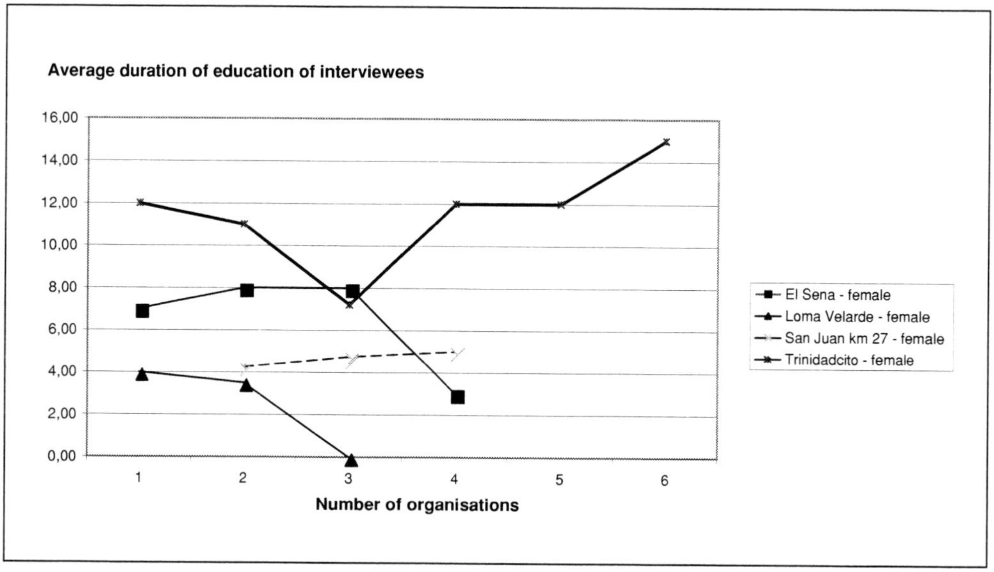

Figure 4-20: Frequency of organisation membership in relation to education in years (average female)

El Sena:	n=9
Loma Velarde:	n=4
San Juan km 27:	n=10
Trinidadcito:	n=13
Total:	n=36

The hypothesis has to be discarded in the case of the data pertaining solely to women. There are examples of women with 12 years of schooling who belong to only one organisation, whereas women with no education at all are members in three.

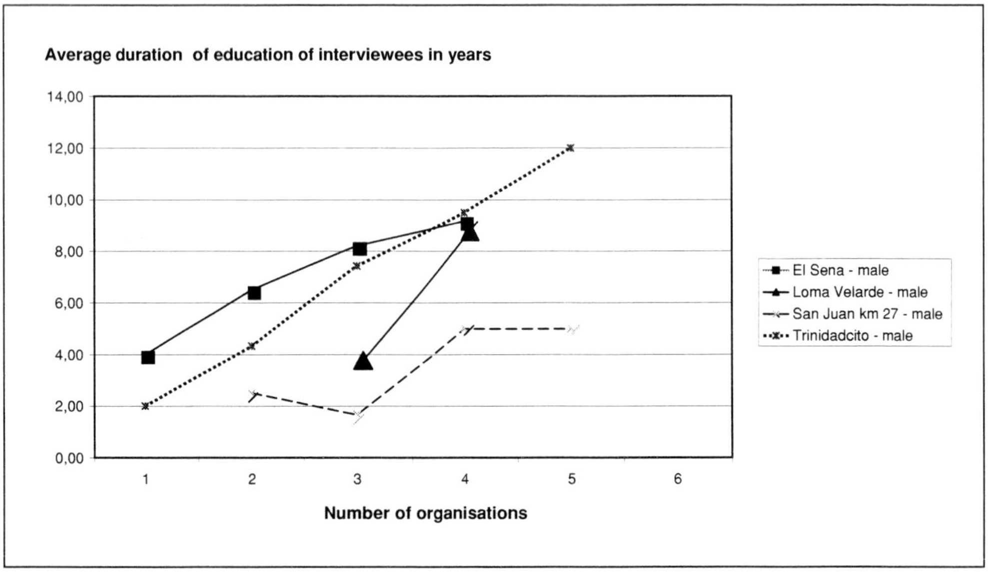

Figure 4-21: Frequency of organisation membership in relation to education in years (average male)

El Sena: n=17

Loma Velarde: n=4

San Juan km 27: n=13

Trinidadcito: n=15

Total: n=49

The data based on all of the male interviewees paints a homogenous picture with a clear trend. The hypothesis that education as a human capital factor is linked to high levels of participation in organisations is confirmed. In this case a higher level of human capital favours a higher level of participation in organisations. This is considered a structural social asset, or social capital in a demand situation where this asset is needed to create benefits.

A World Bank Local Level Institutions Study (1995-2001) in three countries provided empirical findings from Bolivia on the role of local associations in the provision of services to households and the extent to which such associations help households, especially the poor, increase their welfare. The study used a customary reduced form model of household welfare, in which the household social capital endowment was calculated using a multiplicative index. For better comparison with other countries, the results have also been expressed as point elasticities. An important observation is that the magnitude of elasticity showing the effect of social capital is in the same order of magnitude as the elasticity of years of education. The findings show that, even after controlling for ownership of human and physical capital and other relevant exogenous household characteristics, the presence of social capital, as measured in the study, exerts an additional positive effect on household welfare (GROOTAERT 2001: 18). For Bolivia, the World Bank case studies yielded a point elasticity of social capital (referring to household welfare) of 0.13, and an elasticity of years of education of 0.18.

The positive effect of social capital on household welfare (as shown in the aforementioned study) is assumed in this study. The data presented in section 4.2.5 contribute to the identification of the factors that help to build social assets leading to social capital and benefits. The factor 'years of education' was found to have a positive influence on the association membership of men in this study[80]; this does not hold true for women, however. This indicates that there are gender-sensitive intervening factors in the education-organisation link.

This can be construed in different ways; it can be interpreted that female membership in formal organisations either takes or does not take place because of certain societal attitudes in which their educational background does not play any role. This favouring or hindering attitude is expressed, for example, by a husband who does not allow his wife to become a member, or by villagers maintaining male exclusivity in organisations. On the contrary, communities and families may promote female membership in accordance with policies promoted by NGOs and state organisations. Therefore, the attitude on the role of women is more important than their educational background or their capabilities. At the same time, it also depends on the personal attitude of the women themselves and the opportunities formal membership offers them. It may be that women who dispose of good informal networks and are used to relying upon them do not need membership in formal organisations. It may also be that women do not expect any benefits from membership in formal organisations because of the lack of or even negative experiences, in addition to internalised role models which impede membership. It is possible that the costs of membership in terms of time and obligations are deemed relatively high, whereas the benefits may already be accessible through another (male) member of the family. Further investigation of the factors hindering or favouring female association membership is required. It appears that these factors are not related, or only indirectly related, to their educational background.

[80] The effect is assumed because education lies before association membership on the time axis, and higher levels of education correspond with a higher rate of association membership in the data.

4.3 Discussion

Sections 4.2.1 to 4.2.4 have to be taken as the assessment of predefined community elements. These are organisations, institutions, networks and trust as well as performance. Clearly this inventory does not provide a complete picture of the real situation, as there are more elements, and more aspects within the elements assessed that have to be borne in mind. Nevertheless, these elements are the most crucial for the evaluation of capacity at community level. While the focus of this study rested on the community as a whole, consisting of representatives and a population base, a complementary approach would be a capacity assessment of each community individual, their skills, time and wealth, and how far each individual is related to the four elements looked at here. This would require complicated models with many variables and linkages and it is unlikely that such models could reflect the complex reality. The approach presented here provides a tool for a basic reflective community capacity assessment and can be used best when there are several communities for comparison. The four elements together with the fifth dimension, the performance elements – what the subjects actually do with their assets, can be applied in other settings. Other forms of organisation, other types of institutions, etc., such as cultural, political and other differences do not obstruct the application of the framework. Therefore, this is a tool making it possible to draw a picture of the inner life of the community and its workings. This tool makes possible an estimation of its capacity in comparison to that of others.

Figure 4-22 shows the relative communal capacity for each of the four case studies. Relative communal capacity has been calculated as follows: For each social asset the author ranked the four communities; every asset category has been ranked separately (for example, trust, access to information, money in emergencies, long-term credit). The rankings for each category served as a basis for an overall average for each community. The rankings for all four assets were added together to give the overall ranking for the assets continuum: the summed rankings revealed whether a community is located at a high, medium or low level on the continuum. Each element had the same weight in the ranking.

The performance elements were a separate dimension. These were ranked between the four communities, and as a result these performance elements are located at a low, medium or high functioning level. The figure shows each community's situation with respect to the two dimensions social assets and performance elements. The area within the intersecting levels of each dimension represents their capacity. If the surface area for each of the communities is compared, it is possible to determine whether one community has a higher or lower relative capacity than another.

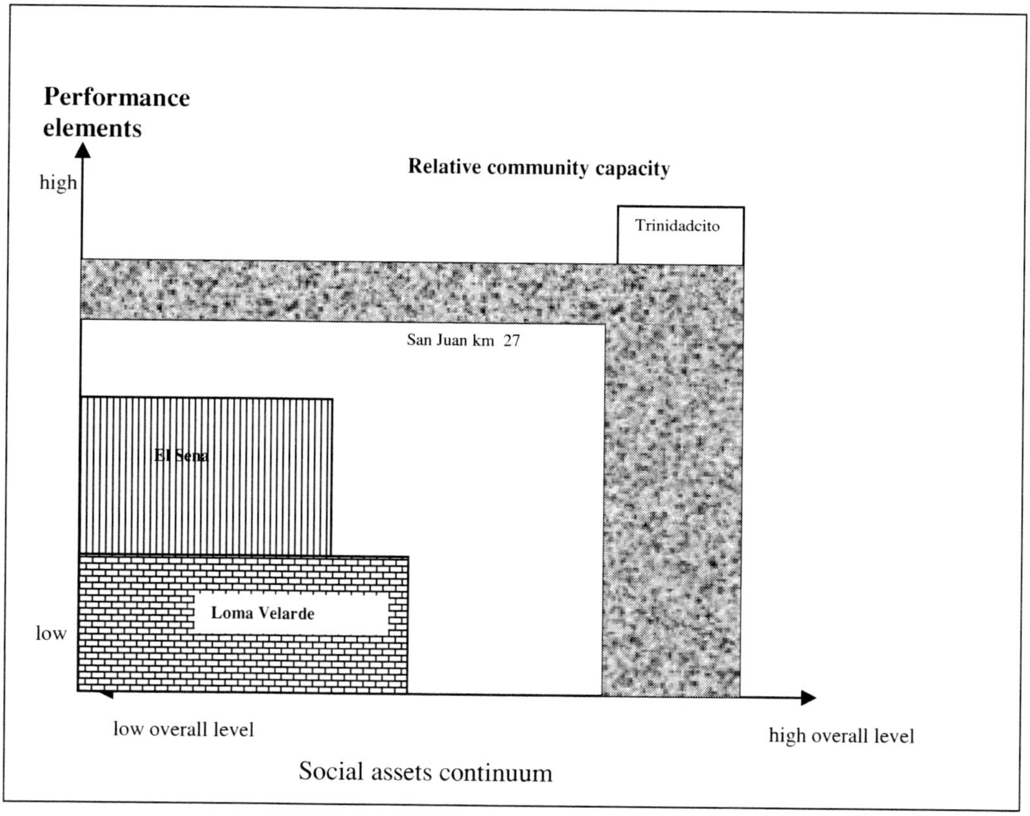

Figure 4-22: Relative community capacity

The surface area of the rectangles expresses the relative community capacity. The higher the surface area, the greater the capacity. Here capacity is a function of the four different elements of social assets and of performance elements. Therefore, in the community capacity ranking Trinidadcito leads, followed by San Juan km 27. El Sena is in third place, and Loma Velarde ranks lowest.

Table 4-5 : Rankings per social asset element

	Organisations	Institutions	Networks	Trust
1	San Juan km 27	Trinidadcito	Trinidadcito	Trinidadcito
2	Trinidadcito	San Juan km 27	San Juan km 27/ Loma Velarde	San Juan km 27/ Loma Velarde
3	El Sena	Loma Velarde	El Sena	El Sena
4	Loma Velarde	El Sena		

The overall ranking for the social assets continuum is Trinidadcito (1, first place, highest capability level), San Juan km 27 (2), Loma Velarde (3), and El Sena (4), with the lowest asset level.

However, in the performance elements dimension the ranking is Trinidadcito (1), San Juan km 27 (2), El Sena (3) and Loma Velarde (4).

As a result, the overall relative community capacity is clearcut, with Trinidadcito (1) and San Juan km 27 (2). Either Loma Velarde or El Sena is third, depending on how much weight one puts on the performance elements or the assets dimension. In terms of the overall capacity comparison they are at a similar level, with each one stronger in one of the two dimensions.

There are competing views on community capacity and its link to well-being in the literature. Assessments focussing on the social and economic well-being of natural resource-dependent communities act on the assumption that a community with a high level of well-being is better able to manage its resources effectively because attention does not primarily rest on survival (Nadeau et al. 1999). But this view is questionable because a high standard of living or happiness does not necessarily lead to civic action. While some argue that well-being is a broader concept that includes capacity, other authors see it the other way round. It is beyond dispute that they are closely related; the question is 'how' they are related.

For the purposes of this study, the author made an assessment of community capacity, which focused on organisations and institutions at community level, as well as on networks and the level of trust of interviewees belonging to a particular community. The performance elements reveal the extent to which community objectives are achieved. Community objectives are divergent from individual goals, and ideally lead to an improvement for all members of a community. In the view of the author, capacity is one side of the coin, and socio-economic factors the other. The coin as a whole makes up well-being. Capacity has more to do with empowerment, competence and readiness than with economic resources. The four elements presented are social assets, which serve as a social capital base. The performance elements are the real situation when social assets produce an output by means of social capital. The author considers this connection to be very important as it draws analogies between different theoretical frameworks and combines them.

Social capital and social asset building require further investigation. Recent studies of the historical development of social capital deliver the empirical basis for the assumption that social capital can only be created through long social processes (see Bray, et al. 2004: 4). The approach proposed by von Twickel (2002), which was used here, distinguishes social capital as relatively short-term in terms of the realisation of benefits, which can only be achieved by means of existing social assets. These social assets underlie the same assumption referred to previously, namely that these institutions, structures, trust, etc., need time to develop. However, in more recent research another argument has been put forward: Social capital (and social assets) can be created in short time periods and can be influenced by public policy. Krishna (2000) observed a relatively quick development of social capital (embodied in functioning and legitimate user committees) during the course of the implementation of the Rajasthan Watershed Development Program in India. A similar observation was made here in the case of El Sena. The strong interest to use the chance which offers the reform process to get secured land property rights has mobilised the construction of social assets and social capital necessary for the representation of a functioning community in a very short time, with outside support of NGOs.

A common future research question emerges from each of the case studies, namely to what extent will social assets and social capital remain stable or, to be more exact, continue to fulfil their respective purpose if they were constructed in short time periods. As results from chapter 3 show, social assets which were developed over longer time periods, seem to continue to contribute to the system, though maybe in a different role. The decisive factors for the preservation of social capital have to be determined in follow-up studies, especially in situations where there is a relatively short-term evolution of social capital.

Apart from these conclusions rooted at the empirical level, the question of how the applied theoretical framework suited remains, as does the transfer of Sen's approach from the individual to the community level. The presented performance elements reveal what the communities succeeded in doing with the commodities and characteristics at their disposal. These characteristics are also made up of the social assets found in their specific features. Institutions, organisations, networks and trust are tools that help to determine the functioning, that is to say the realisation of certain performance elements. Following Sen's logic, the community selection process for performance elements and the implementation constitute the community capability. Based on this capability, not only are performance elements chosen, but characteristics can also be changed, for example institutions. In this study, community capacity is therefore identical to 'community' capability (as transferred from Sen). This works as long as this capability implies collective internal processes in which all individuals have equal opportunities to influence community development, also by means of a legitimate leadership, and to improve the standard of living of community inhabitants. Sen's notions of capability and functioning delivers lines of thought that also apply to communities in the study area, where a community has to act as a legal body. However, the translation of Sen's approach to community level in combination with the selected social assets constitutes only one conversion alternative enacted by the author in congruence with her own considerations. These considerations may not include all of the important aspects or are possibly too general. More attention should be attached to the internal processes of the community, and how they are shaped. The author proposes an intensification of research into the individual-community link, to be increasingly guided by socio-psychological schemes.

5 CONCLUSIONS

This study investigates the realities facing forest-dependent communities in the Bolivian Amazon from different angles. The differing focuses deliver different results. However, these results complement each and together paint a portrait of reality.

5.1 Theoretical aspects

In terms of the theoretical aspects, the investigation provides a contribution through the application of elements of institutional theory, such as path dependency, as well as social capital and related theories, to a broader basis of empirical data resulting in a further analysis of these theories. All in all, the application of these theories proved a useful means to achieve the research objectives. However, the theory did not always cover certain aspects, which appeared to be relevant during the study but proved to have deficiencies in their explanatory capacity. This gave rise to new questions.

The concept of path dependency was applied in this study to the concrete example of rural forest-dependent communities undergoing legal reforms. In the theoretical literature, the existence of path dependency is usually regarded as a factor impeding later developments such as reform implementation. While this constraining hypothesis holds true for some aspects, path dependent elements can also be supportive. As this study shows, rural communities with long[81] histories of experience in internal community organisation have higher capacities to autonomously define local priorities and attain these goals, as well as transform reform requirements into practised policy. In this case, path dependency is deterministic, but in a positive way.

The role attributed to actors 'external' to the community such as NGOs, state agencies or peasant federations is a methodological problem from a path dependency point of view. Their influence on internal processes is manifold. Prior to the arrival of the surveying crews implementing the reforms, the state organisations lacked the staff and the money necessary to assist the (remote) communities in ensuring that the disadvantaged benefit from the upcoming reforms in any meaningful way. Furthermore, other stakeholders, such as the barraqueros who were about to lose land, acted strategically to hamper developments opposing their interests. In several cases the lack of input by state organisations was ameliorated by NGOs and the peasant federation, as well as the church[82]. NGOs carried out information campaigns and organised workshops, the participants of which subsequently further disseminated the information in their regions. NGOs also provided infrastructure and organisational assistance in the communities themselves.

[81] Long is in this case relative. All settlements in the study region are 'young' in comparison to settlements worldwide. In the context of local history, however, long is defined as 15 years or older.

[82] The Catholic Church plays a major role as a mediator in conflicts between the stakeholders at the regional level. This is not of great importance within the communities detailed in this study, but there are accounts of minor church influence, for example, a preacher from an evangelist congregation is said to have told people not to participate in politics.

Therefore, the role of external actors is ambiguous. They can be agents supporting the maintenance of structures from the past; for instance, if state agencies do not deliver the services necessary to drive change, be they information, technical or financial support, as well as when they do not impose sanctioning measures for non-compliance, corruption, etc. However, these 'external' actors can also be elements helping to push the reforms through as can be seen in El Sena, where the community would have lost the opportunity to demand land under the *saneamiento* process, if several NGOs had not worked together and triggered the initiative. On the one hand, the 'intervention' made the implementation of the reforms possible, but at the same time, such external influence may undermine local governance in the long run.

Sztompka (1991: 106) stressed the paramount importance of time for the development of societal structures. In his theory and model of social development, time is explicitly and fully incorporated in the analysis. Archer (1988: xxii) referred to incessant cycles of morphogenesis, in which structure and action operate over different time periods. Structure logically predates the actions that transform it and structural development follows these actions (*ibid.* 22). Sztompka regarded history as a continuous chain of praxis[83] mediated by tradition[84]. "The crucial property of history is the cumulativeness of tradition, the permanently growing scope of received heritage from earlier praxis, constraining but also facilitating (providing enriched resources) for later praxis" (Sztompka 1991: 107).

Transferring this notion to rural communities in the Bolivian Amazon, the heritage elements from earlier praxis the author regarded as important in the context of the reforms were: the degree of internal organisation (prior to the implementation of the land reforms), community action to secure access to resources (prior to the reforms), power distribution and the external organisational input facilitating the reforms. These structural indicators comprise the heritage of the agents (the inhabitants) themselves and certain personal experiences such as migration, former dependency relationships (e.g. to a *patron)*, attitudes, for example, towards organisation, the result of personal experience and knowledge, and also a specific habit related to agriculture and other livelihood pillars. These aspects are closely related to the role of the inhabitants as citizens within a decentralised state and as designated resource managers.

The influence of history is reflected in the evolution and change of institutions and organisation. When classifying institutional issues touched upon in this work according to four levels of social analysis (see table 1-5), as proposed by Williamson (2000), the results of this study are located mainly at level 1, but also at level 2 and 3. In contrast, New Institutional

[83] Praxis as events that "leave effects, material residues, memory traces, structural arrangements, institutional forms etc. which make up historical tradition. They are intended and unintended, recognized and unrecognized, but together they make up real circumstances, conditions, situations for further events (praxis). The network of events extends beyond direct co-presence in praxis, and acquires continuity thanks to the indirect mediation of conditions produced by earlier praxis" (Sztompka 1991: 207).

[84] Tradition represents the results of praxis and conditions for praxis at the same time (Sztompka 1991: 207).

Economics (NIE) literature has principally been concerned with levels 2 and 3. In NIE, informal institutions (level 1) are usually taken as given as they tend to change very slowly and are characterised by social embeddedness. Williamson, North (1991) and other scholars claimed that informal institutions have a pervasive influence on the long-term character of economies and represent in many cases constraints. Therefore, informal institutions should not be taken as given, but understood as a vivid element within the system and be investigated.

The relationship between informal and formal institutions, level 1 and level 2, proved to be clear-cut in the case studies carried out in this research study. The new legal framework in Bolivia (level 2) has through decentralization and land reform created a legally defined community space. While this space exists formally, the interactions within this space, namely within a community, are based almost exclusively on informal institutions (level 1). This can be interpreted as a disconnection from the formal and the informal, or as the formal 'embracing' the informal, whereby on balance agency originates to a greater extent from the informal and, therefore, has repercussions for the extent and the manner in which the formal is implemented.

Agrawal pointed out that democratisation hinges on decentralisation, which "changes the opportunity structures for participation, and makes available to citizens multiple channels through which to access and shape governance and the exercise of power" (1999: 7). In northern Bolivia, formal institutions have delivered new channels, but informal institutions are the backbone of rural community systems. Where there is a link between the informal and the new channels, the informal adopts incorporating the new and generally remains the more influential form of institution in the region. This in turn feeds back into theory. The New Institutional Economics approach of assuming informal institutions as given does not adequately reflect their active role in the system. Although informal institutions usually have a long-term influence, they are also relevant in short-term investigations to the understanding of community systems and their capacity. Informal rules currently regulating political representation and resource use, as well as many other things, in rural communities in Bolivia are in a process of evolution and adaptation, but remain the leading tool for the facilitation of interaction in rural forest-dependent settlements. Therefore, further investigation into the processes related to the formation and change of, and the influence on informal institutions is required.

5.2 Perspectives for independent communities in the Bolivian Amazon

5.2.1 Internal stabilisation?

The rural communities in the Bolivian Amazon are characterised by forest-dependency and at the same time are affected by poverty (defined in UN-terms). The enforcement of the Forest Law and INRA Law have contributed to reducing the disparities in the distribution of natural resources, resulting in a rise in the ratio of land allocated to peasant and indigenous communities. This study, with its in-depth focus on community internal aspects, proves that organisational functioning, power relationships and informal rules within communities mainly define (un)equal resource access and distribution, as well as the (non) functioning of equal opportunity local governance. The community system is influenced by historical path dependencies, which also impact upon present community capacity. Community capacity is crucial to the realisation of community benefits and local resource management.

Ruiz[85] (2005) stated that the reforms failed both to encourage forest users to manage forests in a sustainable way and to govern extractive activities in rural settlements in sufficient detail, nor did they reduce the disparities in the distribution of the resources within rural communities. This supports the findings of this study. The importance of power asymmetries is reinforced by data provided by other researchers[86] in the region. The case studies of Litoral and Puerto Oro by Pereira (2004) emphasise the importance of power relationships, because both 'independent' communities are ruled by powerful families who *de facto* manage all of the natural resources. Hentschel (2002) investigated Santa Maria, which is regarded as the community *par excellence* by NGOs because of the high degree of organisation and the fact that it was home to one of the first community forest management plan initiatives in the region. This community has a long history of independence, the autonomous action of community organisations actively seeking external support from NGOs in order to enhance opportunities through better information, the training of community leaders, etc. This serves as an example of path dependency advancing the implementation of reforms and goes along with high community capacity.

As the results of this study show, communities dispose of different forms of internal organisation and community performance. Depending on the design of the communities' social assets and the collective performance (which is based on individuals), these communities possess a higher or lower capacity to meet the demands of their inhabitants, manage natural and other resources in a sound way and improve well-being in general.

The question of the extent to which the building of community capacities may be endorsed from outside arises. The data show that external endorsement at the micro-level can only take place selectively and in relation to emerging issues. The mere nature of the defined social assets points to a construction process requiring time. If power, management rights, etc., are transferred to the local level, and democratic principles are applied, then state and society have to bear the costs of developments occurring during this construction process. That is the price of democracy. The author holds the view that at the micro-level, living conditions and natural resource management can only be selectively influenced through direct intervention by governmental and non-governmental organisations. The key to success is the local actors in the communities themselves. If governmental and non-governmental organisations intend to ensure that rural communities can meet goals such as poverty alleviation and 'sustainable'

[85] Ruiz study was carried out in the northern Bolivian Amazon within the framework of the same BMZ/CIFOR project and through the University of Freiburg. It involved an analysis of the implementation of the reforms in combination with an analysis of the regional stakeholders and the conflicts between them.

[86] Within the same CIFOR project and a subsequent project.

natural resource management, shorten the construction process for the sake of the people concerned in the respective settlements and lower negative externalities on forests and people in general, then they should engage mainly in the strengthening of civil society at the micro-level by providing a wide range of opportunities for all members of the population. They need to provide opportunities for people to enhance their skills, knowledge and access to capital in order to guarantee a system of checks and balances making possible the rejection of local elites and facilitating management solutions which take into account local needs and are feasible. Such a system would contribute to good governance, improving livelihoods and resulting in forest management solutions that do not depend on permanent external back up. Such a concept is in line with Sen, who defined an improvement in the standard of living or well-being according to the enhancement of the range of choices and the possibility to realise opportunities, which holds true for individuals as well as for communities.

When relating the selection criteria of the case studies and the differences in internal capacity of the respective communities, then there is no general direct relationship to be found. It is logical that, for example, a remote community has higher transaction costs for transport than one close to town. However, the design of social assets and community performance result in both higher (Trinidadcito) and lower (Loma Velarde) capacities, even though both are remote communities.

Whereas geographical remoteness seems not to play a role, 'political' remoteness or relevance is important. Both Trinidadcito and Loma Velarde are located in rural municipalities. While Loma Velarde has only nine households and the respective rural municipality did not function due to a corruption scandal, Trinidadcito has 45 households and is located in a rural municipality where the high population of possible voters counts for a lot. This fact offers a wider scope for community performance. Community capacity, as defined in this study, is not dependent on low or high endowment with natural resources, nor does it depend on the size of the community. There are small, badly organised communities, big and well organised communities and vice versa. Resource management depends on their community capacity.

With regard to the selection criterion 'community foundation history', the case studies prove a direct link to social assets. This holds especially true for internal rule setting and the organisation of the political representative body. The longer a community has been independent, the more internal rule-setting takes place without external influence, and the greater the representation of all inhabitants in the political representative body. In this respect the community El Sena may be classified as an exception, as despite high external influence a community body representing all inhabitants has been created in a short period of time.

By taking into consideration socio-historical factors in the debate on reform implementation and resource governance, constraints and supportive elements can be better understood. It is unrealistic to expect that with the arrival of reforms, the inhabitants of rural communities will become 'new citizens' overnight as the law supposes them to be. They formally possess new opportunities of participation and *de jure* land rights, which imply legal access to natural resources. However, the study shows that the management of resources at local level is in the hands of actors about half of whom are unaware of any legal reforms, whereas only a few individuals are well informed. There are strong information asymmetries, not only between the micro and meso/macro levels, but also at the microlevel itself, which pose a hindrance to broader participation. Without any knowledge of the opportunities, no one can avail of them. Better informed people occupying positions as community representatives can improve local resource management and participation if they hold themselves accountable to those they represent. Those who use formal instruments provided for in the laws as tools for personal enrichment are a manifest hindrance to participation and community resource use opportunities. Communities managed in an abusive way by influential individuals usually lack information, are badly organised and powerless to bargain in the interests of all community members. As empirical results show, the majority of interviewees claim a lack of any political representation of their interests.

This contrasts with the achievements of the *campesino* and indigenous movements at regional and national level. The regional *campesino* movement in collaboration with other regional movements achieved a change in the law, which led to the increase of their land entitlement from 50 to 500 hectares per *campesino* family. Apparently many individuals at the micro-level are not aware of the activities of the *campesino* movement at political level, or that the activities do not coincide with their personal interests (which the author considers unlikely). Another explanation could be that the *campesino* federations are perceived as representing interests opposed to urban-based politics and, therefore, are not perceived as part of the interviewees' 'political representation system'. This means that when the interviewees were asked about the political representation of their interests (without specification of the level), they did not consider their own federations as their political representation.

This can be traced back to the history of the *campesino* movement in Bolivia. There is a dichotomy between the state and its citizens, a disconnection and negatively weighted perception of politics in the eyes of the rural inhabitants. In different eras political parties tried to gain influence in the rural area by founding or supporting existing peasant organisations, leading to their instrumentalisation and fragmentation in the sector, and the loss of the trust of the population base[87]. The results of this study support the assumption that the pursuit of votes in rural areas is still influenced by corruption and the manipulation of rural representatives. *Campesinos* holding a positive view of their representative federation do not classify this organisation in the category 'political' representation. Policy and politics are regarded as something distant, which is decided by corrupt politicians. Their own interests are best represented through contrary methods and involve extreme demands, street blockades and national demonstrations before there is any thought given to sitting down at a negotiation

[87] An extreme example: Fom 1964 to 1969 the peasant movement was under the influence of the army, which was the main 'political party' under general Barrientos (Krempin 1986: 96). Subsequently, peasant consciousness and the desire for independence within the *campesino* movement were high. Current rules reveal a mistrust of the relationship to urban-based political organisations and parties. Demands made in the political sphere are expressed in a reformist manner, for example, by street blockades and by a strategy of confrontation with state agencies.

table. The author encountered this attitude through the participation in workshops and meetings held by peasant representatives and from the interviewees directly. The assumption of a narrow definition of 'political' interest representation, where peasant federations are not included is also backed by the observation that NGOs were almost never classified in the representation of political interests category by the interviewees. In spite of this, however, the interviewees expressed positive attitudes towards the NGOs due to personal benefits derived from certain projects.

As this study shows, the participation of rural inhabitants in municipal and national elections at a formal level is hindered by the fact that a high proportion of the citizens in the research area lack personal identification documents. These are not necessary for communal elections, however. In any case, smart politicians abuse the situation and buy voters by providing them with personal documentation. As the data indicate, the lack of information in relation to legal issues in combination with a negative attitude towards the possible opportunities presented through politics prevents rural inhabitants from getting actively involved.

Although almost all of the communities in the region rely on the forests for their livelihood, knowledge of the new law governing forestry is scarce. At department level, a similar paradox can be found. The forest area of Pando Department (where three of the four case studies are located) exceeds 90% of the total land area, and the main cash income is derived from the collection and processing of Brazil nuts, yet the government of the department (*Prefectura*) has not prioritised the forestry sector even though it is responsible for implementing public investment programmes and projects related to the sector. Instead priority has been given, for example, to the distribution of cattle[88]. In the municipalities of northern Bolivia, the transfer of responsibilities and resources has led to the reinforcement of existing local elites, granting cattle ranchers and timber companies a high degree of influence in local politics (Pacheco 2004: 23).

All four case studies are birds of a feather in the eyes of the law in that they are all independent communities housing rural smallholders. However, these settlements are in many respects heterogeneous. The outcomes of the legal reforms differ in each of these places due to the constraints or supportive elements placed upon them by local conditions. Aspects such as the local institutional and organisational history, power and information asymmetries, as well as community capacity influenced by individuals will shape resource use in the future. The implementation of new laws, and their interaction with existing local rules, is a long and complex process. Critics may, therefore, object on the basis that there is not enough proof of socio-historical constraints and that it is just too difficult to sort out the crucial elements in such a process. Nevertheless, transformation studies have produced clear evidence as to the

[88] The *Leche Para Todos* (milk for everyone) project 2001/2002 distributed cows to communities for the purposes of milk production. The species distributed is common in the region, produces little milk and, therefore, serves better as a source of meat. No capacity building for beneficiaries took place and several animals died (Maldonado 2002: 63). In many cases, forests were cleared in order to create space for the cattle, although the beneficiaries were required to possess 3 to 5 ha grasslands before livestock was granted.

importance of recognising path dependencies in good time. In institutionalism there is a lot of theory on the evolution of institutions, but empirical application, especially of the concept of path dependency, is hard to find. The purpose of this study was to bridge the gap.

Societal issues are not easy to grasp and cannot be explained by simple models. This is not an argument in favour of setting these important issues aside, however. This research was undertaken at a time when communities had to organise themselves in order to gain access to land, which is one crucial turning point in the implementation of land reform. The author views the results almost as a photograph, taken at a certain moment capturing as much detail in relation to the situation of that time as possible. The past is more frequently transmitted by oral accounts than by written documentation.

Since there is no objective truth, only facts that can be made transparent in an inter-subjective way, the author sought to adopt an approach, which made the evaluations as transparent as possible. Despite analytical limitations, there is a clear tendency towards path dependent processes in the independent rural communities of northern Bolivia.

It is important for future studies to take into consideration the result demonstrating that the migration background of the inhabitants (whether they were previously in a dependency relationship or not) is not decisive for community organisation practices, but rather the attitude they adopted as a consequence of their migration experience (what position they assume, whether conformist and passive, or self determined and active). Many families in San Juan km 27 were in dependent employment at one point, but broke away after relatives and friends had informed them that they could obtain access to land in their communities. They dispose of a rigid system of organisation at communal level and are active smallholders. This is also shown by the data in relation to agri'culture'. In other places, such as Loma Velarde and El Sena, this is not the case. With respect to feudal dependency relations, there is a degree of adaptation and conformity, which accompanies a low level of internal organisation. An unequal share of power is the one element that can tip the scales against the prospects of community resource use as intended by the law.

Although all of the communities in the research region are subject to outward migration, and more importantly migration inwards, as well as seasonal variations, it is mostly the processes of the community micro-system that affect the internal system of rule development. As a result, participatory rule making and, consequently, 'good' local community organisation are better established in communities, which have been independent for longer. According to the rule of time, participative and effective internal organisation (which leads to better community resource management) needs time to develop. Outside influences pushing organisation can be effective as a supplementary measure in cases where the need is urgent, but cannot substitute an internal process, which takes place over years. The possible mismanagement of resources during the period in between is the cost society has to bear. The alternative is to ignore democratic principles and for the state to impose authoritarian rules, or for certain stakeholders to again draw control of the communities unto themselves.

The process of land (re)distribution under the reforms has not yet ended. Nevertheless, it is clear that the independent communities in the northern Bolivian Amazon account for a large piece of the cake. This does not refer only to land, but also implies access to vast forest areas. In order to claim land these communities had to prove to the land administration authorities that they were organised. Whereas some communities accomplished this by themselves, others relied heavily on assistance from outside. The need to organise in order to access land under the reforms is just the first step on a ladder, which can ultimately lead to community-based enterprises. Keating (2003) developed a systematic methodology for evaluating and monitoring the management capacity of community-based enterprises. This document is an aid in the identification of the next steps and in sorting through the strengths and weaknesses, which have to be borne in mind. It is highly recommended that similar studies be conducted in other countries and settings in order to find out more about the factors.

Although under law the community owns a common pool resource, the community members must decide what will become of common property, especially the manner in which this resource is internally distributed and managed. This has economic, ecological and distributional consequences and, therefore, social effects. As long as the legal format of decision-making is adhered to and other formal requirements are met, any outcome within rural communities is deemed legal, although it may run contrary to the intentions of the reforms.

5.2.2 Forest use

As northern Bolivian rural communities are endowed with vast forestlands, they will in the future have the option to provide environmental services under the terms of the Clean Development Mechanism (CDM) of the Kyoto Protocol. While there are potential livelihood benefits, there are also many risks for communities. The outcomes depend, for example, on the type of forests used in the carbon projects[89]. As the majority of the rural communities in the research area are located in remote areas possessing few inhabitants, one must assume that the transaction costs associated with organising, initiating and maintaining a forest carbon project over a large area (that is to say with the participation of many communities) will be high. The higher the degree of organisation in the communities and the greater the co-operation in efficient network structures as a direct link from the micro to the macro level the lower the transaction costs, and the higher the benefits.

The natural resource endowment of these communities depends in general on a) the natural conditions, b) the institutional arrangements, and linked to that c) the human impact on the ecosystem. Effective institutional arrangements limit human impact to the framework provided for in the arrangement and no further. By bringing the aspects of natural resource

[89] The possible types of forest for use in the carbon projects are 1) large-scale industrial pulp or timber plantations, 2) agroforestry, community forest plantations, 3) agroforests (forest gardens), secondary forest fallows, 4) forest rehabilitation and regeneration areas, 5) strictly protected forest areas, 6) multiple-use community forestry within protected forests (Smith and Scherr 2002: 4)

endowment and the defined community resource management potential together, the author made a normative estimation of whether the implications for future common property use may be critical, acceptable or positive. Such estimation is open to dispute. However, the development agencies demand that the aspects presented be taken into consideration. An initiative undertaken by several organisations working with rural communities in the study area developed a proposal for investigation, which has as yet not been realised due to a lack of financial resources. Several experts recommended the investigation of internal community aspects and their impacts on natural resource use. They also recommended that the heterogeneity of respective communities and their history be taken into account. This demand evolved due to experiences revealing that the success or failure of policy implementation appeared to be subject to internal factors.

Community forest management plans remain scarce in the study area. Due to the lack of information, organisation and financial resources forest management plans are not drawn up. The high transaction costs, the size of the areas and the value of the tree species do not justify financial investment in a management plan. In communities where such a plan exists, the process was usually financed by NGOs or was supported by a government agency through the provision of a surveyor. The land titling process is behind schedule, and forest management plans are only the second step. Many community organisations do not dispose of explicit strategies or definition processes for strategies that incorporate steps towards formal forest management. In other parts of the country, this process is more advanced. Apart from insecure property rights and dependence on support organisations like NGOs, the communities find themselves in a weak position in the market (Cronkleton and Albornoz 2004: 9). Where there is little organisational experience, the risk exists that forest resources are 'sold' to a timber company by means of contracts as a product of asymmetric business relationships, which jeopardise the natural resource base, and the economic and social benefits for the communities in the long run.

With respect to forest certification, Bolivia ranks high internationally and is first amongst the Latin American countries, with more than 1 million hectares certified. Nevertheless, community-based forest management is complex due to the need to respond to multiple objectives that include social and economic factors affecting the people who settle on managed lands. Peasant and indigenous communities are also interested in the certification process but: "In terms of forest management capacity and political influence, the social sector is the weakest in the certification process and timber companies the strongest" (Quevedo 2004: 16). Once a community initiative has reached a certain degree of organisation and is ready to pursue certification goals, the greatest limitations still remain, namely financial capital, tenure and marketing (CFV and CIEC 1997). Even when communities have achieved the necessary high level of organisation, organisational problems also remain a limitation, alternatively considered high (33%) or low (25%).

Despite the perceived limitations, community-based forest management has potential. In Mexico, an estimated 80% of forests are in the hands of communities with collective land grants[90] (Bray *et al.* 2003: 673). Community-based forest management there has reached a scale and level of maturity unmatched anywhere else in the world (*ibid.*). They manage non-timber forest products and timber for commercial extraction up to cases of finished timber products, which require industrial processes. Communities as the managers of common property forests who utilise larger market opportunities are an unusual species of stakeholder in less-developed countries. While in Mexico the seeds for community forestry were sown during the Mexican Revolution at the beginning of the twentieth century, the Amazonian communities are working according to a later timetable.

The rural smallholders in Amazonia are regarded on the one hand as the cause of forest destruction, and on the other hand as the saviours of the forests. The total area of forests under common property regimes under the stewardship of smallholders makes up a large part of the Amazon. Instead of being an object of development, these smallholders require active participation in order to develop strategies that serve the local people and the forests. Hurtienne and Pokorny criticised the one dimensional view of experts on the perspective of the Amazon and gave three examples of this: 1) the tendency to ignore the potential of an *agricultor familiar* (which in the Amazonian context is a rural smallholder, author's note), 2) a narrow understanding of forest ignoring possible contributions of other forest types (like secondary forests and *matorrales* = undergrowth, shrubbery), and 3) the obsessive use solely of monetary values for decision-making, and the disregard for the great importance of non-monetary values (*ibid.* 2004: 64). While this critique refers to research and policy across the whole of the Amazon, one must keep in mind that the call for the active participation of rural smallholders in decision-making depends on the different institutional settings of the respective countries with a share of the Amazon.

In Bolivia, the formal participation of rural smallholders is possible to a certain extent under the legal reforms. Whether participation occurs at local level, and the extent to which it occurs, depend on factors presented in this study. Strengthening the participation of the poor in political processes and decision-making forms part of the concept of sustainable development. This not only promotes opportunities for increasing the five forms of capital[91], but also facilitates empowerment (World Development Report 2000/2001). The utilisation of natural resources in the Bolivian Amazon underwent boom and bust cycles over the course of history. To date, this primarily NTFP-based utilisation of the forests has ensured the maintenance of an abundant forest cover with a great proportion of primary forest. The historically evolved social structures in which this NTFP use has taken place are in a state of transformation, but are part of the heritage of the rural community inhabitants. This heritage influences local community action in times of legal change and the manner in which poverty alleviation goals (like the enhancement of different forms of capital), sound forest management and capacity building can be achieved. The pressure on the northern Bolivian Amazon is increasing due to road building (also on the Brazilian side), the decline of forest

[90] In two categories, known respectively as *ejidos* and indigenous communities.

[91] Natural, physical, financial, human and social capital, sustainable livelihoods concept by Carney 1998.

resources in other parts of the country, and population growth (increasingly also settlers from the highlands). These factors indicate a trend towards increased timber-use, yet the Brazil nut market will continue to remain important[92].

Regardless of which natural resource is used most in the future, the creation of social, economic and ecological rewards benefiting even the poor parts of the population will depend on community capacity. The conditions can be improved by factors at the meso and macro-level, as touched upon in the study carried out by Ruiz (2005 in preparation). Further results will be yielded in a follow-up project currently being carried out in the research area, which focuses on poverty alleviation. However, in the context of this study, it was not possible to delve more deeply into the current meso and macro-level conditions. It is the community history and the communitiy capacity (as a collective of individuals in one legal body) that tip the scales in favour of benefit creation, enhancement and redistribution.

[92] Barriers on exports resulting from stricter European Union food safety rules jeopardise exportation to the European Union. These hindrances are being tackled by projects designed to secure Brazil nut quality standards, and involve the monitoring of aflatoxin fungus levels prior to exportation in order to adhere to permissible levels.

6 REFERENCES

Agrawal A. 1998. *Decentralization and Development.* Department of Political Science, Yale University, New Haven

Agrawal A. and C. Gibson 1999. "Enchantment and Disenchantment: The Role of Community in Natural Resource Conservation". In: World Development, Vol. 27, issue 4, April, pp. 629-649

Anonymus undated. *Final Report on* the Workshop: Decentralization and Social Policies in Latin America. http://www.idrc.ca/socdev/pub/documents/quito-e.html, accessed 2/26/2001

Archer M. 1988. *Culture and Agency.* Cambridge

Arnold M. 1998. *Managing forests as common property.* FAO Forestry Paper No. 136

Assies W. 1997. "Muchas cáscaras y pocas nueces: Extracción y desarrollo sustentable en la Amazonia". In: *Debate Agrario*, No. 26, pp. 41-57

Atteslander P. 2000. *Methoden der empirischen Sozialforschung.* 9., updated edition, Berlin

Bates R. 1995. "An assessment of the new institutionalism". In Harriss J., J. Hunter and C.M. Lewis (eds.). *The New Institutional Economics and Third World Development.* London

Bebbington A., Kopp A., Rubinoff D. 1997. *From chaos to strength? Social capital, rural peoples organizations and sustainable rural development.* Presented at the FAO workshop on pluralism, forestry and rural development, Rome

Bender D.R. 1967. "A Refinement of the Concept of Household: Families, Coresidence and Domestic Functions". In: *American Anthropologist*, 69 (3), pp. 493-510

Bennington A. 1997. "Social capital and rural intensification: local organizations and islands of sustainability in the Andes". In: *The Geographical Journal*, Vol. 163, No. 2, pp. 1-9

Berge E. 2001. *Contemporary Institutional Theory.* Lecture notes for 3 may 2001. Trondheim

Blanes J. 1999. *Descentralización y participación popular en las comunidades aymarás de Bolivia. Reflexiones sobre el futuro de la modernización del Estado.* La Paz

Blom A. 1998. "The Exogenous – Traditional Institutions and Their Ownership" in: *In Search of Alternatives: Poverty, the Poor and Local Organisations.* CDR Working Paper 98. 10. Centre for Development Research Copenhagen

Bojanic Helbingen A. J. 1999. *Growth, money flows and income distribution of the Brazil nut industry in the Bolivian Amazon.* Paper presented at the third workshop: Contributions of NTFP to socioeconomic development, Hot Springs (1998).

Bojanic Helbingen A. J. 2001. *Balance is beautiful: Assessing sustainable development in the rain forest of the Bolivian Amazon.* PROMAB Scientific Series 4, Riberalta

Bortz J. and N. Döring 1995. *Forschungsmethoden und Evaluation für Sozialwissenschaftler*, Berlin

Bourdieu P. 1976. *Entwurf einer Theorie der Praxis auf der ethnologischen Grundlage der kabylischen Gesellschaft*. Frankfurt a. M.

Bourdieu P. 1980. "Le capital social. Notes provisoires". In: *Actes de la recherche en sciences sociales*, n. 31, pp. 2-3

Bourdieu, P. and Loic Wacquant 1992. *Invitation to Reflexive Sociology*. Chicag

Bray, D., C. Antinori and J.M. Torres-Rojo 2004. *Regulatory Frameworks and Market Relationships in Mexican Community Forestry*. Draft paper for workshop on community-based forestry October 8-9, 2004. Humboldt University, Berlin

Bray D.B., Merino-Pérez L., Negreros-Castillo P., Segura-Warnholtz G., Torres-Rojo J.M. and H.F.M. Vester 2003. "Mexico's community-managed forests as global model for sustainable landscapes". In: *Conservation Biology*, Vol. 17, No.3, pp. 672-677

Brenner R. 1983. *The Human Gamble*. Chicago

Brillantes A. and N. Cuachon (eds.) 2002. *Decentralization and Power Shift. An Imperative for Good Governance. A Sourcebook on Decentralization Experiences in Asia*. Volume I. Asian Resource Center For Decentralization. Working Paper Series of the Center for Local and Regional Governance (CLRG) of the National College of Public Administration and Governance, University of the Philippines, 2002/2

Bukes G. 2000. *Der Zusammenhang von wirtschaftlicher Entwicklung und Demokratisierung. Das Beispiel Bolivien*. Beiträge zur Lateinamerika-Forschung. Institut für Iberoamerika-Kunde Hamburg, Band 3

Burgess R. 1984. *In the Field—An Introduction to Field Research*. London

Burt R. S. 2000." Structural Holes versus Network Closure as Social Capital". Pre-print for a chapter in Lin N. et al. (eds.) 2001: *Social capital: Theory and Research*

Campbell B. and N. Byron 1996. "Miombo Woodlands and Rural Livelihoods: Options and Opportunities". In: Bruce Campbell (ed.). *The Miombo in Transition: Woodlands and Welfare in Africa*. CIFOR, Bogor

Carney, D. 1998. "Implementing the Sustainable Rural Livelihoods Approach". In: Carney (ed.). *Sustainable Livelihoods. What Contribution Can we Make?*. Papers presented at the Department of International Development's Natural Resources Advisers' Conference, DFID, London, pp. 2-26

Castaldo S. 1995. *Le relazioni distributive*, Egea, Milano

CDR - Centre for Development Research 1999. *Popular Participation in Bolivia: Does the law "Participación Popular" secure participation of the rural Bolivian population?* Working Paper 99.6, October 1999, Copenhagen http://www.cdr.dk/working_papers/wp-99-6.htm , accessed 21.12.2000

Cecchi C. 2003. *Public goods and public services. The process of building social capital in the rural areas*. Paper presented in the Gruppo di lavoro su Processi e politiche di sviluppo rurale at SIDEA, XL Convegno annuale, 18-20 september, Padua

CFB – Cámara Forestal de Bolivia 2001. *Bolivia Forestal*. Santa Cruz

CFV – Consejo Boliviano para la Certificacion Forestal Voluntaria - and CIEC – Centro Interdisciplinario de Estudios Comunitarios 1997. *Taller Nacional sobre Planes de Manejo Forestal Comunitarios y Mecanismos de Participación Social en la Certificacion Forestal (Memorias)*. November 28, 1997, Santa Cruz

Chambers R. and M.K. McBeth 1992. "Community Encouragement: Returning to the basis for community development". In: *Journal of the Community Development Society*, 23 (2), pp.20-38

Cheema, G. Sh. and D. A. Rondinelli 1983."Implementing Decentralization Policies: An Introduction". In: *Decentralization and Development: Policy Implementation in Developing Countries*, edited by G. Shabbir Cheema and Dennis A. Rondinelli, Beverly Hills, London, New Delhi, pp.9-34

Chitere O.P. (ed.) 1994. *Community Development. Its Conceptions and Practice with Emphasis on Africa.* Nairobi

CIDOB - Centro de Información y Documentación de Bolivia 1979. *Diagnostico Social del Norte Boliviano. Volumen I.*, La Paz

CIFOR- Centre for International Forestry Research 1999. *Developing Institutions for Sustainable Use of Non-Timber Forest Products. A Request for Targeted Research Funding to the German Federal Ministry for Economic Cooperation and Development (BMZ).* Bogor

CIFOR – Centre for International Forestry Research 2003. *Decentralisation in Latin America.* Bogor

CIPCA Norte 2001. *Porcentajes de personas que tienen documentos de identidad – comunidades del norte amazónico.* Unpublished document by the *Centro de Investigación y Promoción del Campesinado*, Riberalta

Colby B. 1996. Cognitive Anthropology. In: *Encyclopedia of Cultural Anthropology 1*. David Levison and Melvin Ember (eds.), New York, pp. 209-214

Coleman J. S. 1988. "Social Capital in the Creation of Human Capital". In: *American Journal of Sociology* 94 (Supplement), pp. 95-120, reprinted in Dasgupta, P. and I. Serageldin 2000. *Social Capital. A Multifaceted Perspective.* The World Bank, Washington, pp. 13-39

Commons J. R. 1931. "Institutional Economics". In: *American Economic Review*, 21, pp. 648-657

Commons J. R. 1968. *Legal foundations of Capitalism.* Madison

Coomes, O.T. and B.L. Barham 1994. "The Amazon Rubber Boom: Labor Control, Resistance and Failed Plantation Development Revisited". In: *Hispanic American Historical Review*, 74 (2), pp. 231-257

Cronkleton, P. and M. A. Albornoz. 2004. *Forestería Comunitaria en Bolivia: Abriendo Horizontes para Nuevos Actores.* CIFOR, Santa Cruz.

C.S.U.T.C.B. 2003. *Historia del Movimiento Originario en Bolivia por la Confederación Sindical Única de Trabajadores Campesinos de Bolivia.*

http://www.nadir.org/nadir/initiativ/agp/free/imf/bolivia/txt/2003/0125historia.htm, accessed 10.15.2003

D'Agata A. 2003. *Endogenizing Sen's Capabilities: An Adaptive Dynamic Analysis.* Paper to be presented at 3rd Conference on the Capability Approach: From Sustainable Development to Sustainable Freedom 7-9 September 2003, University of Pavia

Dasgupta, P. and I. Serageldin 2000. *Social Capital. A Multifaceted Perspective.* The World Bank, Washington

De Jong, W. 1999. *A comparison of theories on institutions relevant to natural resource management.* Draft for CIFOR, Bogor

DHV 1993: Tenencia de la Tierra en la Región Castañera de la Amazonia Boliviana. Bolivia, Proyecto de Desarrollo Agropecuario, Banco Mundial/Gobierno de Holanda, La Paz

Döring H. 1998. *Kritische Analyse der Leistungsfähigkeit des Transaktionskostenansatzes.* Dissertation zur Erlangung des wirtschaftswissenschaftlichen Doktorgrades der Wirtschaftswissenschaftlichen Fakultät der Universität Göttingen

Etzioni A. 1996. "Positive aspects of community and the dangers of fragmentation". In: Development and Change, 27, pp. 301-314

FAO – Food and Agricultural Organization – 2003. *Multilingual thesaurus on land tenure.* Rome

Favereau, O. and E. Lazega (eds.) 2002. *Conventions and Structures in Economic Organization. Markets. Networks and Hierarchies.* New Horizons in Institutional and Evolutionary Economics Series, Cheltenham, UK

Feierman S. 1990. *Peasant Intellectuals*, Wisconsin

Fink A. S. 2000. "The Role of the Researcher in the Qualitative Research Process. A Potential Barrier to Archiving Qualitative Data". In: *Forum Qualitative Sozialforschung/Forum: Qualitative Social Research* (On-line Journal), 1 (3) December. Available at: http://qualitative-research.net/fqs/fqs-eng.htm, accessed 11/22/2004

Flap H. 2002. "No man is an island: the research programme of social capital theory". In: *Conventions and Structures in Economic Organization. Markets. Networks and Hierarchies.* New Horizons in Institutional and Evolutionary Economics Series, Cheltenham, pp. 29-59

Flores G. 1999. *La ley INRA de Bolivia: ¿una segunda reforma agraria?* http://www.fao.org/WAICENT/FAOINFO/SUSTDEV/SPdirect/LTan0033.htm, accessed 4/4/2001

Girtler R. 1984. *Methoden der qualitativen Sozialforschung. Anleitung zur Feldarbeit.* Wien

Granovetter M. 1985. "Economic Action and Social Structure: The Problem of Embeddedness" In: *American Journal of Sociology* 91, pp. 481-510

Grindle M. S. 2000. *Audacious Reforms. Institutional Invention and Democracy in Latin America.* Johns Hopkins University Press, Baltimore

Grootaert Ch. 2001. *Does Social Capital Help The Poor? A Synthesis of Findings from The Local Level Institutions Studies in Bolivia, Burkina Faso and Indonesia*. Local Level Institutions Working Papers no. 10, The World Bank, Washington D.C.

Haley D. and M.K. Luckert 1990. *Forest Tenures in Canada: A Framework for Policy Analysis*. Ottawa

Hanifan L.J. 1916. "The Rural School Community Centre". In: *Annals of the American Academy of Political and Social Sciences*, 67, pp. 130-138

Helliwell J. and R. D. Putnam 2000. "Social Capital and Economic Growth and in Italy". In: Dasgupta P. and I. Serageldin (eds.): *Social Capital: A Multi-faceted Perspective* World Bank, Washington

Heltberg R. 1999. *New Institutional Economics. A Survey of Property Rights and Natural Resource Management*. Unpublished draft 'Chapter One'

Heltberg R. 2001. *Property Rights and Natural Resource Management in the Developing Countries*. Forthcoming in the Journal of Economic Surveys

Henkemans A. 2001. *Tranquilidad and Hardship in the Forest. Livelihoods and Perceptions of Camba Forest Dwellers in the Northern Bolivian Amazon*. PROMAB Scientific Series 5, Riberalta, Bolivia

Hentschel G. 2002. *Die Veränderung institutioneller Rahmenbedingungen für die Waldnutzung durch Campesno-Siedler im bolivianischen Amazonasgebiet*. Unpublished diploma thesis, Faculty of Forestry, Freiburg University

Hurtienne T. and B. Pokorny 2004. "Blanco y negro o bien colorido: discrepancias en la percepción de los bosques por los investigadores y agricultures familiares". In: Pokorny B., Sabogal C. and F. Krämer (eds.). *Forum sobre bosques, gestión y desarrollo: opciones para la Amazonia*. CIFOR, Belém, pp. 63-72

Ibarra E. 2002. *Private forest use decisions and state forest policy effectiveness in Costa Rica: The role of institutions, private stakeholders and the State*. Dissertation presented at Albert-Ludwigs-University, Freiburg

INE – *Instituto Nacional de Estadística* – 2001. *Censo de Población y Vivienda*. La Paz

Jasek-Rysdahl K. 2001. "Applying Sen's Capabilities Framework to Neighborhoods: Using Local Asset Maps to Deepen Our Understanding of Well-Being". In: *Review of Social Economy*. Vol. LIX, No.3, September 2001, pp. 312-329

Keating 2003. *Guía Sistematica para Evaluar y Monitorear el Desarrollo de una Gestión de Empresas Forestales Comunitarias*. Paper presented during the II Conference on Forestry in Cochabamba. August 2003. Cochabamba, Bolivia

Klamer L., E. Mante (eds.) 2002. *Capabilities in Action. What people do*. Cost 269 –Working Group, http://www.cost269.org/working%20group/DocCapabilities/Ch_1.doc, accessed 11/3/ 2004

Klemp L. 1997. *Ein Volk bricht auf – Entwicklungspolitische Überlegungen zur Zivilgesellschaft in Tanzania,* in: Politik und Zeitgeschichte. Beilage zur Wochenzeitung Das Parlament, B 9/97, 21. Februar 1997, pp. 19-29, Bonn

Knight J. 1992. *Institutions and Social Conflict.* Cambridge University Press, Cambridge

Krempin M. 1986. *Bauernbewegung in Bolivien: die Entwicklung der sozioökonomischen Lage sowie der politischen Haltung und Organisationsformen der ländlichen Bevölkerung in Bolivien unter besonderer Berücksichtigung der Bauernbewegung seit 1969.* Frankfurt am Main

Krempin M. 1997. "Politik und Gesellschaft", in Bruns (ed.). Bolivien, zweite, überarb. und aktualisierte Auflage, Köln, pp. 117-224

Krishna A. 2000. "Creating and Harnessing Social Capital". In: *Social Capital: A Multifaceted Perspective.* P. Dasgupta and I. Serageldin (eds.), pp. 71-93

Krishna, A. and E. Shrader 1999. Social *Capital Assessment Tool. Prepared for the Conference on Social Capital and Poverty Reduction*, June 22-24, 1999. The World Bank, Washington

Kundhlande, G. and M.K. Luckert 2001. *Towards an Analytical Framework for Assessing Property Rights to Natural Resources. A Case Study in the Communal Areas of Zimbabwe.* Staff Paper of the Department of Rural Economics, University of Alberta

Kusel J. 2001. "Assessing well-being in forest dependent communities". In: *Understanding Community-Based Frost Ecosystem Management*, G.J. Gray, M.J. Enzer, and J. Kusel (eds.), pp. 359-384, New York, London and Oxford

Kusel 1996. "Well-being in forest-dependent communities, part I: A new approach". In S. Doak and J. Kusel (eds.): *Sierra Nevada Ecosystem Project: Final Report to Congress, Vol. II, Assessments and Scientific Basis for Management Options*, pp. 361-74 University of California, Centers for Water and Wildland Resources

Lave, J. and S. Kvale 1995. "What is anthropological research? An interview with Jean Lave by Steinar Kvale". In: *Qualitative Studies in Education, 8*(3), 219-228.

Lazarte R. J. 2000. *Entre dos mundos. La cultura política y democrática enBolivia.* Plural / microcosmos, La Paz

Leach, M., R. Mearns and I. Scoones 1999. "Environmental Entitlements: Dynamics and Institutions in Community-Based Natural Resource Management." *World Development*, Vol.27, No.2, pp.225-247

Lijerón Casanovas A. 1998. *Introducción a la Historia Amazónica*, Mojos, Beni, Bolivia

Lin, J. Y., and J. B. Nugent 1995. "Institutions and Economic Development." in J. Bherman and T.N. Srinivasan (eds.), *Handbook of Development Economics, Volume III.* pp. 2301-2370. Elsevier, Amsterdam

Linz J. and A. Stepan 1996. "Towards consolidated democracies". In: *Journal of Democracy*, Vol. 7, No. 2, pp. 14-31

Maldonado Kühne R. 2002. *Natural resource management in a tropical protected area. Conflicts between use and protection in the Reserva Nacional de Vida Silvestre Amazónico Manuripi – RNVSAM, Bolivia.* Unpublished diploma thesis, Faculty of Forestry, Freiburg University

Mandondo A. 2000. *Situating Zimbabwe's natural resource governance systems in history.* CIFOR Occasional Paper 32. Center for International Forestry Research, Bogor.

Mayring P. 1999. *Einführung in die qualitative Sozialforschung*, 4. Auflage, Weinheim

McCracken D. G. 1988. "The Long Interview". In: *Qualitative Research Methods*, Vol. 13, Newbury Park

McKee Chr. 1999. *The Campaign for an Instrumento Político: The latest Developments in the Indigenous Movement in Bolivia.* Paper presented to the Society for Latin American Studies Postgraduates in Latin American Studies (PILAS) 1999 Conference, The Graduate Institute, The University of Hull, Hull, England (4-5 December 1999)

Mertins, G. and Popp, J. 1996. *Experience of Development with Tenure Rights of Indigenous Groups in Andean South America, Example Bolivia.* Study for the Guiding Principles Land Tenure in Development Cooperation. Deutsche Gesellschaft für Technische Zusammenarbeit OE 4250 / Div. 435

Ministerio de Desarrollo Humano/ Secretaría Nacional de Participación Popular 1996. *Apre(he)ndiendo la Participación Popular. Análisis y reflexiones sobre el modelo boliviano de descentralización.* La Paz

Mohoney J. 2000. "Path dependency in historical sociology". In: *Theory and Society,* 29, pp. 507-548

Molina C. H. 2001. Personal Interview, 10th of January 2001 in Santa Cruz de la Sierra

Mummert U. 1995. *Informelle Institutionen in ökonomischen Transformationsprozessen.* Baden-Baden

Mummert U. 1998. „Wirtschaftliche Entwicklung und Institutionen. Die Perspektive der Neuen Institutionenökonomik". In: *Entwicklung und Zusammenarbeit*, Jg.39:2, pp.36-39

Mummert U. 1999. *Informal Institutions and Institutional Policy – Shedding Light on the Myth of Institutional Conflict.* Diskussionsbeitrag 02-99. Max-Planck-Institute for Research into Economic Systems, Jena

Nabli, M. K. and J. B. Nugent 1989. "The New Institutional Economics and Its Applicability to Development". *World Development*, Vol.17, No. 9, pp. 1333-1347

Nadeau, S., B. Shindler, and C. Kakoyannis. 1999. *Forest communities: New frameworks for assessing sustainability.* The Forestry Chronicle 75(5), pp. 747- 754.

Nee V. 1998. "Norms and Networks in Economic and Organizational Performance". *The American Economic Review,* 88 (2), pp. 85-89

Nee, V. and P. Ingram 1998. "Embeddedness and Beyond: Institutions, Exchange, and Social Structure". In: Brinton M.C. and V. Nee (eds.). *The New Institutionalism in Sociology.* New York

Nemarundwe N., W. De Jong and P. Cronkleton 2003. *Future Scenarios as an instrument for forest management. Manual for training facilitators of Future Scenarios.* Bogor, Indonesia

Neumann R.P. 1992. "Political ecology of wildlife conservation in the Mt. Meru area of Northeast Tanzania." In: *Land Degradation and Rehabilitation* 3, pp. 95-98

North D. C. 1990. *Institutions, Institutional Change and Economic Performance*. Cambridge University Press, Cambridge

North, D.C. 1991. "Institutions". In: *Journal of Economic Perspectives*, 5 (1), pp. 97-112

North D. C. 1992. *Institutionen, institutioneller Wandel und Wirtschaftsleistung*. Tübingen

O'Brien, D. and V. Patsiorkowski 2000. *Peasant households before and after the 1998 financial collapse in Russia: further evidence of incremental institutional change*. Paper prepared for the annual meeting of the International Society for the New Institutional Economics, Tübingen, Germany, September 22-24, 2000, pp.1-21

OECD –Organisation for Economic Cooperation and Development undated. *Transaction Costs and Multifuncitionality. Main issues*. Note by the Secretariat of the Directorate for Food, Agriculture and Fisheries, Workshop on Multifunctionalities

Olson G. 1991. *Clifford Geertz on Ethnography and Social Construction*. http://jac.gsu.edu/jac/11.2/Articles/geertz.htm , accessed 10/21/2003

Olson M. 1965. *The Logic of Collective Action*. Cambridge

Olson M. 1982. *The Rise and Decline of Nations: Economic Growth, Stagflation and Social Rigidities*. New Haven

Ostrom E. 1990. *Governing the Commons. The Evolution of Institutions for Collective Action*. Cambridge

Ostrom E. 1994. Neither Market nor State. Governance of Common-Pool Resources in the Twenty-First Century. Paper presented at the IFPRI Lecture Series, Washington D.C.

Ostrom E. 1997. *Private and Common Property Rights*. At a latter date to be published in Encyclopedia of Law and Economics. http://economy.boom.ru/pubs/E_Ostrom_Private_and_common_property_rights.htm , accessed 3/1/2001

Ostrom E. 2000. *Private and Common Property Rights*, http://economy.boom.ru/pubs/E_Ostrom_Private_and_common_property_rights.htm , accessed 3/ 1/2001

Pacheco Balanza P. 1998. *Estilos de desarrollo, deforestación y degradación de los bosques en las tierras bajas de Bolivia*. Serie: Bosques y sociedad N° 2, La Paz, Bolivia

Pacheco Balanza P. 2001. Personal Interview, 11th of January 2001 in Santa Cruz de la Sierra

Pacheco Balanza P. 2004. *Decentralization of Forest Management in Bolivia: Who Benefits and Why?*. Draft for CIFOR, Bogor

Paldam M. 2000. *Social Capital: One or Many? Definition and Measurement*. University of Aarhus, Denmark (written for the *Journal of Economic Surveys* – special issue on political economy)

Pearce D.W. and T.K. Turner 1990. *Economics of Natural Resources and the Environment*. Hemel Hempstead

Peluso N. 1992. "The political ecology of extraction and extractive reserves in East Kalimantan, Indonesia". In: *Development and Change*, 23 (4), pp. 49-74

Pereira L. 2004. *Institutional changes shaping livelihoods of forest-dependent people in northern Bolivian Amazon: a case study of Bolpebra municipality*. Unpublished master thesis, Faculty of Forestry, Freiburg University

Peres C..A., Baider C., Zuidema P., L. H. O. Wadt, K. A. Kainer, D. A. P. Gomes-Silva, R. P. Saloma, L. L. Simoes, E. R. N. Franciosi, F. C. Valverde, R. Gribel, G. H. Shepard Jr. , M. Kanashiro, P. Coventry, D. W. Yu, A. R. Watikinson, R. P. Freckleton 2003. "Demographic Threats to the Sustainability of Brazil Nut Exploitation". In: Science, Vol.302, Dec., pp. 2112-2114

PNUD – Programa de las Naciones Unidas para el Desarrollo 2003. *Informe de Desarrollo Humano en el Norte Amazónico boliviano*. La Paz

Putnam R. D. 1995. "Bowling Alone: America's Declining Social Capital". In: *Journal of Democracy* 6(1), Jan.1995, pp. 65-78

Quevedo L. 2004. *Forest Certification in Bolivia*. Unpublished draft paper presented at the Symposium "Forest Certification in Developing and Transitioning Societies: Social, Economic, and Ecological Effects", Yale School of Forestry and Environmental Studies, 10-11 June 2004, New Haven

Raimondo M. A. undated. *The measurement of trust in marketing studies: A review of models and methodologies*. ISTEI, Milan, http://www.bath.ac.uk/imp/pdf/14_Raimondo.pdf, accessed 9/8/2004

Ribot J. 2002. *Democratic Decentralization of Natural Resources. Institutionalizing Popular Participation*. World Resources Institute, Washington D.C.

Ribot J. 2003. "Democratic Decentralization of Natural Resources: Institutional Choice and Discretionary Power Transfers in Sub-Saharan Africa". In: *Public Administration and Development*, 23 (1), pp. 53-65

Rondinelli, D. and Sh. Cheema (eds.) 1983. Decentralization and Development: Policy Implementation in Developing Countries. USA

Ruiz 2005 (forthcoming). *Institutional change and social conflicts over the forest use in the northern Bolivian Amazon*. Dissertation presented at Freiburg University, Germany

Sánchez de Lozada G. 2001. Personal Interview, 19 of September 2001 in Riberalta

Scherr, S., White A. and D. Kaimowitz 2003. *A new agenda for forest conservation and poverty reduction. Making markets work for low-income producers*. Forest Trends (with CIFOR/IUCN), Washington D.C.

Schlager, E. and E. Ostrom 1992. "Property-Rights Regimes and Natural Resources: A Conceptual Analysis". In: *Land Economics*, 68, pp. 249-262

Schmidt S. 1999. *Institutionenökonomische Analyse der staatlichen Forstwirtschaft in Deutschland. Die Bedeutung formeller und informeller Institutionen*. Schriften aus dem Institut für Forstökonomie der Universität Freiburg. Band 12, Freiburg

Scott A.D. and J. Johnson 1983. *Property rights: developing the characteristics of interests in natural resources.* Resource Paper No. 88. The University of British Columbia, Department of Economics. Vancouver, B.C.

Sen A. 1979. "Equality of What?". In: A. Sen 1982. *Choice, Welfare and Measurement.* Oxford

Sen A. 1985. *Commodities and capabilities.* Professor Dr. P. Hennipman Lectures in Economics, Vol. 7, New York: North-Holland

Sen A. 1992. *Inequality Reexamined.* Oxford

Sen A. 1993. "Capability and Well-being". In M. Nussbaum and A. Sen (eds) *The Quality of Life*, Oxford

Smith, J. and S. Scherr 2002. *Forest Carbon and Local Livelihoods: Assessment of Opportunities and Policy Recommendations.* CIFOR Occasional Paper No. 37, Bogor

Souza C. 2001. "Participatory Budgeting in Brazilian Cities: Limits and Possibilities in Building Democratic Institutions". In: *Environment & Urbanisation*, Vol. 13, No. 1, April 2001

Stahl J. 2003. *Rationalities in Cavineño Livelihood Strategies. A case study from the Bolivian Amazon.* M.A. thesis presented at Freiburg University, GermanyStoian D. 1999. "Change and adaptation as keys to sustainability: Extraction- based livelihood systems in the Bolivian Amazon". In: Council for Tropical and Subtropical Agricultural Research (ATSAF). *Knowledge Partnership: Challenges and Perspectives for Research and Education at the Turn of the Millennium.* Seminar proceedings, 14-15 October 1999. Bonn, pp. 1-12

Stoian D. 2000. *Variations and dynamics of extractive economies: the rural-urban nexus of non-timber forest use in the Bolivian Amazon.* Dissertation presented at Freiburg University, Germany

Stoian, D. and A. Henkemans (2000). "Between extractivism and peasant agriculture: Differentiation of rural settlements in the Bolivian Amazon". In: *International Tree Crops Journal*, Vol.10. pp 299-319

Sztompka P. 1991. *Society in Action. The Theory of Social Becoming.* Cambridge

Ticonas, E., Rojas and G., Albó X. 1995. *Votos y Whipalas. Campesinos y pueblos originarios en democracia.* Fundación Milenio, CIPCA, Cuadernos de Investigación 43, La Paz

Tomaselli I. 2000. *The private sector and sustainable forest management – South America perspective.*STCP – Brazil, http://www.cifor.cgiar.org/fsfm/Papers/OSLO_III_5_PS.pdf, accessed 4/4/2001

Tool M.R. (ed.) 1993. *Institutional Economics: Theory, Method, Policy.* Kluwer Academic Publishers, Boston/Dordrecht/London

Umlauft F. 1898. "Capital und Arbeit in den Kautschukdisricten von Südamerika" In: *Deutsche Rundschau für Geographie und Statistik 20 (11)*, p.481-491

Unnamed. *Modern Mongolia. Reclaiming Genghis Khan* undated. An Exhibit of the University of Pennysylvania Museum of Archaeology and Anthropology, http://www.upenn.edu/museum/Mongolia/section4.html, accessed 8/19/2002

Urioste F. de C., M. and D. Pacheco undated. *Bolivia: mercado de tierras en un nuevo contexto (Ley INRA).* Fundación Tierra http://www.cepes.org.pe/coalition/Paises/Bolivia/Cas_Bol/Document/Mcdo%20de%20tierras%20nuevo%20contexto.htm, accessed 5/4/2001

Von Twickel Ch. 2002. *Beziehungen und Netzwerke in der modernen Gesellschaft: Soziales Kapital und normative Institutionenökonomik.* Münster

Webster N. (ed.) 1998. *In search of Alternatives: Poverty, the Poor and Local Organisations.* CDR Working Paper 98.10, November 1998. Revised papers from the Workshop on the CDR (Centre for Development Research Copenhagen) Research Programme: Local Organisations and Rural Poverty Alleviation (LORPA) Tune, Denmark, 28-30 August 1996

Weinberg, M.S. and C.J. Williams 1973. "Soziale Beziehungen zu devianten Personen bei der Feldforschung". In: Friedrichs (ed.). *Teilnehmende Beobachtung abweichenden Verhaltens*, Stuttgart, S. 83-108

White, A. and A. Martin 2002. Who owns the world's forests?, Washington, D.C.: Forest Trends

WIKIPEDIA 2004. *Postmodernism.* http://en.wikipedia.org/wiki/Postmodern#Brief_outline_of_postmodernism, accessed 11.24.2004

Williamson O. 2000. "The New Institutional Economics: Taking stock, Looking ahead". In: *Journal of Economic Literature*, Vol. 38 (September), pp. 595-613

Woolcock M. 1998. "Social Capital and Economic Development: Toward a Theoretical Synthesis and Policy Framework".In: *Theory and Society*,Vol. 27, No. 2 (Apr.), pp. 151-208

World Development Report 2000/2001. *Attacking poverty overview.* The World Bank, Washington D.C.

WTO/UNIDO 2004. *Implementation of the WTO/UNIDO MoU. Joint Technical Cooperation Programme Responding to the DOHA Development Agenda.* Joint Progress Report. 16 July 2004, http://www.unido.org/file-storage/download/?file_id-25735, accessed 12/13/2004

7 ANNEXES

Annex 1 Eleven characteristics to link tenure and economic behaviour

Kundhlande and Luckert (2001)[93] presented a concept consisting of eleven characteristics, which provided a framework facilitating the linking of tenure to economic behaviour. The questions posed in relation to tenure issues addressed the eleven characteristics: Comprehensiveness, Exclusiveness, Use Designation, Duration, Allotment Type, Size, Transferability, Fees, Operational Requirements, Operational Control, and Security

In the following will be given the short definition for each of those (see Kundhlande and Luckert 2001: 6-12); for further details and specifications see ibid.:

COMPREHENSIVENESS	describes the set of natural resources over which households have control
EXCLUSIVENESS	refers to the ability of a tenure holder to prevent other parties from freely enjoying the benefits of the resource
USE DESIGNATION	limits the types of activities that tenure holders can carry out on a given type of tenure
DURATION	specification of the period over which property rights can be specified
ALLOTMENT TYPE	refers to whether the tenure specifies an area over which a household possesses rights, or whether the tenure specifies volumes of natural resources that may be collected by the household
SIZE	refers to the spatial or volume specification of the tenure
TRANSFERABILITY	refers to the ability of a resource owner to sell, bequeath, or gift an asset (including the benefits generated by the asset) to others at mutually agreed upon terms
FEES	may be payable by households growing and/or harvesting agricultural crops or forest products
OPERATIONAL REQUIREMENTS	Society may require that resource users adhere to certain regulations during the use of an asset, for resource management and in their harvesting practices. Such restrictions may be designed to ensure that management and harvesting practises are consistent with society's goals

[93] Building on work carried out by Haley and Luckert (1990) and Scott and Johnson (1983)

OPERATIONAL CONTROL	Operational controls are the mechanisms for enforcing the conditions of tenures. Such mechanisms may involve policing by appointees selected by villagers, and a system of penalties against those who break the rules
SECURITY	Security may be defined by the perception of a tenure holder concerning his/her ability to capture benefits generated by the resource in the future and whether changes in tenure will occur which increase or decrease the derived benefits

Annex 2 Details on the Popular Participation Law

Note: The expression *Participación Popular* refers not only to the Popular Participation Law, the details of which are given below, but also implies other laws, such as the Administrative Decentralisation Law and others which taken together represent the comprehensive process of decentralisation in Bolivia.

The following text is extracted from:

Mertins, G. and Popp, J. 1996. *Experience of Development with Tenure Rights of Indigenous Groups in Andean South America, Example Bolivia.* Study for the Guiding Principles Land Tenure in Development Cooperation. Deutsche Gesellschaft für Technische Zusammenarbeit OE 4250 / Div. 4350

Popular Participation Law (Ley de Participación Popular)

The Popular Participation Law (Ley de Participación Popular) was passed on April 20, 1994. The authority in charge, "Secretaría Nacional de Participación Popular", belongs to the Ministry of the Environment.

Since Bolivia's return to Democracy in October of 1982, the demands of the population to take part in the democratic decision-making process have been growing, but have found little consideration in the existing State-centered structures. A further reason for the administrative reorganization of Bolivia was the preponderance of the four large cities, La Paz, El Alto, Cochabamba, and Santa Cruz. Before the "Participación Popular", 86% of state allocations were received by these cities, and a large percent of the remaining sum went to the capital cities of the nine Departamentos. At the same time, the national territory was not completely divided into municipalities, leading to a political, economic, and social margina-lization of the rural population and the resulting migration (JOST, 1996: 57f).

The Popular Participation Law deals with the most important new distributions of the political and economic power since the Revolution of 1952 (JOST, 1996:59).

Important Goals of the Participación Popular:

Municipalisation of the land: While only urban municipalities existed before the reform, for the first time in Bolivia's history, rural areas were finally recognized as independent territorial units through the Popular Participation Law. As of November 1995, 308 communities already existed.

Expansion of the traditional competency of the communities through transferral of corresponding resources.

Abolition of the preference to large Departamento capital cities, and the distribution of tax money according to the of number of inhabitants: Besides the regular or extraordinary financial allocations through the Federal budget, the Departamentos have at their disposal separate sources of income, for example highway tax. The most important source of income is the Regional Compensation Fund of the Participación Popular, through which a financial balance between the regions is to be supported through means of the Federal budget (JOST, 1996:65).

The legal recognition of approximately 20,000 OTB (Organizaciones Territoriales de Base), meaning the "Comunidades Campesinas", the "Juntas Vecinales" and the "Pueblos Indígenas", as well as their endowment with control rights dealing with the responsibility of the community (Art. 2). The integration of the indigenous groups, containing over half of the total population, is to be supported through the Participation. This makes the law to one of the most important instruments of indigenous politics.

Article 1:

"The present law recognizes, promotes and consolidates the process of Popular Participation through the articulation of the interests of indigenous, rural and urban communities in the legal, political and economic life of the country. It promotes the improvement of the quality of life of the Bolivian woman and the Bolivian man through a fairer distribution and better management of public funds. It strengthens the political and economic instruments necessary for the perfection of the representative democracy and guarantees equal representation for women and men".

Next to the new Bolivian Constitution, Article 1, 3 and 9 of the Popular Participation Law stipulates the recognition of traditional indigenous organizations and internal management structures (Tentas, Capitanías, Cabildos Indígenas del Oriente, Ayllus, etc.), which lead to an enormous reinforcement of the indigenous self-determination rights. The law serves as an aid in argumentation, especially for the Lowland Indians, who traditionally have a communal organization form and fight against the division of their territories into private plots of land.

Article 3:

As subjects of the Popular Participation, the 'Organizaciones Territoriales de Base' shall be defined, which, according to their practice and status as a farm community (comunidad campesina), indigenous people (pueblo indígena) or neighbourhood union (juntas vecinales), can be registered.

As representatives of the 'Organizaciones Territoriales de Base', Men, Women, Capitanes, Jilacatas, Curacas, Mallcus, Secretary Generals and others, according to their customs and status, shall be recognised.

Article 9:

The joint organizations (Asociaciones Comunitarias) which were secured through the 'Organizaciones Territoriales de Base' shall be recognised according to their customs and status.

Übersicht der bisher in dieser Schriftenreihe erschienenen Bücher

ISBN	Titel	Autor	S.
3935638272	Urbane Waldbesitzer (Band 1 ifp)	Ulrich Schraml Karl-Reinhard Volz	208
3935638337	Naturnahe Waldbewirtschaftung durch private Waldeigentümer (Band 2 ifp)	Claudia Bieling	159
3935638361	Private forest use decisions and state forest policy effectiveness in Costa Rica (Band 3 ifp)	Enrique Ibarra	195
3935638469	Globale Waldpolitik (Band 4 ifp)	Frank Hofmann	309
3935638477	Innovation in der Forstwirtschaft (Band 5 ifp)	Lutz Pickenpack	239
3935638566	Waldbesitzer in Deutschland - Zwischen Tradition und Moderne (Band 6 ifp)	Ulf Härdter	309
3935638647	Modelling Community Forestry in The Gambia (Band 7 ifp)	Alexander Gareiß	178
3935638655	Promotion of innovations in forest based small and medium size enterprises of developing countries (Band 8 ifp)	Christian Held	223
3935638663	Die politische Positionierung der Forstverwaltungen in Deutschland (Band 9 ifp)	Johannes Fischbach-Einhoff	332
3935638744	Institutional change and social conflicts over the forest use in the Northern Bolovian Amazonas (Band 10 ifp)	Sergio Ruiz	258
3935638760	Capacities of rural forest-dependent communities in the northern Bolivian Amazon in times of legal reforms	Carmen Gottwald	170
3935638752	Konflikte in Erholungsgebieten – Ursachen, Wirkungen und Lösungsansätze (Band 12 ifp)	Carsten Mann	256

Jeder Band kann für 19 Euro direkt beim Verlag bestellt werden (s. Impressum).